MY LAST YEAR OF LIFE (IN SCHOOL)

D1606652

KEITH MANOS

BLACK ROSE writing™

ISBN: 978-1-61296-600-7

PUBLISHED BY BLACK ROSE WRITING

www.blackrosewriting.com

Printed in the United States of America

Suggested retail price $18.95

My Last Year of Life (In School) is printed in Adobe Caslon Pro

For all my fellow educators
who demonstrate commitment
to their students and a passion
for their profession.

PRAISE FOR
MY LAST YEAR OF LIFE (IN SCHOOL)

Surprising and honest, Keith Manos gives us a behind-the-scenes look at a teacher's last year in a school he once loved.

~**Sarah Willis,** author of *Some Things That Stay* and *A Good Distance*)

During his last year as an English teacher in a suburban high school, Ethan Miller faces much more than just wayward teens. There are the parents, the school board, and contemporary issues he never could have imagined when he began his career 35 years before. Author Keith Manos's true-life novel takes us through the day-to-day events in the classroom--the teen brawls, the school board trials, and the disturbing issues facing educators today. In the end, Manos has a lot to teach us all about the human condition.

~**Deanna Adams,** author of *Confessions of a Not-So-Good Catholic Girl, Rock 'n' Roll and the Cleveland Connection,* and the novel, *Peggy Sue Got Pregnant.*

MY LAST YEAR
OF LIFE
(IN SCHOOL)

MONDAY, AUGUST 20, 2012 A.M.

On this warm, sunny day as I walk into the Bayview High School cafeteria, I'm dreading this question: "How was your summer?"

I'm not kidding.

The truth is I have heard one colleague after another ask me this same question on this first staff day for teachers for thirty-five years.

How was your summer?

Every year.

For thirty-five years.

How would *you* react?

Please ask me something else!

In fact, that question is so old, so much a cliché, so teacher-oriented (In what other profession is this ever asked?) that I almost regret seeing my fellow Bayview staff members again after two months apart. Yes, I know they mean well and you may think that I'm being too harsh, but as I start this 35th year of teaching – indeed, my *last* year of teaching – I guess I am hoping finally for a different greeting at the beginning of the school year.

Plus, what can I tell them?

I cut the grass.

I cleaned the house.

I read books.

I watched my sons' baseball games.

I attended professional development seminars.

The same things I've done every summer.

I am as boring as the question. Old, too. Not one-room-school-house old, but old enough to remember using a reel-to-reel projector to show movies to students and making handouts with a ditto machine. In fact, no one in the building has worked for the Bayview School District longer than I have. Some of these people might think I dated Eleanor Roosevelt.

Today, when I enter the Bayview High cafeteria, I feel like Forest Gump – you know, in that scene when he walks down the school bus aisle and confronts the glaring eyes of the other kids. Although seats are available, no one, except for one little girl, lets him sit down. In truth, no one glares at me but no one asks me to join him or her either. Most of the faculty is young, and they have their own cliques: The coaches. The young moms and dads. The science guys.

I used to be in a group – single guys who hit happy hour almost every Friday – but that was years ago when my stomach was flatter. When hangovers didn't last for two days like they do now. Plus, those teachers are gone now, all retired themselves or dead, so I'm not in any group now. Nevertheless, I make my face smile and scope out the empty seats, hoping no one says, "Taken."

And if someone does ask about my summer, I tell myself, so what. Just go with it, Ethan, because after today, you'll never hear that again.

Therefore, I walk casually to the last table in the back of the cafeteria and slide down the bench seat until I reach Jack Johnston, a social studies teacher who had dreams years ago of being a MMA fighter. I first met him was when he began teaching at Bayview five years ago; he was eager then to tell me and some of the football coaches about the bar fights he'd had. Today, Jack looks tanned and cheerful, still sporting a military buzz cut and smiling broadly.

"How are ya?" Jack asks.

Thank God.

I have to think for a moment. Then: "Bothered as hell about getting old …and going bald," I tell him. "Look at this," I add, pointing to the emerging bald spot at the crown of my head. "Who am I…Friar Tuck?" I glance down at my stomach just to be sure my belly doesn't resemble Tuck's as well.

Jack's smile turns into laughter, and he glances around our table to see if anyone else heard me. "You're something else, Ethan," Jack says and elbows me in the arm. Then he cranes his neck and goes back to looking around the room. "I wonder if they hired any new tail."

"I don't know," I say. "I'm not in the loop anymore. Why couldn't 'The Bachelor' have been around when I was single? I just can't believe Kyle chose Amanda instead of Courtney."

"Just wondering," Jack says. He's single, and his eyes are now on the small groups of teachers, mostly women, entering the cafeteria at the other end. "Yeah, 'The Bachelor,'" Jack muses. "I'd be perfect for that show."

Gretchen Suchs (pronounced *sucks*) suddenly plops down next to me. I still can't believe she married a guy with that last name. Every year on the students' first day of school since she started teaching eight years ago, she has to warn them not to tease her about her last name. They are simply to call her Mrs. S. Today, Gretchen is looking even skinnier than last year, like she's double anorexic. This makes me nervous; I want to haul her to my grandmother's house and make her eat six plates of spaghetti and meatballs.

She says hi to Jack, frowns, and gently touches my forearm with her bony fingers. "Ethan, do you know yet what you're teaching?"

"I hope it's English, but I wouldn't be surprised if they," and I gesture towards the administrators standing at the front of the cafeteria, "have me teaching home economics. If they do, I'm bringing in my laundry, even my underwear, for the students to wash."

Like Jack, Gretchen smiles and playfully nudges my forearm again. Her elbow feels like a sharp stick. Eat donuts and French fries, I'm screaming at her inside my head. Milkshakes. Pizzas. McDonalds. Anything.

"I'm teaching 9th and 12th grade English again. I get 'em coming and going," Gretchen announces in her theater voice and then squints at me. "I was here yesterday and asked. Aren't you curious about what you're supposed to teach?"

9

"I am," I admit. "I've been teaching tenth grade for the last fifteen years. I hope I'm teaching it again. I'll find out after the opening session concludes." I don't say anything about my bald spot to Gretchen. She would be embarrassed.

For me.

"Ask him now, silly," Gretchen says. She pokes me with her elbow again.

"Ask whom?"

"That guy." Gretchen points to a short guy with glasses standing in the front of the room with the other administrators. "That's Ellis Morgan, the new assistant principal. He's the one who did the schedule."

So I follow Gretchen's recommendation, get up, and weave between three-person groups talking in the middle aisle to get to the front of the cafeteria. I introduce myself to Ellis Morgan, smile, and inquire about my class schedule.

He turns to face me, and his glasses slide a little down his nose. "Your name again?"

"Miller. Ethan Miller."

Morgan retrieves a large black binder from a nearby table, opens it, and skims through the pages. When he gets to my name he stops and lifts the binder for me to see what's on the page.

"Eighth grade?" I examine the paper in front of me again just to be sure. As I expected, I'm teaching four 10th grade classes and now two periods of 8th grade language arts. I keep my voice calm; I'm thinking maybe there's a mistake. "I prepared all summer to teach 10th grade again, and now you're telling me," and I point to the binder, "that I have to teach two eighth grade classes as well? I've *never* taught eighth grade."

"But you're certified to teach it," Mr. Morgan argues quietly. He looks up at me, his face unsympathetic, his eyes drifting back and forth from the binder to me.

I regret showing weakness here to a stranger, but I say, "This has to be fixed. I'm not ready to teach eighth grade. How can I prepare any lessons in one day?"

Mr. Morgan adjusts his glasses and squints again at the page. "I don't think I can change this."

I dig into a shallow reservoir of courage. "Mr. Morgan, is it *can't* or *won't*?"

He stares at me as if in disbelief. "We start tomorrow. How can I change the schedule now?"

Believe it or not, I'm still calm here. "I don't even know what textbook the eighth graders use."

Mr. Morgan glances at the crowd of people behind me and then at his fellow administrators who linger nearby. "It's probably in a classroom somewhere. I would tell you, but I'm new here." He shrugs his shoulders beneath his rumpled suit. "Can't you just have them write stories or something?"

"There's still time to change this, isn't there?" I'm thinking, we're educators, right? Professionals. We know how to do our jobs.

In response, Mr. Morgan glances at the other administrators again, hoping, it seems, for one of them to rescue him, and closes the binder. "I don't think so, Mr. Miller."

I take that as a cue to return to my seat, which I do, although I don't feel my legs moving beneath me. A to-do list grows in my head: Locate the 8th grade textbook, create a syllabus, talk to the other 8th grade teachers, design at least two weeks of lessons, research on-line for 8th grade themes, look up acne medications and hip-hop artists, pray Mr. Morgan changes the schedule.

I review in my head what I know about eighth graders: Massive drama, massive gossiping, massive teasing, massive texting. Get prepared, I tell myself. Don't let them breathe. This is your last year. Your victory lap.

"Well?" Gretchen asks when I sit down.

"Tenth grade and eighth grade," I mumble, kicking myself for thinking my last year would be easy.

Gretchen stays semi-optimistic. "It could be worse. They could make you teach seventh grade."

I look at her and grin. "Yeah. It could be worse."

Only the custodians are missing as we meet this Monday morning in the high school cafeteria – the teachers, secretaries, intervention specialists, aides, bus drivers, and administrators. The entire K-12 staff, over eighty of us, seat ourselves at these long, white, bomb-shelter hard tables that can be folded up into the walls at the end of the school day. My tabletop has been cleaned, but some long-ago student is reminding us in magic marker to "Fuck Bayview."

Most of my colleagues are dressed in shorts and t-shirts, and we contrast sharply with the administrators who are dressed in suits and ties, except for the new elementary school principal, a middle-aged woman who is dressed in a tan pants suit she must have bought in 1984 at a garage sale. She is smiling so much she is either trying too hard to be liked or never thoroughly researched our school system before accepting the job offer.

We are given a simple breakfast of watermelon cubes, stale muffins, and coffee, and I find myself comparing this spread to the meals provided in previous years on this opening staff day: eggs, bacon, ham, hash browns, juice, and coffee two years ago; a sausage casserole and French toast three years ago; four types of muffins, a fruit bowl, and croissants five years ago. My memory fades as I dump little squares of watermelon and a muffin onto my paper plate and return to my table where Jack is already munching away. I steal a glance at Gretchen and privately lament she has only coffee.

Around 8:30 A.M., our superintendent, Dr. Adrian Andrews, stands tall and welcomes us back, and after at least ten minutes of blah, blah, blah soon declares we will "dedicate ourselves to customer service." He never identifies, however, who exactly our customer is. The students? The parents? The Bayview residents?

Dr. Andrews became the superintendent after the previous superintendent was fired last year for charging the school district for the adult movies he watched in his hotel room when he attended a conference in Columbus and for taking office equipment like printer cartridges, a fax machine, and staplers and selling them on Craig's List. He was arrested but not charged after he paid back the school system and forfeited his administrator's license.

Dr. Andrews, in fact, is the fourth superintendent we have had in the past six years (the other ones were also fired or asked to resign). He's a tall, thin man who is always dressed formally in a fashionable suit and a bow tie – today his suit is dark grey – maybe the same suit he wears for his other job as a pastor at a church in downtown Cleveland. Therefore, I'm not surprised when he greets all of us, raises both arms to the ceiling, and asks God to bless the Bayview School District and to help the Board of Education find the money to repair the high school roof.

Today, Dr. Andrews tells us he is excited and grateful to be the superintendent of the Bayview School District. He reveals that he took an $8000 pay cut when he accepted the position and will make *only* $110,000 this year, a declaration, I think, that is supposed to make us admire his sacrifice.

Dr. Andrews inherits a school with problems: Last year, a parent filed a report to the Ohio Department of Education that several middle school teachers discriminated against her son and failed him because he liked to wear girls' clothes, including a bra, to school. That is, on those days when he came to school. He was absent about sixty days. There's even still an unresolved grievance from a female teacher who was denied the use of the bathroom next to the superintendent's office after Dr. Andrews used it once last year after her and choked on the smell.

Dr. Andrews shakes his head, as if ridding himself of a bad memory, and announces he will not allow past events to influence his future plans. What he actually tells us is, "I'm a forward looking person. You can't change the past. If you walk backwards, you'll run into something forward."

What?

He steps away from the portable podium at one end of the cafeteria, surveys the room, and attempts inspiration. "We are gonna work to get outta Academic Emergency; we are gonna get Excellent with Distinction. Rome wasn't built in a day." He is referring to the report card each school gets from the Ohio Department of Education that rates schools under five categories: Excellent with Distinction, Excellent, Effective, Continuous Improvement, Academic Watch, or Academic Emergency. These ratings are based on graduation rates, students' test scores, and student attendance. Last year there were only five other school districts in the entire state – all of them urban school districts – with lower ratings than the Bayview School District, so the superintendent's ambitious announcement causes some of my colleagues to exchange glances and roll their eyes. Does he really think, their eyes tell each other, that we can go from Academic Emergency to Excellent with Distinction?

"Our goal," Dr. Andrews continues, "is to make sure the little foxes are all in place. And if we work hard, we will celebrate hard."

His last statement makes some colleagues smile. When Dr. Andrews notices this response, he grins as well and explains the school board has promised him a $2500 bonus if we improve on the ODE school report card. "We are gonna get ourselves outa this mess. And if we make it," he proclaims, "I'm gonna use that twenty-five hundred dollars to celebrate with you all."

More smiles. Some people even clap. He really has our attention now. I start thinking how he might spend the $2500 on a celebration where all the teachers, secretaries, intervention specialists, aides, bus drivers, and even custodians – almost 90 people – are all invited. Another breakfast? A cold cut and potato salad luncheon? An evening party with a band and beverages? Can I bring my wife?

This has the possibility to be so much better than the way past administrators expressed their appreciation to us. We have received picture frames, monogrammed coffee mugs, monogrammed pens, monogrammed water bottles, stuffed animals, and other items I think I have either lost, thrown away, or given away. I try to keep listening to Dr. Andrews, but I'm thinking about the $2500 party. Maybe beer will be served. I want to email him that I like Bud Light.

Next, Dr. Andrews wants us to know the school system is in financial trouble. He makes us repeat after him: "We are B-R-O-K-E!"

So we do.

Letter by letter, we chant, "B-R-O-K-E."

"We have no money," Dr. Andrews insists. He almost yells this, and I sense he is trying to frighten us now.

No money? If there's no money, how will they pay us? What am I going to do then? How is my family going to get along without my paycheck? I try to exchange a glance with Jack and Gretchen, but Gretchen is staring glassy-eyed at Dr. Andrews and Jack is checking messages and tweets on his smartphone.

Dr. Andrews finishes with, "Bayview might be a small crumble in the water but we have to work together. I want to work with smart people around me so I can be smart. We all must work to accomplish customer service. The goal is to get Excellent with Distinction."

There is polite applause. The bleacher style cafeteria seat is getting very uncomfortable. I have tried leaning forward, stretching back, twisting left and right, but still the discomfort from the hard seat that does not have a back persists as now the president of the board of education approaches the podium. Our board president is Mrs. Gerta Zimmerman, a short, pleasant-looking, middle-aged woman whose bob haircut sways left and right as she ambles to the lectern. I had her son Gordon in class five years ago, a boy I had to penalize three times for plagiarizing his papers. After the third time, she approached me in tears during a conference held in the principal's office, begging me to give him another chance. I didn't, and, according to school policy, he failed.

"How was your summer, everyone?" she asks.

Well, there it is.

From Gerta Zimmerman.

Figures.

Several teachers generously mumble a "Good" or "Fine," and they even smile while I stifle a scream.

Mrs. Zimmerman is either being nosy or concerned – I can't tell which – when she says next, "I'm here because I just want to stay involved, to know what's going on. I wish I could be a fly on the wall in all your classrooms tomorrow when the kids come." She pauses and turns to Dr. Andrews and asks, "How many classrooms are there?"

Dr. Andrews doesn't say anything. He only raises his eyebrows and looks at her in response to the question, so Mrs. Zimmerman turns back to us and says, "Well, I wish I could be fifty flies to be in all the classrooms to see the wonderful job you all are doing...." And then, after realizing bus drivers are in the room, she adds, "And twenty more flies to be on all the buses to see how wonderful a job all the bus drivers are doing." She ends her disjointed, rambling presentation by raising a fist in the air and shouting, "Let's have a super great year!"

We applaud weakly but politely again to her cheerleader finish, and I almost anticipate a chorus of "Go, Fight, Win" will follow. Mrs. Zimmerman steps back from the podium and seems uncertain about what to do next: Sit down? Introduce the next speaker? Leave? She looks again at Dr. Andrews for help, and he rescues her by returning to the podium to tell us a representative of the Metlife Insurance Company will now speak to us. I am reminded of Mark Twain who said, "In the first place, God made idiots. That was for practice. Then he made school boards."

The day's irony continues: This is our first day back, a fresh start to another school year, and suddenly the Metlife representative distributes a funeral planning guide to all of us.

Death? My funeral? Plan for it now?

"Hey, check *her* out," Jack whispers to me.

The raven-haired, slender MetLife agent in a tight skirt also gives each of us a little, stuffed Snoopy, which I, in turn, decide to give to my wife later as a gift even though she will recognize immediately I received it at school today. The funeral planning guide is important, the pretty agent declares. She tells the story of a teacher who got divorced, re-married, forgot to change his beneficiary, and after he died, the ex-wife, not his current wife, received all his retirement funds and inheritance.

So there it is so far on our first staff day of the 2012-2013 school year: The school is in a financial crisis, the president of the school board wants to spy on us, and Metlife is cautioning us that death could be right around the corner. We've been warned.

And I have to teach 8th grade.

Dr. Andrews returns to podium and announces, "Before you leave the cafeteria this morning to go to your building meetings, pick up and sign this paper," and he points to a one-inch stack of papers on a cafeteria table near him. "It adds a moral clause to the contract."

"Moral clause?" Megan Cutler calls out from the other side of the cafeteria. Megan is an excellent biology teacher who also serves as our union president.

Dr. Andrews' eyes search for Megan, and he frowns when he finds her. "The board and I want this added," he declares. "We expect our staff to have high standards."

"But who defines what is moral and what isn't?" Megan demands. "What standards are you talking about?" She looks around the room and bunch of us nod our heads.

"C'mon, Megan," Dr. Andrews pleads. "We just don't want any Bayview staff members strippin' or doin' porno on the Internet. Don't you think that would set a bad example for our students?"

I glance at my colleagues, trying to imagine them naked. Then I think of my own hairy chest and legs. Both images make me grimace. I'd probably put dollars in their G-strings to have them put their clothes *back on*.

"Are you kidding?" Megan asks. We all know she's being rhetorical.

"Who here has the time to strip?"

"Weekends!" Dr. Andrews argues. "Weekends."

Megan frowns and waves a hand dismissively. "Let's talk later."

The meeting in the cafeteria ends, and we have a sixty-minute break before we need to report to the high school library on the second floor where the secondary school principal, Henry Compton, is scheduled to meet with us. As we exit, no one picks up the moral clause amendment paper.

MONDAY, AUGUST 20, 2013 P.M.

The Bayview High School building, where I have taught for 35 years, probably resembles many other school buildings in its size, structure, and smell. Built in 1962 it has two floors in an H-shaped format with one carpeted cross-over hallway; the other hallways have speckled-gray tile floors, lime green walls, and probably the same stale, anti-septic cleanser janitors have been using to clean floors and rooms for decades.

Even though several staff members have not arrived yet in the library, Henry Compton begins his meeting promptly at noon. Mr. Compton, a man with a friendly demeanor and dots of gray in his black hair, shouts his opening greeting, much like Robin Williams did as Adrian Cronauer in the movie "Good Morning, Vietnam." We hear a loud, "Good afternoon, Bayview!"

Twice.

That is because the first time we all did not respond with our own "Good afternoon" with enough enthusiasm. This is Henry Compton's second year at Bayview; he replaced a principal who was fired for dating a custodian and having sex with him in her office during school hours.

After our second good afternoon response satisfies him, Mr. Compton distributes a handout that reveals our students' state test scores from the last school year. He gives us a minute to examine the row of percentages and whether we met expectations or not in various categories and then asks us pointedly, "What does this mean?"

There's a pause and all I can feel is the cold air on my back coming from the air conditioners stuck in the windows of the library. In fact, I'm freezing. His question is like one I would ask my students: very open ended, involving higher order thinking skills. But my mind unfortunately isn't working on a higher order level because all I can mentally address is the fact, even on an eighty-eight degree day outside, I am chilled to the bone inside the library. I am grateful when one of my colleagues takes me off the hook and points out the categories where we did *not* meet expectations: math and science.

I hope no one objects as I get up and turn off one of the air conditioners. When I return to my seat, Mr. Compton is informing us we need word walls in our classrooms, that they are important to helping students succeed on state-mandated tests. Now that I don't have an arctic wind blowing at my back, I am ready to participate. I raise my hand and ask Mr. Compton, "What is the research that says word walls improve students' performance on the standardized tests?"

He blinks several times before he answers. "When students go from room to room," he finally says, "the repetition...the word becomes..., you know." He waves his hand around his head like he is lassoing a fly. "They learn the word."

I don't let him off the hook. "Do you mean, are we all supposed to post the same words? How does algorithm relate, let's say, to English?"

Mr. Compton looks at me for only a moment, his lips parted, his eyes blinking again, his forehead damp, before turning away and announcing to the wall above our eyesight, "Word walls, people. I want to see word walls."

Robert Ingersoll, a 19th century political leader, said, "It is a thousand times better to have common sense without education than to have education without common sense."

Mr. Compton next tries to address several staff members individually but cannot remember their names. He looks at Rebecca Leever, English teacher for the 11th grade, and stumbles before someone whispers her name to him. "Yes, yes, I know...Mrs. Leever." He laughs and then starts to introduce the new staff members, all intervention specialists, but gives up after the first one and just tells them to stand and introduce themselves. This isn't new. Mr. Compton often struggles to pronounce names so many colleagues' names get abbreviated. For example, to Henry Compton, Ander Klyszewski, who teaches sixth grade, is either Mr. Ander or Mr. K.

There are the usual cursory announcements about forms we need to fill out and turn in and the importance of standing at our doors when students exchange classes, but we spend the majority of time discussing school discipline. The discussion gets stuck when the staff cannot agree on whether students should be permitted to use headphones and cell phones in the hallways.

It's finally decided that electronic devices will not be allowed, and Mr. Compton points a finger at the ceiling and declares, "I will tell the students at the first assembly they will not be permitted to have their cell phones in the hallways. I will warn them there will be consequences. There will be no shortcuts about discipline at Bayview High School."

More eye rolling. Last year our Homecoming queen punched out another girl two days before the dance but still got her crown anyway.

Other teachers who have retired in recent years have told me that my final year of teaching will be easy. I have heard them say over and over, "You can do it standing on your head."

Let's see.

In the hallway after the afternoon meeting, as I head out to find an 8th grade textbook, I see Ernie Kelsey outside his science classroom. He is a young teacher and his thin face and over-sized t-shirt suggest he lost about twenty pounds over the summer. He starts grinning at me, as if reading my mind. "I don't even know how to respond to any of this," he admits. "Who is that guy in there? Why didn't Compton introduce him to us?" He gestures in the direction of Mr. Morgan's office.

"It's amazing," I say to him. "But pretty typical. You should know the version of Murphy's Law here at Bayview: If it's possible to screw it up, we certainly will. If it isn't broke here, we'll work on it until it is."

TUESDAY, AUGUST 21

The first day for students.

I believe in Gail Godwin's comment: "Good teaching is one-fourth preparation and three-fourths pure theatre."

I am in room 129, which must have been cleaned in July because cobwebs have already re-appeared along the windows and corners, and dust covers my computer and bookshelf.

I wonder how many students will arrive today with the confidence they can succeed in my class. In *any* of their classes actually. And what rumors about me have they heard? How will they respond to my opening day agenda and teaching style? Will they think I am one of the "cool" teachers?

Probably not.

It's the first day – the final first day of my last year of teaching. I have neatly written the key agenda items on my white board: my general expectations, the homework for tonight (obtain a notebook and folder), and directions for completing a personal information card. I am also ready to distribute the 1st Quarter Course Guide for each English class – except for the 8th graders – along with a grammar diagnostic. In short, today's first class resembles the first day opening I have done for the last twenty years.

Because it works.

Around 7:30 A.M. I offer cheerful greetings as I stand just outside my doorway and commend those students who arrive already with a notebook and folder. To some, I say, "Enter at your own risk," and I interpret their wrinkled foreheads and tight lips to mean they don't find my greeting to be either amusing or clever.

Inside, they see a decorative classroom with posters of a diverse group of authors like Twain, Wright, Steinbeck, Angelou, and Alcott on one bulletin board and a collage of interesting and unusual pictures – kids on a bus, a Japanese garden, the Grand Canyon – on another under the heading "Write about your World."

In short, I am ready to begin year thirty-five.

My first day lesson, in fact, is pretty typical: First, I explain my personal expectations:

Show up on time. Come prepared. Attendance is a key to academic success.

Bring your notebook and folder for each class.

Pay attention, especially when either a classmate or I talk.

Respect each other and me.

I distribute the first quarter syllabus and give them time to read the double-sided paper. Most do not bother with the reverse side but after I ask if they find it to be a helpful document, some nod while others look out the window. I have to remind myself that these students have never listened to Led Zeppelin or have seen anvils fall on Wiley Coyote.

Then I ask them what *they* expect of *me*. This brief brainstorming session produces some typical responses:

Don't give us homework.

Don't lecture.

Show movies.

Let us work in groups.

Let's read fun books, not boring ones.

Go on field trips to the mall.

On the first day I am also always interested in what students have heard about me: the rumors, the complaints, maybe any compliments (although these are very rare). In my first period class, Jenny Wilson, a pretty sophomore girl with caramel-colored skin, says, "I heard you're mean and stuck up."

I offer a good-natured chuckle in response.

But there is more: A sophomore boy asks, "Are you a robot?" The focused look on his face tells me he's not making a joke.

"No, not really," I tell him. "I'm an android."

"You look like you would be in a horror movie," says an 8th grade girl in my period 4 class, who smiles, but I am not certain this is a joke or a serious comment. "Yeah," says Czarina, another 8th grader with dark glasses and straight black hair framing her pale face. "You look like the guy who killed the girl in the movie 'The Lovely Bones.'"

I haven't seen the movie. "Really? Is he a good-looking guy?"

Czarina frowns and studies my face again. "No."

In the back of the room, another 8th grader, Austin, waves a hand. After I point to him he waves a piece of paper and asks, "Can you help me?"

This makes me feel important. I'm needed. "Sure, what's wrong?" I almost run down the aisle to his desk.

He examines the paper one more time and then hands it to me. "My schedule...I don't have a lunch period."

I take the paper and scan the column of his classes. Austin is correct. No lunch period appears on his schedule. "This is unusual," I tell him, and my doubts about Ellis Morgan's skill with scheduling deepen.

I hear, "I don't have lunch either" from three other 8th graders, and my feeling of self-importance disappears. I cannot help them and, lifting Austin's schedule to my chest as if this was a trial and I was holding key evidence, I say, "Take your schedules to Mr. Morgan immediately after this class."

In the lounge at lunchtime Julie Hanson, middle school intervention specialist, tells us she was orienting her six seventh grade students to the school that morning and when she showed them the computer lab, they witnessed two ninth graders naked on the floor having sexual intercourse. Julie tells us the boy, once he and his girlfriend were discovered, pushed the girl off of him, pulled up his pants, and ran shirtless out of the computer lab down the hall.

"I hadn't seen a penis like that since my German shepherd tried humping my leg," she adds.

Julie's seventh graders were so traumatized, many of them wanted to leave school, so she spent the rest of the morning trying to calm them down and calling their parent/guardians to inform them of what their child witnessed in the computer lab.

Some teachers are just frustrated. Art teacher, Melissa Fleck, discovered she has a schedule where she has to teach Art I, Art II, and Advanced Art during the same period. The new Spanish teacher – a woman who's new and whose name I can't pronounce – is teaching Spanish I, Spanish II, and Spanish III in the same classroom during the same period as well.

Directly after lunch in my block 5-8 class, as I hand out index cards, Devin Jones yells at another boy across the room, "You ain't no baller!" so I first try eye contact to quiet him down. Second, I remind the whole group about what they should be doing ("Fill out the personal information cards quietly"). "Dude, I'm buying me some Jordan's." Devin now yells. "You wait."

I approach his desk, lean down only slightly because he is so tall, I'm almost at eye-level with him, and whisper that I am counting on him to stay quiet while either a classmate or I am talking. I ask him to behave and to set a positive example for the other students. "Can you do that?" I ask him.

Devin dips his face toward his desk and nods, but after I return to the front of the classroom, he begins swiveling and gyrating at his desk, as if mimicking a dance. "Hey, ya'll," Devin calls out. "You see the new Usher video?" He stands and starts spinning with his arms in the air.

So I kick him out of the classroom, and at the doorway he calls back over his shoulder, "That's cool. I don't need to be in class. I know enough already."

Of course, I'm hoping my punishment of Devin will convince the other students to behave in class. It's the first day – I have to send a message. Right?

25

But it's possible my message is: Act like a jerk and you get to leave class.

I'm not worried about Devin being unsupervised in the hallway. There must be twenty or thirty students wandering back and forth out there because their schedules are messed up: They do not know which class to go to, so they don't go anywhere, choosing to wander the hallways or to hang out in the library or gym.

Even though the period isn't over, the bell rings. The bell rings, in fact, nearly forty times during the day because although we are on a new bell schedule for an eleven period day, neither the maintenance supervisor nor any administrator, I learn later, knows how to delete last year's eight period day computerized bell schedule and replace it with an eleven period format, so we get the sixteen bells from last year along with the twenty-three bells for this year (an additional bell rings five minutes after the school day has ended to remind students they should be out of the hallways).

I also learn nearly forty percent of the student population has screwed up schedules. One of my English 10 Honors students has two classes in the morning and not another one until my class at the end of the day; seniors are shoved into specials classes, like art, that they never signed up for; and many students have two classes during the same period. Students carry book bags full of supplies because they do not have lockers, and Mr. Compton revealed on the PA they would not have lockers for five days.

I check my emails at the end of the day, and there's one from Dr. Andrews: "Let me personally thank everyone for assisting in providing a smooth opening today. Please feel free to contact me via email with any concerns. Remember, Winners Never Quit, and Quitters Never Win!!! We are in it to WIN!!!"

Henry Compton also sends us an email that begins "Thanks for a GREAT start to a GREAT school year." This statement is followed by sixteen exclamation points. I counted. In addition, he wants us to laminate our daily schedules and post them outside on the left side of our doors. I respond to his email asking him where I can find a lamination machine. He immediately responds that there is a lamination machine at the elementary school, but it is broken. He recommends I "go to a place like Kinko's and get it laminated."

WEDNESDAY, AUGUST 22

The second day of school is always the first day for me to assign seats, so there's the typical grumbling: "Why do I got to sit in the front?" I follow this with a lesson on note-taking: the outline form, Cornell method, two column notes, bullet points. I send students to the board to demonstrate their note-taking methods while classmates watch and I critique: "That's it, Czarina. I like how you use capital letters to indicate main points."

Often – even on the second day – I step outside myself and examine my presence in the classroom. Are my students engaged or simply compliant? The truth is, we teachers never have absolute control over our students, even under the threat of punishment or what we professionally call "consequences." Speaking of consequences, I also preview my "classroom expectations." Five years ago, I called these "Classroom Rules" and twenty years ago it was simply "Discipline."

I inquire, "Did you know that in an 1850 one-room schoolhouse, the girls sat on one side, boys on the other? Only the teacher talked; the students stayed quiet and only read, wrote, or studied. Any violations resulted in students being hit by a switch." Of course, I have to explain what a switch is.

Then I ask my students if they have heard either of Emily Post or her rules of etiquette. No one has, so I challenge them with some etiquette questions: Does the lady's first rule still apply for teens? *Yes.* Should you arrive early for a friend's party? *No, either on time or no more than fifteen minutes late.* For a Homecoming Dance, do the restaurant reservations need to be made in the male's name? *No, either the boy or girl can make them.* They seem to get a kick out of this, and I sense they

28

are ready for my "rules."

Here they are:

1. **Arrive on time.** You must be inside the classroom and in your seat before the bell rings.

If you are tardy, you will receive a detention for the following day. **No warnings.**

2. The following items are **not** allowed in class: cell phones, any electronic devices, food, candy, brushes, combs, or cosmetics. **You get one warning.**

3. **Show respect!** Do not speak while others are speaking, interrupt others, curse, touch others or their property, or tease others. Keep your hands and feet to yourself. Rude and disrespectful behavior will not be tolerated.

4. **Talk only when permitted.** Raise your hand to participate.

5. Never toss paper, pens, pencils, or other objects in class. This is dangerous and a distraction and will not be tolerated.

6. Be attentive. Do not sleep in class.

7. The consequence for vandalizing any property that belongs to me, the school, or a classmate is you being responsible for replacing or paying for that property.

8. You are allowed to leave your seat to sharpen a pencil, throw away trash, get tissue, or use a resource (dictionary). Just do this quickly and without distracting others.

Expectations regarding Class Work

MY LAST YEAR OF LIFE (IN SCHOOL)

1. Complete all assignments on regulation (8"x11") sized, white paper folded no more than one time. **Never write on the backside of the paper**. This makes your work easier to evaluate. Any papers not complying will be returned and you risk receiving no credit.

2. **No late work is accepted.** All assignments are due by their due dates unless you make a prior arrangement with me.

3. If you are absent, you must see me for the make up work. You have the number of days missed to make up the work (i.e., two days missed, then two days allotted to make up the work).

4. Cheating or plagiarizing (copying homework, for example) on any assignment will result in an automatic failure for that assignment.

5. Keep **organized** in your folder all handouts I distribute to you in class. Your folder will be evaluated each quarter.

6. Copy the class objective that is on the white board immediately each day after you get to your seat.

Consequences for Violating any Classroom
Expectation or Expectations regarding Class Work

Students will face, but are not limited to, the following consequences:

1. Conference between teacher and student.

2. Teacher will call parent/guardian and inform them of your behavior and/or performance in the classroom.

3. Referral to assistant principal.

4. Removal from the class.

You are also expected to follow all the guidelines and rules as they are presented in the student handbook while in this class and in this course.

I realize that no matter what rules I put on paper, I need to reinforce them every day. During my first years of teaching, an older colleague advised me to embarrass students to make them behave. He was right; that worked, but now I regret doing it. That is not how I want students to remember me. Therefore, I refrain from embarrassment or sarcasm to control student behavior.

I make sure to cover emergency situations: the mandatory, once a month fire drills; our tornado and lockdown procedures; and my expectations when I am absent.

I show them where extra, road-kill pens and pencils are, the electric pencil sharpener, and my six foot tall, four-sided, twirling book rack full of fiction and nonfiction books. I even have one student sharpen a pencil so they can hear how loud it is and why I prefer they sharpen their pencils before class begins so we do not have the distraction.

We practice the way I distribute and collect papers – quietly and efficiently. This fails, however. They cannot help but talk to each other, to grab papers from their classmate's hand, and to ask questions immediately about something they read on the page before I can explain it to them all. So we try again with another handout, but the noise level is only slightly lower and complaints about snatching are repeated.

There is even show-n-tell today. I distribute an essay plagued by grammar errors, and after hearing their comments like, "This sucks" and "Who wrote this?" and "Was this written by a third grader?" I explain that substandard work is unacceptable in this class, that excellent work on papers and tests takes effort. Unfortunately, many students do not really know a strong work ethic, so I tell them how I determine when a student works hard:

Written work is thorough.

Homework is done on time.

He or she has read the whole book, not just part of it.

He or she asks questions in class and participates in all discussions.

I tell them if they work hard in both school and in their careers, they will be successful. "Yeah," a student chides from the back of the room, "my dad worked hard twenty years for his company, and they laid him off."

Except for that comment, everything seems positive. No one complains about the rules. I even ask if they find them to be fair and heads nod. They then stick these "Classroom Expectations" handouts in their folders and get ready for the next item on the agenda.

I demonstrate how they are to raise their hands – the elbow next to their ear – and then we practice, raising hands by doing "the wave" to the left and right in the classroom.

Class concludes with this: their first writing assignment.

How would you spend one million dollars?

This assignment always works. In the past, nearly every student turned it in the next day. I use it to get better acquainted with some aspects of their personal lives and to discern their writing skills at the beginning of the school year.

So ends my second day at Bayview High, and later at home I check my email, especially my Education Digest newsletters. I want to stay updated with the trends and dialogue associated with my profession, even if this means I have to sift through dozens of spam messages offering products to make my penis bigger.

Sipping a cold Pepsi at my desk at home, I check a NEA newsletter and read a *Baltimore Sun* report that Education Secretary Arne Duncan, speaking to about 800 Baltimore County English teachers, stated that "teachers should earn more and there should be more focus on educating the whole child." The *Sun* quotes Duncan saying, "You didn't go into teaching to get rich, but you shouldn't have to take a vow of poverty either. We desperately underpay educators in this country. We are losing so much talent, and I think the consequences of that are devastating."

FRiDAY, AUGUST 24

The day starts with sweat. Colleague Jennifer Stimson asks me to help her take textbooks from the book storage room to her classroom on the second floor. So I do. It takes me nine trips to lift a stack of eight McDougal Littel algebra textbooks each time, balance them against my chest, walk up the stairs, carry them down the hallway into her classroom, and finally dump them on her windowsill. I thought Jennifer would also carry some, but by the third journey back and forth I realize I am on my own.

Two male colleagues pass me and joke, "Hey, Ethan, are you getting your Pilates for the day?"

It takes me over twenty minutes to lift and transport those nine stacks of books, and I am sweaty and exhausted by the time I'm done. Jennifer, still seated at her desk in the corner of her brightly lit classroom thanks me without looking up.

I'm thirsty, but the water fountain near my classroom doesn't work. Its metal surface is desert dry. I'm not surprised. It didn't work last year either. The nearest working fountain is down by the gymnasium, but in fifteen minutes students will enter my classroom and I still have to write the academic objective and lecture notes on the white board.

I know my schedule. Ten minutes after ten A.M. – that's when I'll get a drink and use the bathroom. Ten after ten, I promise myself. Hang in there.

I start to write my learning activities on the white board and just as I begin listing the words protagonist and antagonist for my Honors class lesson, David Grasser (Mr. G), a short, balding social studies teacher of fifteen years who rarely shaves, interrupts me. He drops a box full of papers on my classroom floor, sticks his hands on his hips, and asks, "Is this yours?"

I put my black marker on the tray, stroll over, and examine the box's contents. "No."

He joins me in gazing at the box full of old papers and handouts, but his face is more perplexed than mine. "Are you sure?" He reaches down and lifts a single paper off the stack inside the box. It is a handout I distributed last year. "Isn't this yours?"

"Yes, but...." Now it makes sense to me: The box is full of paper from last year's paper recycling campaign, and David wants it out of his classroom. The paper in his hand is one I distributed last year and a student must have tossed it into the box. The rest are not. Nevertheless, I take the paper from David, drop it back in the box, and say, "I'll take care of this, David."

"Okay, great," he says. "I thought this was yours." He nods, satisfied, and leaves my classroom. I go back to the white board and make a mental note to dump the box in our recycling bin outside later in the day.

Checking my emails at home that evening I learn from my NEA newsletter that in Chicago, which has the third largest student population in the country, the Chicago Teachers Union (CTU) is threatening to strike. According to the *Chicago Tribune*, the deliberations between the two sides "remain far apart on teacher compensation, performance evaluations and job security."

I close out my emails and start work on new lesson plans for my 8th graders: We're going to explore the merits of space travel, debate the need for the government's expenditures to fund NASA, view some YouTube videos of the space station, write some for or against editorials, and read some science fiction. All in one week. I have until Sunday night to design these lesson plans, connect them to the Common Core standards, and construct meaningful assessments. In addition, I need to grade over 60 essays written by sophomores, explaining how they would spend one million dollars. I hope my wife has not made any weekend plans for us.

MONDAY, AUGUST 27

Rain falls heavily this morning. Which is fine. My grass needs watering and it cools off my classroom, which has neither air conditioning nor fans.

The faculty gets updated class rosters from Ellis Morgan in our mailboxes, but mine cannot be correct. At least a half-dozen of my English 10 students are listed in two different classes. Alas.

I linger as usual by the doorway to greet my students as they enter Room 129 for first period. I smile and look them in the face.

"Pull up your pants, Marcus. Dress code."

"Good morning, Charkita."

"Welcome aboard, Darren. I'm pleased you remembered to bring your notebook today." Then I lean toward him and whisper, "But you forgot to zip up, though."

Since today's lesson for my sophomores is about revising their one million dollar essays based on my markings and comments, I let them see how *my* former high school and college instructors graded my papers.

"Check these out," I say and distribute about eight different papers around the room, like it's show-and-tell.

The point?

See, I experienced the same thing as you. My teachers marked up my papers as well. This is what English teachers do.

My papers go up and down the aisles during my first period class, and students are relatively quiet until Marcus yells, "1976!"

I realize he has discovered a date on one of my papers. Marcus, like the rest of his classmates, has been trying to determine my actual age since the first day of school. Though I am actually 58, I told them on the first day I am 75.

"Were you born in 1976?" Marcus adds. "That makes you," he pauses, doing the math in his head, "that makes you like thirty-six. I *knew* you weren't seventy-five." He smiles broadly and fist bumps Jimmy who sits next to him.

I smile back at him and tell him that paper was from my college days. When I was, in fact, at Cleveland State University getting my Masters.

Marcus stares at the date on the paper and then at me. "Yeah, but that still only makes you around forty then."

For a moment I wonder about Marcus's grade in math and then direct students to open their writing portfolios and examine their essays on how they would spend one million dollars.

"What do you think," I ask, "about my markings and comments?"

Marcus nods his head. "You cool...I feel what you doin' here, Miller."

Tina is more critical. "You sure are picky."

"You're right," I tell her. "I am picky...but I hope I'm being helpful."

Tina sighs and nods her head.

Every class works on revising their papers, but this gets interrupted during the 5-8 block when Darrielle Thomas needs to see the nurse. After I tell her the nurse is not in her office today, Darrielle's eyes droop, and she sags at her desk, so I suggest she go to the main office instead. Ten minutes later a tall female security officer escorts Darrielle back to my classroom and, after Darrielle has returned to her seat, whispers to me at the door, "Darrielle gets all up into herself, so's she got to leave the classroom."

I can only look at the security lady. Probably too long because her eyes get all crinkly when she realizes I don't know what she means. Plus, I wish I knew her real name. All the students call her Mrs. T because she has these broad shoulders and wears a lot of gold jewelry around her neck inside her blue polo shirt that has SECURITY on the back. There is a rumor that she once made the practice squad of a WNBA team.

I still stand awkwardly at the door, distracted somewhat by the growing conversations behind me, but I'm curious now. I want to know more about Darrielle's condition. "What does that mean?" I ask.

Mrs. T glances over my shoulder, probably at Darrielle and says, "She gets all clasterphobia. I seen them types in prison. You should move her next to the window."

After Mrs. T leaves, I direct Darrielle to sit at a desk by the windows. She moves to her new desk, but her eyes continue to droop.

Although school has been in session for a week, Ebony Burrell arrives for the first time to my period 5-8 block. In fact, she's fifteen minutes tardy. Within minutes she calls out that she has to blow her nose. She leaves her seat, grabs a tissue from the box I have on top of a cabinet, walks into the hallway, and blows her nose. Even with the door closed, we still hear the foghorn sound in the classroom. Connor Reese, who sits closest to the door, is so amazed by this sound he jumps up. "Do you hear that?" he asks, laughing. "That's like a truck horn. That girl must have all kinds of snot in that nose." His eyes dart back and forth from Ebony outside the closed door to his classmates, who grin back at him, lean up, and try to peer through the door's window themselves. Connor laughs loudly when Ebony blows her nose again. His classmates join him. Revising the "How I Would Spend One Million Dollars" papers will have to wait.

"Okay, Connor, sit down," I demand. "Leave Ebony alone."

After she returns, Ebony then asks me over and over to go to the bathroom. It's like this: "Can I go to the bathroom?" Two second pause. "Can I go to the bathroom?" Three second pause. "Can I go to the bathroom?" Two second pause. "Can I go to the bathroom?" I keep telling her to be patient because I know this routine from her. I had her in class last year; this is her second year in English 10. Ebony, however, cannot be patient and walks out of the room without permission.

From my classroom phone I call the main office and inform the secretary that Ebony is wandering the hallways without a pass.

"What you want me to do about it?" the secretary asks bluntly.

"I guess to let security know."

"There ain't no security here for me to tell."

I pause. "Okay, never mind."

In my last class of the day, my English 10 Honors class, I begin class by pointing out that we will be investigating and discussing themes from Twain's famous novel, *The Adventures of Tom Sawyer*, one of the two novels they had to read over the summer. "With whom does Tom have the best relationship?" I ask brightly to begin a discussion.

Karl's hand is up halfway through my question, and I decide to reward his enthusiasm by calling on him. To be honest, even after I had finished asking the entire question, only two other students raised their hands.

"With his father Sid," Karl answers proudly.

"Sid is not Tom's father, Karl," I say.

Karl's face darkens. "Then who is he?" He thinks I'm teasing him.

"His brother."

"Then how come he's in the book if he's not his father?"

I do not answer him – in fact, I do not know how to answer him.

We do some roleplaying. I ask for volunteers to demonstrate how Tom and the stranger boy confront each other on the street. Tierra and Martin volunteer. They come to the front of the classroom and circle each other, raising their fists at times as if ready to fight.

Then students do some timed freewriting: I say, "Write a much as you can and as accurately as you can about the humor in the novel." I wander the aisles, peek over shoulders, and discover students struggling to fill in more than several lines of writing. No one writes about Tom and Joe playing with the tic during Sunday school or Tom's argument with the new boy on the street, and I begin to suspect many of them may hot have read the entire book. Next, I try debates:

Is Aunt Polly a good parent to Tom?

No hands go up.

Should Tom feel guilty about keeping quiet about the murder of Dr. Robinson? Why or why not?

Here again, most of the students simply look at each other or at me, as if waiting for the correct answer. I encourage them with, "There's no right or wrong to this. I only want to hear your own viewpoints."

Even with this encouragement, only two students, Tierra and Joe, a talkative, stocky boy whose father Jim teaches science on the second floor of Bayview High, respond. Both think Aunt Polly is a decent parent but too unaware of Tom's mischief. I originally planned to use a Socratic Seminar for this but any type of discussion would amount to possibly six or seven students out of 24 being able to comment cogently on the book. They were told yesterday to bring the novel to class, but only six students do today.

I try next to deal with the humor, the colloquialisms, and the characterization by re-reading some dialogue, but my lesson begins to crumble. Although I adopt, even exaggerate the Southern dialect as I talk, mimicking both Tom and Huck as they discuss forming a gang, I notice heads perched on hands, quiet conversations in the back of the room, and some students doodling in their notebooks.

These are my Honors' students?

My mind races for an activity to bring them back – another role-play? Another debate? Writing an epilogue? Even in year thirty-five, I am struggling with planning activities to fill an eighty-minute block.

I cut short my reading the dialogue between Tom and Huck and decide on a debate. "Is Tom a heroic character?" I ask.

Some students claim he is but they do not cite his appearance in court to save Muff Potter or his decision to take the blame for the ripped page in the teacher's book or his rescue of Becky Thatcher from the cave because – I feel almost certain of this now – they have not read that far into the novel. Tom is a hero, they believe, because he got the other boys to paint Aunt Polly's fence. That's it. There are few arguments against this, and I know what they are thinking: What else do we have to endure today before we can leave? I know – in fact, I knew this thirty years ago – that no teacher's lesson plan, regardless of its depth and diversity, is safe from student sabotage. For this day their answers to my open-ended questions are limited, and most cannot reference the novel because they did not bring it to class.

I spend the rest of the period trying to make the novel relevant by comparing Tom's teenage behavior to their own: Do his conflicts with Aunt Polly resemble the problems they might have with their own parent/guardians? Tom hates going to school and even pretends to be sick one day to stay home – Have you ever done that? Do you blame him for running away? Several students respond politely: Yes, they have arguments with their parents and would prefer to stay home from school, but no one has ever wanted actually to run away from home. I think we all feel grateful when the bell rings ending the day.

Will it be the same, I wonder, with *Fahrenheit 451*, the other novel they had to read over the summer? I make a note to remind them to bring Bradbury's novel to class by Thursday.

That night at home I help my son Christopher with *his* summer reading assignment for his Honors English 11 class at South High School. He asks me to edit the paper he has written about *Nineteen Minutes*, a Julie Picoult novel. I read the teacher's directions: She wants a five-paragraph essay with a catchy introduction, a summary conclusion, and a second paragraph that summarizes all the plot events in the novel.

How can an entire novel be summarized in one paragraph?

It takes me two hours to finish editing his paper. Christopher's organization is terrible; his sentences lame; his selected quotes off target. I fix it all. Yes, I know he should do his own work, but I cannot help myself. I am a skilled editor.

Christopher is asleep by the time I finish, so I leave the paper on the kitchen counter with a note that tells him to read the entire essay to be sure he can respond successfully to any questions the teacher might pose to him after she examines it.

It's midnight, but before I go to bed myself, I read my NEA newsletter on-line and discover that in Pennsylvania, "with a cut of almost $1 billion in education spending statewide, Pennsylvania school districts eliminated more than 14,000 positions through furloughs or by attrition - leaving the positions of retiring teachers unfilled, according to a survey released in May by the Pennsylvania Association of School Administrators and Pennsylvania Association of School Business Officials. With the cuts, 70 percent of districts increased class size."

The news is worse in Maryland.

At Perry Hall High School in Baltimore County, Maryland, according to the *Baltimore Sun* newspaper, on the first day of classes "a student shot in the cafeteria was left in critical condition and another student was taken into custody as the suspected gunman." The *Washington Post* reports that students in the cafeteria at first thought the sounds of gunfire were "entirely benign - someone opening a bag of chips or perhaps slamming a nearby door," adding, "the shooting turned the first day of classes at the county's largest high school, with almost 2,200 students, into a crime scene, with police helicopters whirring overhead, distraught parents trying to reach their children and students diving under cafeteria tables."

The shooter/suspect is a fifteen year old who was grabbed by a school counselor and pinned up against a vending machine but not before getting off two shots with a shotgun. According to the Associated Press, the boy's father admitted "his son had been bullied" and that is why he had done the shooting.

It's now way past midnight, and the rain continues to fall.

TUESDAY, AUGUST 28

At school during a morning "discipline" assembly for 9th and 10th graders in the gym, Henry Compton does not begin with a welcoming smile; instead his scowl suggests he's grim, almost upset, even before he says anything. This suspicion is confirmed when he points at a student in the stands, prompting the obligatory "Who me?" repeated over before the exact student Mr. Compton is pointing at is identified. When Derrick Simms, a pleasant young man with glasses, one of my Honors students, realizes *he's* that student, Mr. Compton orders him to move from the middle of the bleachers to the front row. The situation worsens when Derrick nearly trips on the way down, causing much laughter and a chorus of catcalls.

Mr. Compton's mood worsens. "I'm sick and tired of it already," he tells them. "All this back talking and bad behavior. And I told you I didn't want cell phones in the hallways or classrooms." He refers to the student handbook and its 36 rules, which were given to students as they entered the gym, which seems cavernous now with only 120 students in it. "It's on you!" he says. "You better know theeze rules." He then directs them to a rule in the handbook, which unfortunately does not have numbered pages, so he advises them to turn to the page that is "towards the middle, towards the back." As students hunt for some rule about electronic devices, at least a dozen students around me begin to lose their pages because the handbook has been stapled incorrectly. Paper falls onto the bleacher floorboards and stays there.

Martin, another one of my Honors students, keeps raising his hand. He is only about five foot four, skinny, always in good spirits, smiling. Mr. Compton ignores him and cautions the students, "You

43

need to find out what you need to do to graduate." Then he concludes by making them all say out loud several times our school motto: "Be prompt, be prepared, be polite." However, each time he changes the order and some students call out the wrong words. When he sees a husky ninth grader, who's dressed like he just finished raking leaves, not repeating the "Be prompt, be prepared, be polite" slogan, he calls him out, brings him to the gym floor, turns his back to the rest of the students, and says something to his face no one else can hear.

Phil Oster, our director of school security, is next. He's got an NFL linebacker appearance with a bald head, thick chest, and strong arms. He is big on conflict mediation, and, in truth, Phil has resolved a lot of students' issues before they escalated into a loud argument or a physical confrontation. I have heard his speech every year at an assembly like this one. "Let's keep it real," he says. "You are here to get an education. Raise your hand if you want to get suspended." Thankfully, no hands go up. "Dumb question, right?" He encourages them to talk to him if they have a problem, if they are being harassed or bullied, if they ever feel unsafe in the school.

I look around at the 120 9th and 10th graders in the bleachers, their faces blank, indifferent, or withdrawn, especially the quiet kids who sit at the top of the bleachers against the gym wall. These are the kids who do their homework and actually study for their tests. They get it about being prompt and prepared for class.

I worry about them: how they feel about this school and their place in it. I have discovered that many A students unfortunately hide their achievement from classmates. They are embarrassed about their academic success when the norm seems to be to accept being mediocre, even a failure, if that is the trend. Why go against the crowd? The way to popularity, it seems, is to make a C your top grade.

Mr. Compton keeps looking at the gym's open doorway because Assistant Principal Morgan is supposed to be the next speaker, but he never shows up.

The assembly ends, and I eavesdrop on students' conversations as they exit the gym because I'm wondering if they truly listened to Mr. Compton. What do they remember about what he said? Did they find Phil Oster's advice to be helpful? Will they actually read the handbook?

They are not talking about any of that. Most of them are asking to borrow the math homework or to get some gum or to "text me later." I look back and see the empty bleachers are littered with the "rules" handbooks.

That night I finish assessing my English 10 Honors' students' tests on their summer reading and then enjoy hearing my son Christopher say that he thinks about me sometimes during his math class at South High School because his teacher shares my corny sense of humor. I like hearing this, and I begin thinking about my colleagues at Bayview High and how I could brighten a fellow teacher's day with an amusing email or words of encouragement. I know this would be a positive and worthwhile action – for both of us, so I make this a goal for tomorrow.

WEDNESDAY, AUGUST 29

Sipping on my morning tea, I read an interesting article in the Cleveland *Plain Dealer* today that tells a story about the Cleveland Municipal School District CEO Eric Gordon who had to call a parent and apologize "for instructing her young child to report to a hole in the ground instead of an actual school. As it turns out, Shanesha King was originally informed that her six-year-old son Eugene should report to Almira Elementary School almost four miles from their home. The two major problems for Ms. King and Eugene were that, one, they were told school began on Wednesday, almost a week before the actual start time for kindergarten, and, two, the school building had been demolished two years ago." The news reporter, Phillip Morris, wrote, "Maybe this sort of bureaucratic debacle and incompetence is another reason why so many of our children are being left behind."

A student who has shown no real concern for her grade even though the school year is just over a week old is Ebony Burrell. Remember her? She is the large sophomore girl who needs to blow her nose in the hallway instead of the classroom because it sounds like a train engine. She cannot just chuckle at a joke; her laugh is nearly a scream. She wants to talk and call out and socialize during class regardless of who else is speaking. Whatever or whoever meets her disapproval is "retarded."

When she disrespects my orders to be quiet today in class and announces my handout is retarded, I kick her out. I worry that there will be many days like this. I tell her to go into the cafeteria across the hall, but in truth I do not care where she goes. I just want her out of my classroom. Later, during my lunch period, I call her mother and

46

leave a message on her cell phone: Ebony's behavior is disrespectful, she comes late to class, she cannot stay quiet, she teases classmates, she is rude to me.

I've got my 8th graders working on the vocabulary related to the science fiction story "Each an Explorer" by Isaac Asimov: words like desolate, navigation, telepathic, and spores. I can show them pictures of a desert, a brain, and a dandelion. And I'm pleased when they seem to enjoy reading about the astronauts Chouns and Smith.

At Bayview High we have our weekly Professional Learning Community (PLC) meeting where students are dismissed early and all the teachers meet in the library at the close of the school day to discuss and plan academic programs. This meeting, however, ends up being about the overall schedule, which is still screwed up after a week, because outspoken 8th grade science teacher Allison Means waves her hand as if signaling a hot dog vendor at a baseball stadium and calls out, "I'm sorry, but I have to bring up the pink elephant in the room...this new schedule. It isn't working."

Henry Compton stops passing out a paper that has the title Moral Clause at its top and one sentence on it: "While I am an employee of the Bayview School District, I will behave in a moral way." Beneath the sentence is one line for a signature and another for the date. He stands straight and looks at Allison. "What's wrong with it?"

Allison's voice is sharp. "Why did we switch from an eight period day? This eleven period schedule is screwed up."

The rest of us learn that 8th grade math teacher Tom Black has 39 students in his class but only 32 desks. Since seven students have to stand, he rotates them each day so different students are standing on different days. Allison has 42 students in her 8th grade science class so some have to sit on the windowsill. Suzanne Smith claims she is doing a disservice to the 40 students in her 8th grade social studies classroom. "I'm doing the best I can," she exclaims, "but I know parents will be upset with me because I'm not helping their child. I agree with Allison. This schedule has to be fixed. I don't care how, I just want it fixed."

Cindy Greenlee, a seventh grade language arts teacher, stands and holds back her tears. "This is so wrong, so wrong," she chokes out. "I have forty kids in one period and ten in another. How does that happen? How does that happen?" She remains standing, hoping for a response but when Mr. Compton only shuffles the papers in his hand she slumps back onto her seat.

Mr. Compton wags a finger at us. "Let's be professional," he orders. Nothing more is said about the schedule, and I'm surprised when Allison gives up, too.

Next, Mr. Compton wants us to know the fire alarm is not working. The system is, in fact, so old the company who installed it has gone out of business and the parts to repair the fire alarm system cannot be found. We are not to worry though. They are paying a night custodian overtime to be on daytime "Fire watch." In short, he is being paid to just walk (sorry, I split the infinitive) the hallways and to call out fire if, in fact, we have one.

We're reminded to turn in forms, including the Moral Clause one, to his secretary. The meeting ends without any plan to fixing the schedule. As I walk out, I overhear Mr. Compton say to Mr. Morgan, "Why do they keep talking about this?" Mr. Morgan only shrugs in response.

Teachers at Perry Hall High School in Baltimore County, Maryland would find our problems trivial. At the end of the day I read on-line that the *Baltimore Sun* today reports "Robert Wayne Gladden Jr. has been charged as an adult with attempted murder in the shooting Monday at Perry Hall High School that resulted in the wounding of another student." Gladden is a withdrawn kid who had been bullied, and his attorney says, "The bullying his client endured pushed him to a breaking point." One witness said, "Some kids were throwing food at Gladden in the cafeteria - and not for the first time."

Allegedly, on the morning of the shooting, Gladden updated his Facebook status hinting that it would be "the last day of my life." His victim, Daniel Borowy, is still in critical condition. Gladden's attorney says that Gladden "brought the shotgun to school to intimidate bullies and did not aim it at classmates or intend to harm anyone."

Thirty-five years of teaching, and I guess I have been fortunate never to have confronted a student with a gun, although in past years some students have brought them to school.

I close up my laptop and think back to my first year of teaching: one of my morning junior English classes when a shaggy-haired boy named Troy, who always wore a sleeveless denim jacket with a hooded sweatshirt underneath even on warm days, came storming into class. He was failing my class because he never showed up with anything but that denim jacket and his bare hands, which he used that day to throw a chair across the room at the far wall. I took him to the office where a lenient guidance counselor convinced me to give him a break. Troy, the counselor quietly informed me, was having "problems at home."

And that's when I remember that I was going to send an encouraging email or note to a colleague. Allison – along with Tom, Suzanne, and Cindy – certainly needs one.

THURSDAY, AUGUST 30

This morning I read in the newspaper that the Associated Press reports, "South Dakota students are used to extreme cold and having classes called off because of winter blizzards, but the weather that caused their school day to be cut short Wednesday was intense for a different reason: the triple-digit temperatures." Dozens of districts closed schools, according to the state superintendent, for "the safety and welfare of students and staff members. It's tough to learn in an environment when a room is 100 degrees."

Today, however, school is definitely in session at Bayview. There's a stifling blue sky, the temperature outside is in the mid-eighties, and a humid breeze drifts in through the open windows of my classroom, making it feel like it's over ninety degrees – typical August weather here in northeastern Ohio – and foreshadowing the struggle I expect to have all day trying to quiet complaints from over-heated students. I even wish for a moment I worked in South Dakota.

The day begins with a 7:30 A.M. emergency staff meeting in the library. After we all have settled into the hard wooden seats, Henry Compton thanks us seventeen times (I count) to express his gratitude for our patience and hard work during these first two weeks of school. I check my colleagues and no one is listening to him. Nevertheless, Mr. Compton's face is all smiles and blinking eyes as he speaks, and when the florescent light glints off the new specks of gray in his black hair I have a brief pang of sympathy for him. The truth is my colleagues are still pissed off at him and Ellis Morgan for the messed up schedule, which has affected 7th and 8th grade classes especially.

"No bells today," Mr. Compton announces next. "We will exchange classes without any bells from now on." He even hops a little, like an evangelical preacher, and points at the clock on the wall as if the bell originated from there. Clearly, this news makes him very proud. He wags a finger at us and adds, "This is not an experiment."

To be sure, the bells have been an issue. For the first two weeks the bell to begin and end classes rang over forty times for an eleven period day because no administrator could figure out how to delete last year's computerized bell schedule for an eight period day.

I want to ask Mr. Compton if he is certain every classroom clock is synchronized so that all teachers dismiss students at the same time, how we are to determine tardies, whether he fixed the problem of the exchange time between periods 9 and 10 (Period 9 ends at 12:53 and period 10 also begins at 12:53). My inner voice nudges me: "Go ahead and ask. So what if you embarrass the principal and assistant principal? What can they do to you now?"

But I chicken out and stay quiet. It's your last year, I tell myself. You're retiring in nine months. This time my inner voice gets practical: *What difference would it make, Ethan? Better to stay keep your mouth shut to make the meeting end sooner.* Still, I feel the shame grow hot on the skin of my face.

Social studies teacher Suzanne Smith doesn't care when the meeting ends or whom she offends. From behind me, she bursts out, "Another 'experiment'? What about the experiment with the new schedule? I've got thirty-eight seventh graders one period and then forty eighth graders the next period in a classroom that has only thirty desks." She takes a breath. "Where am I supposed to put them? Huh?"

The superintendent, Dr. Andrews, dressed today in a white shirt, plaid bow tie, and a black suit, suddenly enters the library and hears Suzanne's complaint. He quickly exchanges glances with Mr. Compton and Mr. Morgan, who suddenly finds something interesting on the top of his shoes. Although Mr. Morgan constructed the schedule, Dr. Andrews steps in front of Mr. Compton and takes charge of the meeting. "It's dazzle, not us," he tells Suzanne. He's referencing DASL

[Data Analysis for Student Learning], the scheduling program we have been using to assign teachers their periods and students their classes. He then uses the word "rectify" at least a dozen times as in, "We plan to rectify the problem with the schedule as soon as possible."

"When?" Suzanne almost screams. I can tell she's near tears, and there is a wave of murmuring at tables in the back of the library. Then, hoping for encouragement or at least some nods of sympathy, Suzanne looks left and right at the other middle school teachers sitting at her table, but her fellow colleagues keep their eyes on the table or the wall. They've accepted defeat. Their dropped faces are silently telling her you can't beat city hall.

Standing in front of Mr. Compton, Dr. Andrews looks even taller than his six feet four inches. His eyes take in the whole room. "I admit we are experiencing some glitches, but we've got to keep these problems in-house." Translation: *Do not reveal any of our problems to community members or parents.*

"But what's being done to resolve the scheduling problems?" This comes from Allison Means, who never stays quiet.

Dr. Andrews nearly yells his response: "Do you think we sit behind our desks twiddling our thumbs? We're not, you know. We're working on this every day. I only took a thirty-minute lunch yesterday." He exhales loudly, as if demonstrating his exhaustion. "The computer...the system will not allow us to re-enter the schedules. It's DASL. We can't figure out how to enter the wheel. It just won't work."

Only a thirty-minute lunch? This guy is really suffering. Plus, I don't know what he means by "the wheel" and almost tune out when suddenly Suzanne calls out again, "Not good enough!" She stands and waves her arms. Now she *is* crying. Her eyes are wet, and she's sniffling, and Kathy, the librarian who we now call a media specialist, walks over and gives her some tissues. Suzanne takes them, slouches in her seat, and receives a soft pat on the back from Julie Hanson sitting next to her. I'm worried about Suzanne, but I get distracted by Kathy, who decides now to deliver a whole box of tissues to Suzanne. I can't help wondering when during my last thirty-five years of teaching we started calling librarians media specialists.

Allison Means senses momentum building and jumps in again. Allison is the kind of teacher who tells students, "Keep your hands where I can see them." Unlike my long list of rules, she has only three: Be on time, Clean yourselves, Don't dress like a slut.

Allison reaches her hands above her head. "My stress level is here," she exclaims, referring to the location of her hands a foot above her head. "My stress level is so high my heart is beating out of my chest. I feel like I could have a heart attack right now. This is going to affect my attendance!"

Mr. Morgan, standing behind the superintendent, for some reason grins at this and turns and tries to share his smirk with Mr. Compton who ignores him.

Meanwhile, Dr. Andrews turns on Allison. The veins in his neck push against his stiff white collar, which, in turn, makes his bow tie thrust out a little. "Are you saying you are not going to come to work because of the schedule?"

"No," Allison declares. "I'm saying my stress level is up to here." She lifts her hand again over her head. "I'm trying to teach science to thirty-nine eighth graders without any lab equipment in a room with no sink, no tables, and only twenty-eight desks. It's frustrating!"

But Dr. Andrews wants to argue. He asks her again, "Are you saying you are going to stay home because of the schedule."

Allison does not respond. It only took a few minutes, but Allison gives up, too. "No, I'm not saying that." She drops her hands, dips her head, and settles back in her seat.

Lisa is the thin, anemic-looking, new substitute Spanish teacher, who was hired after the first Spanish teacher quit because of the stressful workload. Megan Cutler, who sat in on the interview, told us later that Lisa was hired because she spent a week in Mexico last summer. Today, Lisa gestures timidly with a pale hand to get Dr. Andrew's attention. After he grudgingly acknowledges her, she points out she has students taking Spanish 1, Spanish 2, and Spanish 3 all during the same period in the same classroom. "How am I supposed to teach them all?" she asks.

Dr. Andrews glares at her. "Who are you?"

"Lisa Sturm," she answers. "Spanish."

Mr. Compton whispers in Dr. Andrews' ear and then pulls away from him. Dr. Andrews nods his head and turns on Lisa: "You are only a substitute teacher here. You don't know the dynamics of the Bayview Schools. Don't you know you have to differentiate?"

Lisa goes quiet and focuses her eyes, as many others are doing, on the tabletop.

My face has cooled – maybe it's the air conditioning – and my inner voice has finished chastising me for wimping out before. I raise my hand and use some of my courage.

Dr. Andrews points at me. "Yes, Mr. Miller."

I look past him to Mr. Morgan, who is in charge of the schedule, "I have read in your emails, Mr. Morgan, that we are your *partners* in education, and if that is true, how can we partner with you to help you fix this schedule?"

He does not answer. Instead, his shoelaces get his attention again.

I don't let him off the hook. "*Can* you fix this schedule? Can it be revised so my colleagues don't continue to have these problems?"

Mr. Morgan looks up: "You all will have the same schedule you have now. I am just trying to figure out the wheel. You know, no one told me about the wheel when I took this job." And he does not talk the rest of the meeting.

I still don't know what *the wheel* is.

Suzanne tries one more time: She points out that we have the long Labor Day weekend ahead and recommends, almost demands, that the schedule be fixed by Tuesday.

"Don't you mandate me to do anything," Dr. Andrews tells her, raising an index finger to the ceiling. He stares at Suzanne until someone points to the hallway where students are passing left and right and announces that students are going unsupervised into our classrooms. This makes the meeting break up, and we all file out of the room and hustle to our classrooms. I decide right then to talk to Allison later.

Later, as my last class – my English 10 Honors class – begins, I focus on Larry Scott, a tall, quiet young man, who like many others, did not do the summer reading. The lack of check marks in my grade book next to his name indicates he has hardly participated since the school year began. Even worse, his mind wanders in class. ADD? I often have to repeat directions to him and use cues to keep him focused. Over a week ago I gave him the novel *Fahrenheit 451* so he could read it and improve on the F he got on the first test. He had not done his summer reading because he never got the book.

Today, when I see he does not have the book in class after being told to bring it, I ask why.

"I don't know," he says and looks out the window.

I join him in looking out the window at the lawn of the house across the street – more specifically, at the huge oak tree whose wide branches put nearly the entire front yard in shadows. I wonder, in fact, if Larry notices that, too. Behind me, the other students are waiting.

So I stroll back to the white board and point out the objective for the lesson, which reveals our goal to identify the themes and motifs in *Fahrenheit 451*. Teachers need to post academic standards and then assess students to see if the objective has been achieved.

I direct the students to freewrite on selected characters from the novel, and minutes later, Larry is still trying to find a pen or pencil. I give him a pen from my pocket and a couple more minutes go by before he can finally locate paper he hasn't doodled on. It takes him even more time to write a single sentence.

I ask students to debate the value of books (channeling Captain Beatty from the novel). Larry has stopped writing to spin my pen on his desktop. I move to stand in front of his desk, which is in the first row, stop the spinning pen, and ask him to repeat a classmate's comments about Captain Beatty. His eyes widen. "I didn't raise my hand."

"I know, Larry. I'm just calling on you because I'm interested in hearing what you think about Captain Beatty." I'm encouraging active listening. Larry has been a passive listener – if he has been listening at all – for too long.

He crosses his arms over his chest and says, "I didn't say anything."

"I know you didn't. I'm asking you to tell us your reactions to what *David* said."

"Who?'

I point to a boy two seats away from him. "David. I know you haven't read the whole book yet, but I think you could comment on what David has said about Captain Beatty."

"Who?"

"Captain Beatty...What did David say about him?"

His eyes widen again. "Which one is that?"

I resent myself here for giving up, but I stop probing Larry with questions and allow him to drift away from us. Indeed, when I call on Chris to repeat David's characterization of Beatty, Larry returns to staring out the window. I make a mental note to talk to Larry after class, and then I feel guilty when I forget to do this after the students leave for the day.

The school day over, I rush to Mr. Morgan's upstairs office and request a moment of his time to explain that Larry Scott is struggling in English 10 Honors, that the work, especially in writing, could overwhelm him. Mr. Morgan does not understand why I am concerned about this. Larry, it seems, is also in Honors Biology and Honors Geometry.

"But I'm concerned he might struggle with the material in *my* class," I repeat.

"Well, he's taking two other Honors classes." He shows me his schedule as if I might doubt this.

"Nevertheless," I try again, "I'm not certain he should be in this class. He originally was on my regular English 10 class roster anyway."

"He's taking Honors' classes in science and math," Mr. Morgan repeats, his eyes on the computer screen. "I don't think I can move him back."

I realize now Larry is staying in English 10 Honors. Ten years ago this problem would have been corrected immediately. Today, however, both Larry and I will have to make some adjustments.

I leave Morgan's office, walk down the tiled hallway to the other end of the school, and sneak into the nurse's office. I know she will be gone, and I am there to steal Band-Aids. I do not feel guilty about this. I need them because I dread those moments in class when a student asks and I do not have one. What typically follows are tormented pleas to go to the nurse, to go to the office, to call mommy or grandma about the little nick in their finger. Band-Aids are like gold in a school.

FRIDAY, AUGUST 31

Friday. Blue and white day. Mr. Compton, who told us to wear blue and white each Friday to demonstrate our school spirit, shows up in a dark suit. Only his shirt is white.

I am dressed in tan khaki pants and a royal blue coaching shirt from my days as a wrestling coach. Most of the faculty, in fact, has blue shirts on. An exception is Rebecca Leever, a 11th grade English teacher, who is wearing a white blouse, a short black jacket, and a red skirt. When I tease her about not wearing blue and white, she tells me, "No one is going to tell me what to wear."

During the exchange of classes, I stand at my doorway and watch students walk by me left and right. When she passes me this morning in the hallway heading to another class, I smile and tell Ebony Burrell, "You're going to have a great day today."

"Yeah, maybe," she responds sullenly and quickens her pace down the hallway.

In my 5-8 block class with Ebony, I distribute a model essay on class clowns. I explain that it was written by a student at a school where I used to teach.

"I wish you still did," says Ebony out loud.

Gene Simmons of Kiss is a former sixth grade teacher. He says that performing either as a teacher or a musician puts one in the spotlight. "In one you are in front of an audience who may not want to be there. In the other, you're in front of an audience who worships at your feet."

I never get a chance to meet with Allison Means. She's absent today.

Tonight I find out from my son Christopher that he got a 90% on his Picoult paper. Ten percent was deducted for grammar errors (run on sentences). I edited that paper; I know there are no run on sentences. But what can I say to the teacher? I would have to admit my participation in writing his paper.

I watch the late night news and learn that the Chicago teachers are getting closer to going on strike. The anchor person makes the point that 11,000 Chicago public school athletes would suffer the most from the strike because "no classes at CPS schools means no organized practice or games for fall sports teams, according to IHSA rules. Besides, 90 percent of CPS coaches also are CTU members so effectively they would be crossing the picket line if they attended any informal practices players have planned."

I have walked a picket line twice in my life. The first time was with my brother and a hundred other Northwestern University students protesting the Vietnam War in 1970 and the second time was when my colleagues and I went on strike on May 2, 2007. After my union leaders announced the strike, I arrived the next day at 5:30 A.M. at Strike Headquarters, ready to do my part.

Why? Because crossing the line was *not* an option and we teachers needed to stand-up to a superintendent who at the time wanted to eliminate our right to file any grievance. Negotiations had dragged on for ten months, so my union followed through with our threat to strike and on May 2nd we began picketing at school entrances. We had heard rumors that the superintendent had already received authorization weeks ago from the school board to hire replacement personnel and uniformed security.

Even before our vote to strike even took place, union president Megan Cutler requested that several of us come to school one Sunday morning in late April to verify a rumor that replacement teachers were being hired. About seven of us arrived at the school and found a sun-splashed parking lot full of cars, which signaled that people, indeed, were inside interviewing for our jobs.

When I saw one well-dressed woman leave her car and walk to the school building, I called out to her: "You know, you are taking a job away from a family man."

"Yeah?" she barely glanced at me. "Well, this is $175 a day for someone who doesn't have a job." Then she continued into the building.

When teachers go on strike, complaints against us intensify. To the community in general, whether it is Chicago or little Bayview, a strike to them means the teachers must not really care about the students. The public's viewpoint is that if we were truly concerned about our students, we would never abandon them like that. When the Bayview teachers went on strike in 2007, a belligerent parent asked me, "What message are you sending?"

"Integrity," I answered, looking directly into her eyes. "I'm living up to my word. That's the message I'm sending to my students. If you say you are going to do something, then do it. If I didn't, then how could I teach them? I want them to see I am a man of my word."

Three weeks later, after I nearly received a $150 ticket for public disturbance (I was carrying my picket sign across an intersection) and a colleague was arrested for crossing the school driveway with his picket sign on his way to use the bathroom at the nearby City Hall (he did not know the police had decided to arrest anyone crossing the entrance), I decided I had had enough.

Without telling Megan Cutler, I phoned Darnell Cook, a school board member I knew personally, and explained that I was calling on my own to see if we could meet. Later that evening, as we sat at his kitchen table and drank Pepsis, we lamented over the length of the strike, the replacement teachers in the school, and the lack of progress with negotiations. He mentioned his son, whom I had taught years ago, and we reminisced about his high school basketball games. Our common ground reminded both of us of how we — and not the superintendent —were connected personally to the school and the community.

From his leather briefcase, Darnell produced a copy of the original contract and a copy of the superintendent's proposals. "Let's see if we can make sense of this," he said, looking at the collection of papers on his table.

Darnell asked what objections the union had to the superintendent's contract; his tone was curious and low key, as if we were discussing the best pitchers in the major leagues. He listened and scribbled notes on the superintendent's proposed contract - once writing "NO" next to the clause "eliminate any teachers' right to file a grievance."

By 10:45 we had discussed each item in question on the master contract and the superintendent's proposals. Darnell promised to speak with the two other board members who were not part of the superintendent's negotiation team. A weekend passed and on Monday, Darnell and the other board members showed up on the picket line to inform us that the superintendent agreed to delete his proposals and bring us back into our classrooms. On May 28th, nearly four weeks after our strike began, Megan signed a new contract for us. Ten months of negotiations, almost four weeks of picketing, and one arrest did not achieve what Darnell and I settled in one evening at a kitchen table.

And one month later, the members of the Bayview Board of Education voted 4-1 in favor of firing the superintendent.

WEDNESDAY, SEPTEMBER 5

I probably should be angry, but I'm more surprised as water slides down my back, tickling my skin. *Why is my neck wet? Is the roof leaking again?*

Some of my 8th graders laugh as I wipe the back of my neck with a handkerchief, turn from the Smart Board, and look up at the checkered ceiling tiles to check if, in fact, water is dripping from somewhere. *But there hasn't been any rain.* The laughter continues, and now I cannot stop the slow wave of embarrassment that is making my face get warm and my eyes narrow. *Why are they laughing at me? If not drips from the ceiling, then what?*

This is a prank, I conclude, and quickly take my eyes off the ceiling to scan my classroom of 8th graders. Fortunately, I'm in time to see wide-eyed and ashen-faced Dylan, sitting in the second row and still holding the stubby, green, plastic squirt gun. *A squirt gun? In class?*

Getting shot by a squirt gun in the classroom has never happened to me before. I don't even have a **No squirt guns** on my list of classroom rules. Nevertheless, I walk slowly to Dylan's desk, extend my hand to him, palm up, and say in my low teacher's voice, "Give that to me."

I'm anticipating an apology; instead, Dylan pleads, "Will I get it back?"

I ignore the other students' snickering and extend my hand, still palm up, again at his face. I straighten my posture. I keep my tone and demeanor formal, like I was preparing to salute an air force general. "Just give it to me," I repeat.

Dylan hands me the plastic squirt gun. "But will I get it back?"

"I don't know," I tell him.

His voice is whining. "I wasn't aiming at you."

"That doesn't matter." I turn my back on Dylan and walk to my desk with the squirt gun and, holding it now, I sense it is half-filled with water. *Who else did he squirt?* I open my top desk drawer and pull out a discipline referral. I will have to write an explanation of Dylan's misbehavior – the squirt gun – and turn it in to Mr. Compton. I will have to call Dylan's parent during my lunch break. I will have to remember never to turn my back on an 8th grade class again, even to use the Smart Board.

Dylan sees me with the referral form. "Ahh, c'mon, Mr. Miller...I won't do it again."

I turn from my desk and face him. "Why would you even bring a squirt gun to school?" The question slips out before I can take it back. For a moment I forget the futility of reasoning with an 8th grader.

Dylan gives me the appropriate 8th grade answer: "I don't know."

I put the squirt gun inside my desk drawer and return in the same slow walk to the front of the classroom. "Let's get back to learning how to use transitions in our writing," I say and give them "the look." You probably know what I mean by "the look": pursed lips, narrowed eyes, clenched cheeks. It seems to work because they return to their notebooks and continue writing sentences using words like therefore, furthermore, and however.

Later, in my last period of the day, my English 10 Honors class, as his classmates silently read "There will come soft rains," a short story by Ray Bradbury, I work one-on-one with Larry Scott to help him understand *Fahrenheit 451.* I have prepared some key questions for him to discuss with me, a jumble of eight plot events for him to arrange in the correct sequence, and a half-dozen illustrations, drawn for me by my artistic wife the previous weekend. Her drawings depict scenes and characters from the novel for Larry to identify – for example, the electronic dog on a city street, Captain Beatty arguing with Montag, Montag's house burning down, and three others.

I start with the illustrations. "Larry, what scene is this in the novel?" I place on his desktop the illustration of Montag scorching his own house.

Larry examines the drawing for a moment and then looks up at me. "It's a fire."

"Exactly, but of all the fires in the novel, which one do you think this one could refer to?" I point to the figure of Montag on the paper. "Who is that, for instance?"

Larry's eyes return to the paper. "A man."

"But which man from the novel?"

"The man with the flamethrower."

I am not going to give up this time. "Yes, the man is holding a flamethrower. He's the main character in the novel. What is his name?" I smile but Larry doesn't see it because his eyes remain on the paper.

"Montague."

"Close...You're thinking of *Romeo and Juliet*. His name is Montag, and guess whose house he's burning here?"

Larry shakes his head. "I don't know."

I pause and realize my wife's illustrations will have to wait. Then I try a discussion question: "Who liked watching television?"

"My little brother."

"No, I mean in the novel. Which character often absorbed herself with television shows?"

"I don't know."

I pause, gently rest my palm on his shoulder, and peer down at his dusky hair. "Did you finish reading the novel, Larry?"

Larry looks up at me and blinks. "Not all of it."

I take my hand off his shoulder and sigh. "Where did you leave off?"

"I don't know."

"Well, just let me know when you do finish." I pick up the illustrations from his desktop. "Use this time now to continue reading."

Larry blinks again. "I don't have my book."

"Here," I hand him my copy. "Use mine." Then I finish class by roaming the aisles to check on the progress the other students are making with "There will come soft rains" and to answer any questions.

We teachers have another PLC meeting in the library after school, and the theme for this one is differentiated instruction. As we enter Mr. Compton hands each of us a packet of stapled papers about it, and after I sit and examine the handout I see terms like Compacting, 4-MAT, Constructivism, Inferential Thinking, and Tiered Instruction written on the top page.

I want to do the right thing and make a personal plan to research each of these terms and apply them somehow in my classes, even if it is my last year. Mr. Compton smiles, waves the extra copies of the stapled packet above his shoulder, and asks us how we differentiate in our classrooms. No one says anything at first but soon some of the middle school teachers mention activities like word puzzles and word searches, videos, Internet games, and drawing pictures. Gretchen Suchs says she allows re-takes on tests. Next to me, David Grasser ignores the discussion and marks wrong answers on his students' American Revolution quizzes.

Mr. Compton assigns groups of teachers to research various aspects of differentiated instruction in order to present to the whole group in one week. I am in-group #1 and our topic is Content. High school Earth science teacher Jim Simmons, who announces that he attempted Tiered Learning last year, volunteers to take the lead and present for us next Wednesday. The other four of us gladly nod our approval.

THURSDAY, SEPTEMBER 6

I distribute a handout on clichés to my sophomore Honors class, and I think to myself: This is the last time I will ever hand this paper out. In fact, this entire school year will have me making copies of handouts for the last time. I think I'm like most teachers: We love having closure.

As sunlight streams through the open windows and bounces off students' desktops, I begin with survey discussion questions. I call on Joe Simmons because I know he's interested in attending culinary school after he graduates. "Joe, have you ever heard, 'Oh, that's easy as pie'?"

"Yeah," he nods.

"Have you ever tried to bake a pie?"

"A couple of times."

"Not so easy, is it?" I smile as Joe shakes his head.

I turn my attention to the other side of the classroom where volleyball player Tierra and football player Luis, an undersized linebacker, sit. "What about you athletes. Has a coach ever told you to give 110%?"

"Every day," Luis answers.

"But it's impossible!" I say. "In fact, your body can take no more than sixty percent exhaustion...And for all of you leaving this school and declaring you have a ton of homework, stop it. Your homework does *not* weigh a ton. These are clichés and hyperboles."

I stroll back to the other side of the classroom. "Jazmine, can I pick on you...use you for my example?"

Jazmine nods, and I approach her desk in the front, stare at the ceiling, and add a singsong tone to my voice. "Have you ever felt you were on cloud nine, Jazmine?"

"Maybe," she smiles a little, but before she can continue, I say, "Why not cloud *thirty-nine*, Jazmine, or even cloud one hundred and eighty-six?"

There is some brief chuckling, and I sense I have their attention. I then direct them to examine the list of clichés on the handout and replace them with either a more conventional or creative expression. I let them work with partners to transform the clichés – expressions like armed to the teeth, beat around the bush, bite the bullet, bury the hatchet, second banana, and monkeying around – into less trite phrases as I walk around checking their work and assisting when needed.

At the end of the day and after nearly three weeks into the school year I feel I have enough information about each of my students to start calling their parents or guardians to inform them of their son or daughter's progress in my class. I think they deserve to hear my observations of their child – their behavior, their attentiveness, their skills as readers and writers, and, of course, their grade. It's about being accountable and being a professional. I've even told the students that I'm going to call their parents, so there are no surprises. That's why I sit at my desk in my now quiet classroom and start poking the buttons on my desk phone.

Several parents are suspicious after I introduce myself and explain the nature of my call. "What did he do?" some ask angrily right away.

I hope they hear my smile through the receiver as I try to calm their concerns and talk instead about how consistent their son or daughter has been with completing homework or how often he or she participates in discussions or how attentive he or she has been in class.

When I ask if they observe their child reading at home, most parents groan, "I don't have time for that. Just tell me his grade."

So I reveal the current grade and hide my disappointment that no one asks, "What is he/she learning?"

Of course, I remind them how they can access their child's grade on-line on the school's website. Although the school mailed information sheets about this to all the parents in August, I discover my recommendation here is new news for many of them. Probably because I suspect that many students, who arrive home before their parents get the mail, remove any envelopes with the school's address and toss them into the trash.

It takes me an hour and a half after the actual school day has ended to make about nine calls, not including the voice mail messages I leave on four parent's phones and the two phone numbers which are disconnected. I will continue my calls each day, using time during my lunch period as well, until I have contacted the parent/guardian of each student. I do this, in fact, each semester and lament that none of my own children's teachers ever called me.

MONDAY, SEPTEMBER 10

Outside we finally have wonderful weather: blue skies, puffy clouds, gentle breezes. This morning I turn on my computer and check my emails. There's one from Henry Compton informing me that Dylan Graham has been suspended for three days for his squirt gun incident, and there's another from the superintendent asking us to serve on the Levy Committee. Levies are election ballot items that if passed will increase the taxes for property owners (mostly home owners) to fund the school system.

This makes me think of all the school committees I have been on since I started teaching. I have been on six student discipline committees, seven curriculum committees, three curriculum mapping ventures, three calendar committees, ten recognition committees, a career orientation committee, six school improvement committees, and now this will be my fifth levy committee. My supplemental positions have been freshman football coach, assistant varsity football coach, head wrestling coach, athletic director, student council advisor, speech/debate team advisor, literary magazine advisor, drama director, and an after school tutor. I answer the superintendent's email with a positive reply: I would be happy to serve.

During my last class Hank Rogers, an assistant basketball coach, knocks on the door. I can see him peering into the classroom through the little glass window near the top of the door. Actually, Hank is stooping because he's so tall I would only see his neck otherwise. I am giving directions to the students about the quiz on being concrete with their nouns so I do not go to the door right away. He knocks again.

More loudly this time.

I quickly finish the directions, open the door, and ask Hank what he needs. He looks down and shuffles through some papers in his hands, which I readily see are student schedules. He asks, "Is Karl in this class?" He looks down again. "And David and Mark?"

I tell him they are but they are taking a quiz.

"A quiz?" He peers at the papers in his hands again. "Do you have Jermaine here?"

I have to look up at him. "Jermaine is in my period 5-8 block class."

He nods, finally recognizing this on the paper in his hand. "Can I talk to them?"

"Is there an emergency?" I ask. In truth, I know what this is about. This is not the first time a coach has knocked on my door to talk to an athlete. "They're taking a quiz," I remind him. "Can you talk to them at the end of the school day?"

"When is that?"

"In about fifteen minutes."

He pauses, calculating the time in his head. "Yeah, I can do that."

At the final bell, if we had a bell, Hank returns to my room and the five of us – Hank, the three boys, and I – get in a huddle by the whiteboard.

"How they doin'?" Hank asks.

I jump on this. "Well, they all need to be more serious in class. They spend too much time off task socializing, and often I have to repeat directions to them to be sure they know what they should to do next. Sometimes they will raise their hand to participate during a discussion and when I call on them, they realize they have no idea what the question is, so I have to repeat it for them. I mean, I think they're good kids and certainly have potential to do better, but they simply need to be more serious about their academic performance in English."

"So...they're not getting A's?"

I look at him, wondering if he is listening to me. "No, they are not."

One of the sophomore basketball players in our huddle is Mark, a lean and soft-shouldered fifteen year old whose large feet suggest he will grow even taller than his current 6' 2". I have kept a weekly dialogue (mostly by email) with Mark's parent, Ms. Gibson, and with Mark himself since the beginning of September. He was neglecting assignment deadlines or turning in incomplete work. He even struggles to follow the margins on his notebook paper.

Even worse, although I have warned him repeatedly to stop doing that, Mark tries to sleep in class. I thought at first he was ill or working late at a part-time job or exhausting himself in previous classes, so after class one day, I asked him why he kept putting his head down on his desk. "You're an *Honors* student," I reminded him. "Honors students don't sleep in class."

"I know," he mumbled, a hint of apology in his voice.

"Then why?" This came out almost as a plea, and I remember my voice sounding feeble as we faced each other in the empty classroom.

Mark's eyes drifted to my open classroom door. "I like to stay up late and play video games or watch TV, I guess." His eyes stayed on the open doorway, and I knew then like I know now what he's thinking. Escape. Soon, he's telling himself, I will be out of here and on my way home. Call of Duty – Black Ops. Gears of War. Sniper: Ghost Warrior 2. They're all waiting for me.

I nodded my head slowly, desperately hoping an inspirational message would float its way to the front of my brain and then out my mouth in a different tone of voice: one that was encouraging and endearing because I want to be that kind of teacher, the kind that says, "Get your shit together" and the student's attitude changes for the better. But all I said that day was: "Well, okay, but I wish you read a book instead."

Seconds later, Mark did escape into the hallway, quieter now that the majority of students had exited the school. And I slowly weaved my way between students' desks to my bookshelf in the back of the room to re-stack some literature textbooks, disappointed now with myself that thirty-five years of teaching experience still hadn't provided the motivational words I should have expressed to Mark that day.

Today, Mark shoves his hands into his pockets, and his eyes drift to the open door again as Hank continues speaking, telling the boys, "You'all got to get the A, you know. You'all can do it." I'm jealous now. Hank is offering the inspiration I should have provided. In the hallway, other students are shouting at each other and slamming lockers. Again, I recognize the look on Mark's face. Any teacher would. He's sensing Hank is running out of words and the lecture will end soon.

Battlefield 4.

Lost Planet 3.

Madden NFL 25.

They're beckoning him.

Hank turns to the boys, lifts his arms, and tries again. "School's important, you know. You'all can't get that basketball scholarship unless you got the grades."

They keep their faces toward the floor and nod obediently. David's left hand rustles around in his jeans pocket, and I hear clinking keys. Maybe coins. Karl's shoulders sway a little left and right, maybe in rhythm to a hip hop song playing in his head. Mark stands mute and hunched, and I notice for the first time the stubble on his chin. This makes me curious: Has he started shaving yet?

At this point I recognize my contributions are no longer needed in this team huddle so I start cleaning my white board, arranging desks for group work tomorrow, and locating the handouts I need for the next day. My opportunity to be inspiring has passed. Instead of being that motivating teacher, the one students remember and talk about with fondness at their twenty year reunion, today I'm just an old guy shoving desks into groups of four.

Behind me, Hank finishes his lecture, and the boys hustle quickly out the door. When I turn to him, Hank rolls his eyes and then gives me a pleading look. "All I can do is tell 'em," he says and then heads out the door himself. As he exits, I feel somewhat relieved and a little less jealous – Hank sounds like me now.

At home this evening, ABC news announces that the Chicago teachers' strike has begun. "The showdown is pitting the powerful teachers' union against Chicago's mayor, President Obama's former Chief of Staff, Rahm Emanuel. Chicago teachers are fighting for better pay and benefits, but the sticking point is a new plan to base teacher evaluations in part on how well their students score on standardized tests. The unions argue that would put teachers at a disadvantage and possibly cost them their jobs."

I read online that the Chicago *Sun Times* reports that "Sunday night's drama was a roller coaster for teachers, parents and students wondering whether school was on Monday morning - whether students would be greeted by teachers in classrooms or on picket lines. Teachers have been asked to picket outside their own schools." 'Teachers' unions, including my own, across the country are watching this strike in hopes the outcome will be favorable to the Chicago teachers. Unfortunately, the National Education Association, the largest teachers' union, has lost 100,000 members since 2010, leaving it with a membership of about three million. The NEA projects it could lose 200,000 more by 2014 probably due to lay offs and retirement. Like me.

TUESDAY, SEPTEMBER 11

We receive an email this morning from the superintendent that our school will honor the victims of the 9/11 tragedy with a minute of silence which will begin at 8:46 A.M., the time the first building was hit. We are then to discuss with our students the positives of this event.

The positives?

I immediately recognize this as a problem. Students will be exchanging classes between 8:44 and 8:48 A.M. In addition, this event occurred when almost all our students were infants. To be politically correct, should we also have a moment of silence for the soldiers who lost their lives at Pearl Harbor or the victims in Oklahoma City or even more globally, the Japanese citizens who were incinerated by the atomic bombs we dropped on Hiroshima and Nagasaki? Last year my sophomore students read the great nonfiction book *Hiroshima* by John Hersey, and we addressed that issue.

Mr. Compton comes on the PA at 8:51 when nearly all students are inside classrooms, makes a brief reference to 9/11, and announces we will have a minute of silence. So we do.

Except the minute stretches to nearly four minutes, and the whole time I am wondering if I should end the moment of silence on my own, but Mr. Compton finally comes back on the PA and thanks us all.

THURSDAY, SEPTEMBER 13

Fellow English teacher Rebecca Leever, who is also vice-president of our union, knocks on my door in the middle of my lesson on concrete vs. abstract diction (I'm showing the students Abbott and Costello's "Who's on first?" skit on YouTube), and after I join her in the hallway tells me very discreetly that an 8th girl has turned in "an incident report" claiming I "make her feel uncomfortable in class by looking at her in a sexual way."

"No kidding," I say.

"No kidding."

"What student?" I ask.

"I really shouldn't tell you that."

Rebecca advises me next in a low voice not to speak to any administrator about this unless I have a union representative with me. When I press her, she finally tells me the girl's name and I recall the girl's behavior the previous day when she got frustrated with me for cautioning her about doing another teacher's homework during my class. The girl, I was told earlier in the quarter, also has oppositional defiance disorder. I thank Rebecca for the information and tell her I will ask Allison Means to join me if Mr. Compton calls me in about this issue.

In my Honors class, after my lesson on using hyphenated modifiers to highlight description, always-friendly Tierra White says in front of all her classmates, "You are a really good teacher, Mr. Miller. I like how you prepare us to write better. I never knew about this before."

I thank her for the compliment, and three quarters of the class breaks into applause. I wave my hands to calm them but I am both surprised and pleased by this.

At the end of the day I walk upstairs to Allison Means' science classroom and ask her to join me if I am, in fact, called in by an administrator about this 8th grade girl's incident report. She says of course, but not to worry about it now because she and middle school math teacher Tom Black have fixed Ellis Morgan's mixed up schedule. Starting Monday my two eighth grade classes have been replaced by seventh graders. The new class will be called Test Prep, so maybe, I hope, that will solve the problem with the eighth grade girl.

So now I have to prepare lessons for a Test Prep class. I translate this to mean working with the seventh graders on identifying study skills, deciphering multiple-choice questions, completing extended response essay questions, and debating the usefulness of cramming. I leave Allison's classroom and return to my room to hunt through my metal cabinet for the folder on Test-taking Skills. I will use the weekend to create these new lesson plans and a syllabus.

I attend tonight in the high school library a Levy Committee meeting run by Gus Zimmerman, chairperson of the committee and husband to Gerta, the board president, who is also present. During this meeting Mr. Zimmerman never refers to Gerta as his wife but calls her Madame President and speaks to her in an odd, objective way.

This meeting is attended by six parents (two arrive 45 minutes after the meeting starts), both building principals, the treasurer, five teachers from the secondary school, two from the elementary school, six bus drivers, and one man who claims he is the chaplain to the local Democratic party and is there promoting his publication company for our levy literature.

For another odd reason, Mr. Zimmerman brings up the fact that too many parents are taking their children out of the school district. He claims there are multiple reasons for this, but the main reason is the lack of technology in both the elementary and secondary school classrooms. A parent speaks up, "If you have a world-class classroom, people will come back."

"We need computers," another parent adds.

"They better hand out condoms with those computers, if you want the kids to come back," says another parent, an older man who rubs his chin when he's done talking.

Mrs. Woods, a single mom with a daughter who is a junior (she introduces all this about herself to the group), recommends that students should stand out in the street at intersections and hand out literature about the levy, much like firefighters do to raise money for M.S. research.

"They could get killed if they do that," Mrs. Zimmerman declares.

"Madame President," Mr. Zimmerman says to his wife, "address the chairperson first before speaking."

She gives an embarrassed smile and says, "Sorry, Mr. Chairperson." Still smiling, she glances around the table, as if we all are in on some private joke. "I think the children could be in danger standing out in the street."

"Maybe, Mr. Chairperson," Mrs. Woods counters, "they could stand by the side of the road."

Mr. Zimmerman turns to Mrs. Woods and reminds her that the last time the school district had the kids near the road, they goofed around on tree lawns and set a bad example for the school district. In fact, a couple of boys mooned some of the cars going by. Mrs. Woods argues that community members need to see the students front and center of any levy promotion, but David Grasser, the social studies teacher, tells her that the last time students went door-to-door they were treated rudely by the residents, which provoked some male students to urinate on their lawns.

After another debate about the levy's theme – should it be Support our Schools or Save our Schools – Mrs. Woods gets upset when her choice of Save our Schools is rejected and leaves.

The school treasurer informs all of us some hard facts: The school has a deficit of $870,000, there is $4.5 million in delinquent property taxes, and there are over 700 empty homes in Bayview. People, it seems, move in, stay six months to a year, and then simply abandon the home without ever paying any property tax, which could be used by the school system.

A question is asked: What happens if the levy does not pass? The treasurer says the school district will be visited by the Fiscal Commission of the Ohio Department of Education who will categorize us as either under Fiscal Caution, Fiscal Watch, or Fiscal Emergency. No one asks her to make distinctions between these labels which themselves alone sound frightening enough.

A suggestion is made to ask local businesses to fund the cost of creating our literature. Mr. Demetrius Allen, a parent whose son graduated a several years ago, exclaims, "You better hurry up because the businesses in Bayview are closing up fast."

Mr. Zimmerman glares at Mr. Allen. His voice is steely: "No businesses have closed."

"There's empty buildings on Chardon Road," says Mr. Allen. "I was kinda making a joke, but I know what I've seen."

"I think you're exaggerating that," Mr. Zimmerman states. His face is tense.

Mr. Allen sits up straight in his wooden chair and inches forward a little. "You want to go take a drive with me?" He returns Mr. Zimmerman's glare.

Mr. Zimmerman ignores him and pretends to examine some papers on the table in front of him.

An elementary school teacher suggests we get the word out for the levy by using Twitter, Facebook, YouTube stories, and blogs. No one, however, volunteers to arrange this.

The meeting ends with five of us staying to create the language that we will use on lawn signs, brochures, and flyers. I offer my recommendations about keeping the bullet points parallel ("Begin them all with verbs") and less wordy. Everyone readily agrees to let art teacher Melissa Fleck create the graphics and to let me edit the language for these documents.

FRIDAY, SEPTEMBER 14

Devin Jones's behavior has not improved: He continues to twist and turn at his desk as if attempting dance moves. He neglects his assignments. He calls out. Today I hear, "A book just dropped! A book just dropped!" and minutes later "When does this class end?" and then "I need to pee. I need to pee."

During my lunch period I call his guardian, who is his grandmother. "Mrs. Leroy, I feel badly telling you that neither Devin's behavior, nor his grade has improved in English 10."

She breathes, then whispers "Oh, Lord," and then more loudly, "I guess I'll talk to him again."

I try a positive: "He certainly has a lot of energy. I just wish he'd channel it into his school work."

She says, "He wants to play football."

Football? I tell her the season started back in August, that the team plays their third game tonight. Then I repeat that Devin has not been completing either his in-class assignments or his homework.

"So can he still play football?" Mrs. Leroy's asthmatic voice comes over the receiver like a prayer.

I grip the receiver a little more tightly before I respond. "I don't know, Mrs. Leroy. You'll have to ask the coaches."

"Okay, okay, I will. Thank you, sir." She hangs up, and I realize we never addressed improving Devin's failing grade.

The end of the week is a mix of relief and regret. I hope all the skills I have taught this week – researching skills, to be exact, to the sophomores – have been helpful. Usually I do exit cards at the end of a class – i.e., how did this lesson help you? Or what did you find most helpful today? – to find out, but because today's lesson on how to find sources and construct a Works Cited page went almost to the bell – if we had a bell – in each class, there was no time for students to complete exit cards.

The day ends, and I have this egocentric fantasy that my sophomores will tell younger students, "You really learn a lot in that class. He's a great teacher."

But I doubt they will ever say this. Instead, I suspect their comments are more critical, even more derogatory, but I do not know for sure.

At home I read online that in Chicago the teachers' strike is a week old now, but both the CTU president Karen Lewis and the school board president David Vitale are more "positive" about reaching a resolution than they were before, according to the Associated Press. The *Chicago Tribune* reports that union leadership is scheduled to meet today "where the more than 700 delegates can vote to end the strike, pending approval of the contract by the union's full membership. If the delegates vote to end the strike, student and teachers will likely return to class Monday."

Good news, of course, but teachers across the nation are watching this to see the outcome, especially contract language regarding teacher evaluations. If the Chicago teachers concede, then it is possible for boards of education across the country, including mine, to evaluate teachers almost exclusively on students' test scores.

MONDAY, SEPTEMBER 17

Bobby Hunter, a young man who struggled at first to write coherent essays last year in my English class and who now attends a local community college as a post-secondary enrollment student, stops me in the dimly lit hallway as we pass each other at the end of the school day. He tells me he's getting an A in his English class at the community college. "Because of you, Mr. Miller," he says.

"That's great," I say. "I'm glad I helped." This is good, although surprising, news. In truth, I am always wondering if my lessons are worthwhile.

"You really did, Mr. Miller, especially with the writing long essays." Bobby smiles broadly and adjusts the straps of the backpack on his shoulders. The goatee he's trying to grow seems out of place on his young face.

"Wonderful news, Bobby! I appreciate you telling me that. Thanks! And congratulations."

Bobby starts to back up. "Well, I just wanted you to know."

I nod my chin as if acknowledging royalty. "Your news is a highlight to my day, sir. Again, I appreciate it. By the way, I'm curious. What kind of papers did you have to write?"

Bobby stops backing up and frowns. "Something about gun control."

"A persuasive paper, huh?"

"I think." He smiles, his memory concluded, gives me a little wave, and moves on down the hall toward the glass exit doors.

TUESDAY, SEPTEMBER 18

I am more familiar with today's weather than the bright, sunny days we have had recently. From a ceiling of charcoal-colored clouds a pouring rain shifts back and forth between a drizzle and a downpour. My students take furtive glances out the window. A girl in my first block class by the window complains she is cold so I suggest she move to the other side of the room. She doesn't, however.

During my planning and lunch periods I continue my calls to my students' parents. After I provide a brief progress report, I hear stories about kids who suffer from various illnesses, problems related to divorce, Honors' students who hate to read, other kids who hate to write.

After I tell Brenda Wright's mom that her daughter, who barely has a D because her papers are plagued by nonstandard usage, needs to use spell check or enlist the aid of a proofreader, I hear her sigh heavily.

"That girl is so depressed right now. She's not taking her medication."

"Really? In class, she's always smiling, always cheerful."

"I'm thinking of taking her out of that school."

I move the receiver to my other ear. "I recognize that as an option, but you should talk to our guidance counselor first. His name is Al Schmidt."

"Oh, I talked to that Mr. Schmidt over and over. He's no help. He put her in Honors at the beginning of the year. I didn't want her in that class; I wanted her in Regular English."

"I remember..."

She interrupts. "He says Brenda got a B in English 9 Honors last year, so he put her in Honors this year. That was wrong."

My mind goes to Gretchen who teaches English 9 Honors. *Brenda got a B? How did that happen?*

"I'm not voting for that levy neither." Mrs. Wright's tone shifts. Her springtime voice becomes icy. "That school is not helping my daughter."

"I understand your concerns, Mrs. Wright, but..."

"I'm not blamin' you, you're doing what you gotta do," she says. "But my daughter is not happy there."

We hang up, and I make a note to check with Gretchen about Brenda getting a B last year. I can't confront her. I just have to ask.

Another Honors student who is underperforming is Martin, a skinny boy whose crooked mouth seldom lacks for words. Today, before class begins, he asks about his grade so I check my grade book and tell him he has an F. Martin glares at the grade book in my hands as if his eyes could, like Superman's, make it go up in flames. Then he demands I let him go to the guidance counselor so he can drop the class. Ironically, he is one of my most active students and participates daily. He just can't pass any test. I refuse his request because I don't even know if Al Schmidt is even available. This frustrates Martin who stomps back to his seat. "This class sucks!" he says under his breath.

The teenager inside my head wants to respond with, "Yeah? Well, maybe *you* suck!" The adult occupying my body, however, says nothing starts his lesson on conflict in fiction.

Irony.

I attend another Levy Committee meeting tonight where only three teachers, all high school teachers, and three parents show up, not counting Mr. and Mrs. Zimmerman who do not even have a child in the school anymore. The administrators are absent.

We discuss and evaluate the levy literature again, along with a calendar of events, like football games and community events, where brochures and yard signs can be distributed. We will also put blue and white (our school colors) ribbons on all the trees near the street to emphasize the need to pass the levy. One parent suggests we put the blue ribbons on mailbox posts, but Mr. Zimmerman says that may be illegal.

"What if they don't have a tree in the yard?" that parent asks.

Mr. Zimmerman shakes his dome-like head a little and lifts his hands, palms up. "I guess they'll just have to go to the next yard. I don't know. Let's just get it done."

There is a desperate hope that news reporters and television cameras will show up at these events and broadcast the plight of the school district and the needs of our students. However, as before, no one volunteers to contact any television station or newspaper.

This levy meeting takes place at the Bayview Faith Church where we all sit around a large conference table, and I find myself sitting directly and awkwardly across a ten-foot mirror. I feel a little unnerved by this because every time I glance up and examine my reflection I think, "ugly." My face is ashen, and my head looks like a doorknob is stuck on my shoulders. I force myself to sit up because when I take these brief looks I sadly observe that my shoulders are slumped over my chest. It's like an out-of-body experience. I think, as if another Ethan is saying to me, "Look at yourself...that lousy posture, your doorknob head, a face the color of old milk. Why are you even attending this meeting? It's your last year?"

I do not answer myself.

I am tired when I get home later that night. My wife and sons have already gone to bed, so I make a sandwich and watch the news alone. News stations are broadcasting the end of the Chicago teachers' strike. The CTU delegates, representing 29,000 teachers, voted to suspend the strike and return to teaching Chicago's 350,000 students. The teachers will get a 17% salary increase over four years, but 30% of their evaluations will be based on their students' standardized test scores. Would you want 30% of your job security based on how a nine, twelve, or fifteen year old kid is feeling on test day?

I sit in the family room, finish my ham and mustard sandwich, and watch the CNN news report about the strike. I inwardly applaud the Chicago teachers for showing the courage to stand up to the Chicago school board and politicians who want to use standardized tests to evaluate teachers. Either way, after months of negotiations and a seven-day strike, the Chicago teachers will be back on the job.

WEDNESDAY, SEPTEMBER 19

I read this morning an Associated Press article today that refers to "jubilant" CTU delegates who "were eager to get to work and proud of a walkout that yielded results." The Associated Press quotes the mayor of Chicago calling the deal "an honest compromise" and noting that during the strike, "tens of thousands of parents were forced to find alternatives for idle children, including many whose neighborhoods have been wracked by gang violence in recent months."

In my classroom, I feel very disconnected from gang violence as I begin a lesson on plagiarism with the seventeen sophomores in my first period. They all seem in good spirits – most are smiling – so I use this positive mood to begin the lesson by asking how they would define plagiarism. Then I single out Charity, who is often absent from class but today seems energized and alert, and compliment her for always being so respectful, polite, and cooperative in class. "You truly show a lot of the qualities teachers like to see in students," I tell her. This makes her blush a little, and then I drop the bomb. "But even though you do all the right things, except attendance, as a student in this class, I will fail you if you plagiarize your research paper!"

My intent is more to shock than to threaten, and Charity's jaw does drop slightly. Charity – and even the rest of the students, I think – get this point when I add that most plagiarism in schools happens by accident and the simple objective of today's lesson is to prevent that accident. Next, I survey them to discover what they have learned about plagiarism in the past and discover most know it as "copying someone else's work."

Then I distribute an essay about the discovery of the Greek island of Knossos by an English archaeologist named Arthur Evans and tell the sophomores I wrote it. The Knossos essay also makes detailed references to the mythological tale of King Minos and the Minotaur. I let them read it and ask: "Is this plagiarized?"

No one claims it is, although I copied it word for word from a website. Indeed, they are surprised when I tell them I did commit plagiarism.

"Really?" Marcus asks. "But you're a teacher."

"True, but do you think I have ever traveled to Knossos, or that I personally knew that Dr. Arthur Evans discovered that island? I did not, and I never cite my sources in this paper."

I then lecture briefly about plagiarism – how it is recognized, that most students plagiarize by accident, and why it should be avoided (academic integrity). I distribute two contrasting essays on the same subject – one is plagiarized and the other possesses correct citations. Can they identify which is the plagiarized piece now?

I sit at a student desk on the left side of the classroom, lean back, and start to read the first essay. When I look up to see if my students are following along, I note that they are, and I feel this is a good start. Today's lesson is working so far.

Hurray!

A minute later, Jenny Wilson, dressed today in tight jeans and a buttoned down pink shirt, leaves her seat and walks toward me smiling as I continue to read one of the essays in the front of the room. I smile back, thinking she is going to throw some trash away or sharpen her pencil, but instead she heads toward Tina Wills, who sits near the door. I look down to continue reading one of the essays and suddenly hear one of them say, "You a fucking bitch." Seconds later, Jenny and Tina sprint at each other in front of the room. I swivel in my seat and try to jump between them, but I can only wrap one arm around the waist of the nearest girl, Jenny, and extend my other arm towards Tina to keep her away from Jenny and me.

"I'm going to fuck you up," Tina yells at Jenny as I try to squeeze Jenny against my hip to shield her from Tina's swinging fists. Jenny screams and tries to kick Tina.

As both girls throw punches at each other, I get some glancing blows on my head, and when Jenny's thrusts at Tina cause Jenny and me to tumble to the floor, Tina, aiming for Jenny, kicks me in the side. I ignore the dull ache below my ribs; my more urgent goals are to get to my feet, to protect the other students, to stop this fight. On my knees now, I watch Tina grab a textbook off the floor and throw it at Jenny, and we duck just in time. The book sails over both our heads and bangs into the white board. Tina looks for something else to throw, and I yell to the other students to get security.

I get back to my feet and keep an arm around Jenny's waist and my back to Tina, who has started swinging again, to shield Jenny from her fists. I feel grateful when Charity starts to pull Tina away, saying, "Don't do this, Little Bit. Don't do this." I continue to struggle with Jenny whose elbows keep popping into my side as she swings back and forth at Tina.

"This is wicked," Marcus calls out gleefully.

The other students – some standing, some sitting – watch Jenny, Tina, Charity, and me with animated expressions, as if fireworks were going off, and groan when the two security personnel – Mrs. T and Oscar Smith– finally show up and help me separate the girls and pull them into the hallway. Mrs. T, in fact, puts little Tina in a full nelson, pushes on her thin neck, and lifts her body completely off the ground to get her to stop swinging. Tina, her feet now dangling off the tiled floor, stops her kicking and screams, "Let me the fuck go. Let me go!"

Oscar holds onto Jenny's arms and follows Mrs. T, who sets Tina's feet back on the floor but keeps the full nelson locked on her neck, to the office. I hear more profanity as the girls, Oscar, and Mrs. T stomp down the hallway.

I walk back into my classroom where desks have been jostled and a half dozen textbooks are scattered on the floor. My other students are debating good-naturedly who caused the fight and who received the most punches. It takes me several minutes to calm them all down and to get them to agree that we can continue with the lesson on plagiarism. The fight is still fresh in their minds, however, so hardly any of them pay any real attention to my directions to return to the two essays.

I sit down, take a deep breath, and pick up one of the essays off the floor to read again.

"The fuck I am!" That is what I hear first.

"Okay, let's go, bitch!" This comes next.

The verbal threat comes from Mona Nelson, and it's directed at Michelle Cochran, two thick-waisted girls dressed today in jeans and sweaters. Their desks are right next to each other, and they shove them aside to lunge at each other. The scene is all too familiar, and I yell for them to stop. Neither does.

They start throwing punches at each other in the aisle and stagger to the front of the room where Michelle yells, "I'm gonna kill you, bitch."

I get between them, wrap my arms around Michelle's heavy middle this time, and drag her away from Mona, who herself is being pulled now by Charity again and Jimmy but not before I get some kicks in my back. Michelle, raging to get at Mona, tries to twist her way out of my body lock. Her hands push at my shoulders and then my face. I smell perfume and sweat. Michelle threatens me, "You better get the fuck off me. I'm gonna fuck you up, too, if you don't get the fuck off me." To emphasize this point, she shoves her forearm into my jaw, and the long bone feels like an iron bar against my cheek.

I keep my voice even. "Not until you calm down, Michelle." I lean my chest into her until her back is against the classroom wall.

In response, Michelle swings at my head and pushes harder with her forearm into the side of my face. I duck the punch and keep her pinned against the white board wall.

I am grateful again when Oscar and Mrs. T return to my classroom and remove these two girls. Oddly, Oscar Smith, a burly, forty-something, assistant football coach shows no surprise at the scene in my classroom as he grabs Michelle's wrists and pulls her away from me. Mrs. T already has Mona in the hallway, and seconds later they escort both girls in the direction of the office.

I look down and notice my shirt is rumpled and ripped slightly where my sleeve meets the shoulder. My pants are dusty from tumbling on the floor. Mostly, though, I'm exhausted. It's only my first class of the day.

My classroom again is in disarray, and a dozen students rehash with each other what they just observed. This time they debate who won that fight, but most of them are in agreement that the four girls put on quite a show. One student thinks Tina provoked Jenny in some way from her side of the room by mouthing the word "bitch" as I was reading the essay. Charity announces that she thought she heard Mona call Michelle a whore. No one asks if I got hurt.

I need a drink of water, but I am hesitant, however, to leave my classroom to go down the hallway to the nearest fountain (Will another fight break out?), which is all the way down by the gym. I do so anyway. Let them fight, if they want to. I even stop in the restroom to tuck in my shirt and readjust my tie.

Back in my classroom, students watch me pick up books and papers scattered on the floor and straighten some desks. No one offers to help. They stare dumbfounded at me when, believe it or not, I return to the two research-oriented essays to see if they can detect which one is plagiarized. I want to get back to the lesson, to re-establish a normal learning environment, to do the job I am actually paid to do. However, several minutes later, my lesson is interrupted again. This time by a phone call from Henry Compton. He tells me to complete the discipline referrals for the four girls, and I tell him I will once I finish my class.

"The parents are coming," he says through the receiver. "I need them now."

"Now? You want me to stop teaching?"

"Yeah...I need those forms now."

So I stop teaching, pull the forms from a desk drawer, and complete all four of them. This leaves me with only five minutes of the eighty-minute block left for my lesson on plagiarism. My mind is frazzled, so I don't even bother. I collect the essays, and after I dismiss my students at the end of the period, I feel like I cannot continue through the school day.

I stay, however, and muddle through my class of 7th graders as they read a nonfiction article off the Tweentribune.com website and write an extended response answer to a question. After the fights, the heads-down quiet and straight rows of desks make the classroom feel strange. I'm grateful that I can put them on autopilot for one period.

This feeling changes, however, when Ebony Burrell comes screaming into my period 5-8 class. I mean *screaming*. She's angry at another student about some money she claims is owed to her. After I tell her to be quiet, she yells back, "You not goin' tell me what to do. Ever!" As before, I kick her out. I just cannot take any more of that kind of behavior. "That fine, that fine," she yells, turning her back on me as she goes out to the door. "You don't have to tell me twice."

I start the plagiarism lesson again, and although the fights, the forms, the frustration are still swimming around in my head, I decide I can do this. You are a competent teacher, I tell myself. A professional. These students deserve your best effort. I hit the re-set button in my head and start.

In this class I single out Amber this time for my opening quasi-threat about plagiarism, only to be interrupted by Phil Oster, our director of security, who hands me a form at the door that says "Incident Report" at the top. He tells me I need to fill it out, and I promise I will at the end of the day when I have time. He also suggests I fill out assault charges against Michelle, but I look him in the eyes and tell him I won't do that. After he leaves, I put the form on my desk and hand out the Knossos essay to this class. Unfortunately, I am again interrupted by the ringing phone. I pick up, and it's Mr. Compton. This time he asks me to complete the Incident Report form.

"I will," I say into the receiver. "Phil gave it to me. I'll work on it after my last class."

"I need to attach it to the referrals. I need it today...within the hour."

There is this pause, and I wonder if he is going to ask about my welfare, to find out if I'm okay. He does not ask about me, however, so I sigh and say, "Okay, I'll write it up during my lunch."

"Oh, thank you, thank you, thank you, Mr. Miller," he responds in his Adrian Cronauer voice and hangs up.

Consequently, I spend my lunch time period at my computer writing a narrative about the fights that occurred in my classroom that morning. The word must have spread because several colleagues visit me and ask how I am doing. I tell them I am physically fine but emotionally spent. Jack, who teachers down the hall from me, tells me I should complete an assault leave form and press charges against the girls. He wants me to set a precedent for other teachers.

What I want to do is go home, but I change my mind when I discover that I would in addition to the paper work I have done already, I would have to complete a workers' compensation from. I am sick of filling out forms and decide, therefore, to stay. I complete the Incident Report, take it to Henry Compton's office, and then teach my last class.

Finally, at the end of the day in my quiet classroom I clean my white board, prepare my handouts for the next day, and sit at my desk ready to turn off my computer when the pleasant silence is jarred by the ringing phone. I notice with great dismay the outside number on the display. It's Tina Will's mother, who, surprisingly, is in a pleasant mood and views today's events involving her daughter as the silly and immature behavior of young girls. But then she asks me, "Who started it?"

I have to think. "I have no real idea," I finally answer. "The fight seemed to happen spontaneously. I could not tell you which girl started it."

"Okay, okay..." Then her tone becomes more serious, even philosophical. "You know, Mr. Miller, you need to get tougher on those kids. You need to beat on them more."

I do not respond. I just hold the receiver to my ear and wait for any other advice she might offer. But after I discover she has finished, we say goodbye, and I hang up the phone.

Science teacher Ernie Kelsey drops in to tell me that students in his class were amused I struggled at first to deal with the girls because they think I'm really strong. "Yeah," he smiles, re-living the memory of his students' comments. "One of them said you were the toughest teacher in the school, being a former wrestler and all, so he was surprised you couldn't hold them apart, one in each arm."

"Amusing." I try to smile for him.

Ander Klyszewski also stops in, and I realize right away he has no idea what happened in my classroom this morning since he immediately begins venting about the problems he is having with his sixth graders: He wants to talk to me because I'm an English teacher and have taught for over thirty years, and he is in disbelief that his 6th graders have no clue what a noun is, that they cannot spell, and that they have no idea what plot or conflict are in fiction. "You're going to have your hands full when you get them in a couple of years," he warns me before leaving.

He does not know this year is my last.

No one does.

And finally, Gretchen leans half of her skinny body in my doorway on her way out and asks if I will be coming to school the next day.

"I don't know," I say. "I just don't know."

I recollect Robert Anthony who said, "Some people drink from the fountain of knowledge, others just gargle."

THURSDAY, SEPTEMBER 20

It is 7:25 A.M. and Mr. Compton catches me in his outer office while I am making enlarged copies of my handouts for Darrell Roberts, the boy in my period 2-3 block who has limited vision. Mr. Compton beckons me into his office and then quietly says, "Close the door." His face looks taut, like his skin has been squeezed over his cheekbones.

Assistant Principal Morgan is sitting across from him. He does not acknowledge or even look up at me when I enter and close the door. All I see is the top of his wispy gray hair.

Mr. Compton peers up at me over the glasses that have slid down his nose and asks, "Are you all right?" His face is a question mark.

I tuck the handouts under my arm and look at him for a brief moment. Then: "Physically I am fine."

"Are you sure? Did you go to the hospital? Did you see a doctor?"

I realize now what he is after. "No, I did not go to the hospital. I did not see a doctor." I want to tell him about the article in the *New York Post* several weeks ago that reported, "School-violence stats have hit an all-time high since detailed record-keeping on fights, crimes and other incidents began in 2005, according to new State Education Department data." Incidents have "skyrocketed by more than 50 percent since 2005, to 68,313 incidents." But, of course, I don't.

"Okay, okay," he says. "Good. Just checking on you. Are you sure you are all right?"

I nod weakly. "I'm sure." I look one last time at the top of Ellis Morgan's head – his thinning gray hair – and notice he's taken notes on what I said. Then I open Mr. Compton's office door and leave.

FRIDAY, SEPTEMBER 21

I need a day off so I take one. I am not ill or injured; it is what most of us might call a mental health day: a day off to relax and relieve the stress.

Should I feel guilty for doing this?

Like I said, physically I am fine. However, emotionally and psychologically, I remain distressed. The two fights on Wednesday and my administrators' apathy about my welfare have left me feeling ineffectual, like I'm dried up inside. True, I have broken up fights before, most often between boys, but in those incidents my principal immediately asked if I had been injured in any way. Especially after my hallway tussle years ago with Terry G.

I will always remember Terry G., a psychotic young man who enrolled at Bayview High School about fifteen years ago after leaving a juvenile detention center. All we teachers knew about Terry was that although he was eighteen years old he only had earned enough credits to be classified as a sophomore. The administrators who enrolled him kept secret that Terry had been previously incarcerated for beating up and robbing an old man in Cleveland.

During my first week with Terry in English 10, he was polite, friendly, and cooperative although he did no class work or homework. He said, "Yes sir" or "No sir" a lot to my questions to him in class and would most often sit quietly in his seat staring straight ahead. By the second week, however, his attendance became sporadic, and when he did attend, he usually arrived late and became argumentative if I issued a detention.

A rumor soon went around that Terry was trying to start his own gang at Bayview – possibly Bloods or Crips. He, in fact, had threatened a girl who had joked with other girls, calling him an idiot for thinking he could start a gang in suburban Bayview. It was probably mistake for a Tonya to share her opinion about Terry with others because he let it be known he was going to "get her" for it. The administrators claimed they could not act upon a threat that was, in truth, only a rumor, and, indeed, Terry to that point had not violated any school rule that could prompt a suspension. Even worse, Tonya's friend Shakira decided to bring a knife to school in case Terry tried to harm her girlfriend.

My confrontation with Terry actually started with me breaking up an altercation between Shakira and Bernard, a sophomore who had signed on as one of Terry's gang members and was himself diagnosed as Severe Behavior Handicapped (now it's called Emotionally Disabled). Shakira and Bernard were screaming profanities at each other in the hallway in front of my first floor classroom right after the lunch period during an exchange of classes. Even after I intervened, they kept cursing at each other nearly face to face.

I stuck myself between them with my back to Shakira. I faced Bernard to get him to shut up since he was the louder of the two. I found out later that Shakira had pulled out her knife behind my back, ready to use it if Bernard got past me. She hid the knife again when I turned to tell her to follow me upstairs to the principal's office. My presence as a teacher meant something then, I guess, so they obediently accompanied me as I took their elbows and escorted them to the stairs to the upstairs' principal's office.

Word of mouth must have helped Terry learn about this incident because just as Bernard, Shakira, and I neared the office door on the second floor, Terry came sprinting down the empty hallway at us, screaming at Shakira, "I'm gonna kill you, bitch. Ain't no one doin' shit to my homeboy."

I almost shoved Bernard and Shakira through the open office door and positioned myself in my wrestler's stance to take on the charging

Terry.

"Stop," I yelled at him. But he was too enraged, too out of control to stop, and he crashed into me when I met him head-on in the middle of the hallway. We tumbled to the grimy floor, and I rolled him underneath me and pushed his stomach to the floor. My wrestling background came in use: I put him in a wrist and arm bar hold as he thrashed and bucked beneath me. When I straddled his body, using my weight to keep his belly to the floor, Terry screamed from beneath me, "I'm gonna fuck you up, Miller. You get off. I'm gonna fuck you up for this." Terry kept pushing up against me, his elbows stabbing at my sides, but my grip on his one wrist was solid and I hooked a leg to keep him from crawling away from me.

The principal heard Terry's screams, came out of the office, saw the wrestling match on the hallway floor, and darted back into the office to call the police. A single officer arrived five minutes later, handcuffed Terry while I still held him, and then took him away.

I saw Terry G. only two more times in my life after that.

The first time was when I had to appear in Cuyahoga County juvenile court a month later to testify, under orders from the administration, as to the school's assault charge against him. Terry was at the defendant's table about twelve feet away from me as I sat in the witness chair in the half-filled courtroom. Instead of an actual judge, a court referee administered the hearing, and the young prosecuting attorney with stringy hair and a long skirt, I learned later, was trying only the second case in her life. When she asked me to recount the events of that day with Terry G., I honestly related all the events as I remembered them.

When it was his turn to question me, Terry's lawyer, a bearded, thirty-something type whose body seemed packed into a yellow shirt and navy blue suit, asked me under cross-examination, "Did Terry actually hit anyone?" He stayed seated next to Terry and eyed me coolly.

"No."

"Did he physically harm another student?"

"No. I stopped him before he could."

"Then is it your habit, Mr. Miller, to throw students to the floor?"

The question surprised me. "I didn't throw him to the floor. He crashed into me and we fell."

"Why would you, in fact, even confront Terry in the hallway?"

"He was threatening another student." All this seemed clear to me, why not him?

The lawyer stared at me across his long wooden table. "How did he do this?"

"He said, 'I'm gonna kill you, you fucking bitch.'" I thought this would lessen his apparent confusion, but it did not.

He checked his notepad. "So, you grabbed him because he used profanity?"

I leaned forward on the hard, wooden witness chair. "No, I grabbed him because he was sprinting down the hall at me ready to attack another student."

The lawyer looked again at his notepad on the table and then at me. "Could he have been cursing for another reason?"

It went on like this for several more minutes before this lawyer finally finished trying to make the apparent point that Terry, in fact, was the victim here, not anyone else. When he said, "No more questions," I stepped down from the witness chair and returned to my seat in the gallery. I was as angry with my administrators for making me testify as I was at the defense attorney for making me out to be the aggressor. I vowed then never to allow myself to appear in juvenile court again, even if a school administrator ordered me to do so.

I found out later that Terry's punishment was three months in a juvenile boot camp where the inmates were trained to adopt traits such as compassion, loyalty, and friendship. He was released from that boot camp a month before the school year ended.

The second and final time I saw Terry was in July, three months after his release from the boot camp – and six months after I wrestled with him on the second floor hallway at Bayview High School – when

I watched by complete coincidence the 6 P.M. news and saw a report on Terry G. and another young man. They had been found guilty of robbing, shooting, and killing a Korean grocer in a Cleveland neighborhood. Both were being sentenced to life in prison for the robbery and murder of the grocer. Over a year after that, someone told me Terry had died in prison, murdered himself by another inmate.

That summer, I told my Terry G. story to a neighbor, a police officer, who told me he would never be a teacher. He explained he has been called to schools because of student fights, and he no longer has any tolerance for disrespectful kids. His badge allows him to put his hands on kids if necessary, but he recognizes teachers are almost forbidden to do that.

So today, I sleep in until 8:30 A.M. (I typically awake at 5:30 A.M. and get into my classroom by 6:30 A.M.). I eat a bowl of granola cereal and take my yorkie for a walk in the fresh air. Another neighbor, Tom, is walking his dog, too. He starts shaking his head as he nears me, and as our dogs piss on another neighbor's tree lawn, he reveals that he just lost his job as a delivery truck driver.

I listen to Tom grumble for a while about his ineffectual union and then return home with my dog. At least I have a job, I tell myself; at least I have a job.

Maybe Macbeth is right when he says, "Life's but a walking shadow, a poor player/ That struts and frets his hour upon the stage/ And then is heard no more: it is a tale/ Told by an idiot, full of sound and fury, signifying nothing."

All we do signifies "nothing"?

We are heard "no more"?

I certainly hope not. There can be no fatalism in the classroom.

That's why when I get home on this day off from school, I take the leash off my yorkie, sit at my kitchen table, open up my laptop, check the Common Core State Standards for the seventh grade, and go to work on more lesson plans for my seventh grade class.

WEDNESDAY, SEPTEMBER 26

I return today to my lesson about plagiarism – this time, how to cite sources in the body of a paper. I have adopted education guru Madeline Hunter's model of instruction, beginning with an anticipatory set activity; today it's a Marzano technique, and I distribute four different paragraphs where information has been taken from the same source. The students need to compare and contrast each paragraph to see if they can identify the two paragraphs that are plagiarized.

"It's paragraph A," exclaims Devin Jones in my period 5-8 block. He starts gyrating at his seat, almost as if he was riding a roller coaster, his finger poking at the handout as if his fingernail was the tines on a fork and the paper was a piece of meat. "And B!" he calls out. "And C...and D. They're all playjerized." His index finger pokes at each paragraph in turn, and when I tell him to raise his hand to speak in class, he does so immediately, and repeats, "It's A, B, C, and D, Miller. They're all playjerized. These cats cheated."

"First, Devin, stop talking like Sponge Bob. And again, raise your hand so I can call on you."

Devin gives me an exaggerated wink. "Yeah, I got you."

"Also, not all the paragraphs are plagiarized. Anyone else want to try?"

Connor raises his hand, and I after I acknowledge him, he says, "A and B."

"Why A?" Thank goodness, I'm thinking. This might turn into a legitimate discussion. Even Connor is engaged.

"Because there's a bunch of words I don't know."

"That's some unique reasoning." I swivel to include the rest of the class. "By show of hands, who agrees with Connor?"

No hands go up.

"Who disagrees?"

Still no hands. Maria, in the front of the room, giggles silently about something Amber whispered to her and drops her head onto her folded arms. Ebony peaks at text messages on her cell phone. Connor begins moving his desk like it's a bumper car until I walk over and stop him by putting my hand on his shoulder.

I turn to the entire class. "Again, who disagrees with Connor?"

Only Devin raises his hand. "I still think it's all of them, Miller. Take it to the bank."

Now I survey the room with my eyes. It's one of those looks teachers give before saying something they think is profound. "Actually," I declare, using my lecture-voice, "the plagiarized paragraphs are B and C. Note how there are no citations. And Devin, you are still talking like Sponge Bob."

I agree with Chicago journalist Sydney Harris, who said, "The whole purpose of education is to turn mirrors into windows."

The next activity is a favorite for the students and me as I seek a volunteer to role-play a Grammy winner at the awards ceremony.

Devin volunteers immediately and nearly runs to the front of the classroom. "I want to thank my manager, my crew, all my fans...." He pauses, wondering, I'm sure, who else to thank. Then in closure he simply throws up his arms. "I want to thank my fans, I love you all."

As if on cue, his classmates applaud. I clap, too.

Maria lifts up her head and raises her hand to volunteer, and after I call on her, she strolls blithely to the front of the classroom and dramatically uses her hand to brush the hair off her shoulders. She then gushes thank yous to her agent, producer, publicist, hairstylist, and, of course, her fans. "You rock," she says at the end.

"Maria, I wish we had a drama club for you. You'd be great on stage," I tell her.

She smiles in response, returns to her seat, and puts her head on her arms again.

"Here's the point," I tell the students. "These performers give others credit. You have to do the same when you write a research paper. If you don't, that's plagiarism."

This is going well, I tell myself. I march proudly to a side table and pick up a small stack of handouts, which are models showing how website sources are given credit accurately in the body of a paper.

"God, too many handouts in this class." It's Jermaine's voice behind me, complaining, I think, not to God or to me but to a classmate.

When I turn back to the students, papers in hand, although only seconds have passed, something has happened in the room. My students' faces are bland, even sullen, and the momentum of the lesson suddenly dissipates, like air going out a punctured balloon. I still hold the handouts, but now they seem impractical. But if not these one-page research papers I still hold in my hand, then what?

I attempt an incentive. "I'll be evaluating you at the end of class," I warn them, pointing a finger, "to see if you can identify a plagiarized piece of writing." An end-of-lesson assessment is another Madeline Hunter technique.

"A quiz?" Connor grumbles.

Maria joins him. "You didn't tell us we were having a quiz, Mr. Miller."

I take away my pointing finger. "Not really a quiz," I stammer. "More like a...status check...to see if you understand what is a plagiarized piece of writing...and what isn't." I punctuate this with a flimsy smile.

"So is it a quiz or isn't it?" Maria demands.

I pause. The assessment, I realize, is not an incentive or a challenge to them; it's a threat. I didn't encourage them; I threatened them. That's why I say, "No, it isn't a quiz. It's a checkup...like going to the doctor for a checkup to make sure we're in good shape."

I consider my response to be creative, even encouraging, but their blank faces tell me otherwise. I set the research paper handouts on a nearby student desk that is empty and try to remember other articles Madeline Hunter wrote on how to generate a student-centered classroom, but my brain has gone foggy in that area. Nevertheless, I try again: This time, a discussion.

"Who has seen the movie *Titanic?*" I ask.

Half of their hands go up.

"That was a retarded movie," Ebony calls out.

I ignore her. "Does it remind you of another story?"

No hands.

I wait ten seconds, then another ten seconds, hoping the extra time helps them process their thoughts. Devin yawns and puts his head down on his desk. Darrielle looks out the window.

"It's *Romeo and Juliet,*" I finally announce, "on the ocean. You know...Jack and Rose fall in love, she's supposed to marry another guy, they are from totally different families." I stroll through the aisles and gesture with my arms. "Jack sneaks into the upper class dinner party, there's a fight, they decide to die together at the end...." I stop my stroll at the front of the classroom and spread my arms. "And it's a tragedy, isn't it? So, should we accuse James Cameron of plagiarizing Shakespeare, who, by the way, copied from Chaucer?"

Still no hands. I wait ten seconds again and then: "Do you all remember reading *The Tragedy of Romeo and Juliet* last year?"

I almost jump when Connor raises his hand. "Yes, Connor. What do you think? Do the two stories seem alike?"

Connor shakes his head. "Romeo and Juliet weren't on a boat. And they had swords and things."

I glance quickly at the wall clock. "You're certainly right, Connor." Then I reluctantly lift the model research papers off the desk and wave the stack in front of my chest. "Let's try this," I say. "These are research papers with website citations. Let's see if you can figure out if they are accurately cited or not."

A skilled teacher would have been ready with both remediation and enrichment activities in advance. I like to consider myself as a master teacher, and I have neither of these for today's class.

As the students read the research papers, I remember the words of John Gardner: "Much education today is monumentally ineffective. All too often we are giving young people cut flowers when we should be teaching them to grow their own plants."

As I promised, at the end of the class, my assessment is another handout with a previous (and nameless) student's paper. Has he committed plagiarism? Explain why or why not. I collect this when they finish.

Near the end of my last class, I see Ellis Morgan lingering outside my classroom door, and when I dismiss the students for the day, he enters in a hurry.

"Mr. Miller, your schedule has been changed," the scheduling guru announces.

"Again?!"

"Yes. We need to move two seniors out of Art 1 during period four. You're going to teach them," he pauses to check the paper in his hand, "creative writing. Creative Writing 1, to be specific. You'll teach Creative Writing 2 second semester."

"But I teach seventh graders Test Prep during fourth period."

"We're moving them, too. I have to get them into the wheel. They'll be in choir or gym or something else."

"So now it's Creative Writing? It's been twenty years since I taught creative writing."

He checks the paper again. "Creative Writing 1, yes, and you'll help supervise a study hall ninth period instead of teaching those seventh graders."

"What do you want me to do with just two seniors in Creative Writing 1?"

His eyes go from me to the bulletin boards and eventually back to me. "I don't know, writing poems and stories and things, I guess." Then he leaves.

I admit I'm not disappointed about losing the seventh graders. On the third day of class I stopped my lesson on writing sentences with prepositional phrases to deal with a young man who was trying to jump into the trashcan and a young lady was teasing a classmate by calling him "pizza face."

Tonight at home, as my wife watches television, I sit again at the kitchen table, my new office because I get claustrophobic working in the basement, and start work on lesson plans for Creative Writing 1. It takes me three hours on my laptop, but I hammer out two weeks' worth of lessons on creating dynamic characters for fiction, presenting details related to setting, and using figurative language. I decide to take a brief break, and when I check out my NEA on-line newsletter, I discover that 2012 Republican presidential candidate Mitt Romney complained that it is "an extraordinary conflict of interest" that teachers' unions donate money to the Democratic party, and President Obama responded, "You know, I think Governor Romney and a number of folks try to politicize the issue and do a lot of teacher bashing. When I meet teachers all across the country, they are so devoted, so dedicated to their kids."

THURSDAY, SEPTEMBER 27

During my last block of the day, my Honors class, I pull Monique, a five-foot tall basketball player, into the hallway halfway through the period. I have reached my highest level of frustration with her because she cannot stay quiet. I say, "You simply cannot keep talking while I am delivering directions to the class. We have talked about this before, Monique. I cannot tolerate it anymore."

She gives me a plaintive look. "But it's what I do. I talk. I'm afraid if I don't keep talking, I won't be able to swallow."

I process that for a moment – *if I prohibit her from talking, am I putting her health at risk?* I look down on her and decide to wave her comment away with my hand. "It has to stop, Monique. Your socializing is getting in the way of the lessons, of you getting your work done."

She looks up at me. Her face is without expression. "I do my work."

"No, you don't, Monique. You talk when you shouldn't be, and you *don't* do all your work. I just checked everyone's prewriting for your persuasive essays and yours was not completed."

"I was shooting hoops at a friend's house." She glances up and down the empty hallway. "But it almost was."

I keep my voice level. "No, it wasn't. In fact, if this keeps up, you might fail this quarter and be ineligible for basketball altogether."

She stops checking out the hallway and stares up at me. Her eyes widen. This is new information to her. "How?"

I have this brief vision that I am joining Monique at a turning point in her life, that I will now make profound statements that point her in the right direction. But all I say is, "Because you will fail this class and then possibly be ineligible."

Monique stiffens and turns toward the classroom door as if to go back inside, but I stop her by blocking the entrance with my arm. I'm desperate now. "Do you understand what I'm asking you to do? I don't want you to end up being ineligible." I immediately regret saying this, but I cannot take it back. I should know better than to use a grade as a threat; that is not a way to motivate students. This makes me an enemy in her eyes, not a teacher. However, I also cannot take back my statement; that would make me appear ineffectual.

She takes her eyes off me and stares unblinking into the classroom where her classmates are reading and analyzing the persuasion strategies in an editorial advocating the need to increase funds for space travel. "I do my work," Monique mumbles and takes a step toward the open door.

"What about the talking?" I ask.

Her voice is glum. "I won't talk."

I drop my arm and step away from the door to let her walk back inside the classroom.

I attend another levy meeting tonight, this time in the school's board conference room. Only two other teachers show up this time – both are elementary school teachers – and neither volunteers to do anything. Only one of the ladies even says anything at the meeting. She asks if teachers will have to go door-to-door and drop off any literature if it's raining and implies that she won't do that. Other than the four officers of the levy committee, no other parent shows up, and the total number of attendees is nine, including the superintendent.

Mr. Allen arrives late with twenty white t-shirts that have "Vote Yes on Issue #13" on the front and back in blue ink. He proudly passes them out to the group.

Mr. Zimmerman, our chairperson, spreads out a shirt and lifts it in front of his face. "They should say, 'Vote *For* Issue #13,' he tells Mr. Allen. "These are wrong."

"It doesn't say Yes and No on the ballot," Mrs. Zimmerman adds. "It says For or Against."

Mr. Allen grimaces, collects the shirts, and gruffly stuffs them back into the box. "The next batch of shirts will say that...*For*," he tells us, and, head down, he closes up the box. When he finishes, he has more to say: "If this levy does not pass, Bayview will turn into a ghetto next year. People are saying, 'It's over with...Just close that school down.'"

Mr. and Mrs. Zimmerman ignore this and move onto the next topic: Getting the literature into voters' hands by both mail and a door-to-door effort. Looking at us, Mr. Zimmerman declares, "The kids should do that for us, you know. They're a lot cheaper than postage." He grins when he says this, as if he's just delivered a Jerry Seinfeld punch line.

Then Mr. Zimmerman brings up the need for a phone script to be used to call Bayview residents and solicit their votes for the levy. Without a pause, he looks directly at me. "Is this something you could write, Mr. Miller?"

In fact, they're all looking at me now, so I say, "Of course, Mr. Zimmerman. When do you need it?"

This time he looks at his wife and plants his palms flat on the table. "When do you think we'll need it, Madame President?"

Mrs. Zimmerman's eyes go wide. She is unprepared for this question. Her gaze shifts from her husband to me and back to her husband. "I don't know...How about by October first, so we can start calling people?" Although the question is directed to me, she keeps her eyes on her husband, the levy chairperson, as if hoping October 1ˢᵗ is the right answer.

I realize that I have the weekend ahead of me. I have my English 10 Honors persuasion essays to assess, but I will use either Saturday or Sunday night to write the phone levy script. "Sure," I tell the group. "I'll have it ready by October first."

One of the committee officers suggests someone should go into the nursing home down the street to coax the aides and nurses to vote for the levy, not the residents. These elderly people, it is believed, have no clue about the candidates or the issues. Allegedly, the aides and nurses then tell them who and what to vote for.

After another thirty minutes of blah, blah, blah, which includes a fifteen-minute debate about where the lawn signs should be placed on the property and on what roads, only six people remain. During the debate, the Democratic Party chaplain marketing his literature services leaves and a few minutes later so do both elementary school teachers.

FRiDAY, SEPTEMBER 28

I have a conference in my classroom at the end of the school day with Ebony Burrell, her guardian Mrs. Jackson, and Phil Oster about Ebony's behavior in class. Phil, in fact, has to track down Ebony in the hallways because she had originally refused to come to this conference.

We all sit at students' desks in a little circle, and I tell Mrs. Jackson that Ebony has been disrespectful to me in class. I let her read a discipline referral I had filled out – but not turned into Mr. Compton – about Ebony after she arrived late yesterday, yelled in class, teased classmates, used her cell phone, walked out of the room without permission, and said my grading methods were "all fucked up."

"I never said that," Ebony almost yells.

I continue: "She also said, somewhat, I think, as a joke, 'I hope you are still here when I leave this school because I'm gonna come back and cuss you out.'"

"I never said that either." Ebony slaps her hands on the desktop.

Ms. Jackson, a tired-looking black woman in a large cream-colored overcoat, lowers her face and slowly shakes her head as I say this. Then she declares, "It will end on Monday." She turns toward Phil and tells him as if he was the only other adult in the room: "I don't have time for all this...I got two little ones at home."

"I understand what you mean," I interject, trying to sound sympathetic although I am hoping for more certainty that Ebony's disrespectful behavior is going to end. "Ebony simply cannot act this way anymore."

Phil nods as if in agreement with me and says to Ebony, "You seem to be getting along with everyone in the hallways and at lunch, what's going wrong in Mr. Miller's class?"

Ebony admits that, yes, she hates the class and the school, but, no, she claims, she does not act that badly.

Phil says, "I see you've made some friends in the school, you just have to fix your classroom behavior."

"I don't like this school either," Ms. Jackson tells us. "I'm trying to move back to Cleveland Heights by November."

I suggest Applewood, a counseling service, for Ebony, that Applewood worked with two students last year and helped them. I inquire if she wants me to complete a referral form for Ebony. Ms. Jackson gives me her approval and tells me I should contact her if Ebony misbehaves again. I thank her but declare that from this point on I will simply complete a discipline referral if Ebony violates any more rules.

Ms. Jackson does that slow head shake again. "You do what you need to do, you fill out any form you want."

MONDAY, OCTOBER 1

We have our annual Homecoming Candidates Assembly in the morning and the entire student body – grades 6-12 – crowd into the gym to see who will be named the 9th grade count and countess, the 10th grade duke and duchess, the 11th grade prince and princess, and the three finalists for the 2012 Homecoming King and Queen. The seven senior girls who are Homecoming queen candidates smile a lot as they sit nervously on white plastic chairs on the risers on stage. The seven senior boys sit with legs extended casually and arms slung over the backs of their chairs, a cool pose that does little to hide their true desire to be named the 2012 Homecoming King. The winner will have bragging rights for the rest of the school year.

Parents of each member of the Homecoming Court have also been invited to attend this event but only four show up. One of these parents, a father whose name I do not know, sits several rows ahead of me in my colleague Rebecca Leever's chair, making her stand throughout the thirty-minute program. I stand, too, because all the seats in my section are taken by students.

There is a glitch when the microphone sounds scratchy, and another father, a stocky man in a denim jacket, leaves his seat, goes backstage, walks up to the podium while a student presenter is speaking, and begins adjusting the microphone right in front of her. No one complains about this because his adjustments work, and the scratchy feedback disappears.

This reminds me of last fall when our football team played at Fairport High School, which has a bowl-shaped football stadium and the visitors' bleachers are only ten feet away from the players and coaches on the sideline. No fence or rope separates the fans from the team on the visitor's side.

That night, our last football game of the year on an unseasonably warm late October night, was against the Fairport Skippers, who had only one win. We were winless at the time. No students or faculty members came to watch the game, and only ten Bayview parents were there (it was easy to count them).

Even worse, only three of six cheerleaders showed up for the bus, and their advisor did not come either. The three girls cheered alone on that night – "Pump, pump – pump it up!" and "Let's go, Bayview...Let's go!" – to the ten fans.

Half way through the second quarter the cheerleaders were joined by one of our player's chubby grandmothers who lined up with them in her royal blue sweatshirt, which made her look like an M&M cartoon character, and tried to imitate the girls' kicks and arm thrusts as they cheered. After awhile, when grandma and the girls realized no one was cheering or clapping other than me to their cheers, they gave up and just sat in the bleachers and ate the popcorn that I bought for them at the concession stand.

After Fairport took the lead in the third quarter, one of the player's fathers left the bleachers, joined the team on the sideline, and began to help coach the defense. Neither the head coach nor our athletic director asked him to return to the bleachers and watch the game like the other spectators. Unfortunately, his coaching did not help as Fairport went on to win the game, leaving Bayview High School 0-10 for the season.

Today at the Candidates' Assembly we do not have enough chairs for all students to sit so the 6th, 7th, and 8th graders have to sit in the metal bleachers on the side, which are only four rows. These kids are hunched over and jammed shoulder to shoulder. To ease their discomfort they talk to each other and keep on talking no matter how many times their teachers shush them to quiet down.

Students cheer, clap, and call out their names when the three senior girl finalists for Homecoming queen and the three senior boy finalists for king are finally named. Four of them stand at their chairs and smile broadly to the crowd, but the remaining girl and boy are so excited to have been selected they start twerking on stage – to tremendous cheers and stomping from the students in the audience – until Rebecca Leever, who has been standing the whole time and is the closest faculty member, rushes forward to the stage, waves her arm at them, and yells at the boy and girl to stop. Thankfully, they do, but now a hundred students in the audience boo Rebecca as she returns to her spot against the wall. I suspect the twerking incident can almost guarantee that girl to become queen and the boy to be king after the voting is done at the end of the week. Last year, the punch-out girl was voted queen, and two years ago, during the Homecoming dance in the gym, our queen snuck out, broke into the computer lab down the hall, and stole a laptop to do her boyfriend's on-line homework.

After school that day, Allison Means and I sit at students' desks in my classroom twenty minutes after the students are gone and she tells me a story: She was making copies outside Mr. Compton's office that morning and overheard him talking to the superintendent. Mr. Compton had his telephone on speakerphone so she heard them arguing about ink – that is, the color of the ink that teachers must use to complete school forms when they're doing so with a pen.

The problem?

Dr. Andrews, our superintendent, wanted Mr. Compton to be sure all the teachers filled out every form in either blue or black ink only. Mr. Compton was concerned about what he should do if a teacher began the form in blue ink and then finished it in black, or began the form in black ink and finished it in blue. What should he do then? Moreover, was he obligated to sign off on the form in the same ink color the teacher used? Allison, her frustration showing in her hunched shoulders and slight frown, reveals that this conversation went on for twenty minutes.

"I don't believe you," I say. "Twenty minutes? C'mon!"

"Okay," she admits. "But it was at least fifteen...fifteen minutes about blue or black ink on a form."

That I do believe.

WEDNESDAY, OCTOBER 3

In an email today and at our PLC meeting at the end of the day, Mr. Compton demands we have borders on our bulletin boards. Why?

No one knows or asks. However, if any teacher neglects this demand, according to the email, he or she could be considered to be insubordinate. Therefore, after the meeting ends we all scramble, especially me, to find borders for our bulletin boards. Jack and Rebecca lend me some of their extra border material, and I spend 45 minutes cutting, trimming, and stapling the flimsy border paper around the edges of my bulletin boards.

THURSDAY, OCTOBER 4

Open House for grades 6-12...This event has been hastily announced and organized. The evening is supposed to begin with Mr. Compton speaking to the parents in the gym from 6:00 P.M. to 6:30 P.M. Parents can then wander the school, check out the classrooms, and meet the teachers. This event seems more for public relations than to prompt any academic achievement. Mr. Compton reveals to me that he is hopeful 200 parents show up. The parents were first notified of this event in a phone broadcast three days earlier, where they were told the Open House was not for personal conferences. It was only for seeing the classrooms and meeting teachers. However, since by contract the teaching staff is not obligated to work past 3 P.M., only half of my colleagues, including me, show up.

I arrive just before 6 P.M. and open my classroom door, turn on the lights, and admire for a moment the new blue borders around my bulletin boards. Exactly at 6 P.M. I stroll into the gym and count 32 parents who are there to listen to Mr. Compton's speech, but neither Mr. Compton nor Mr. Morgan are there. I return to my classroom to be sure my handouts are ready to go, and indeed, my syllabus and evaluation policy for each class are still stacked neatly on two students' desks.

When I return to the gym ten minutes later, the parent count is up to 36 but no administrator is there yet. Finally, at 6:16, Mr. Compton, with Mr. Morgan in tow, walks into the gym, clamps both hands on the sides of the wooden podium, and welcomes the parents.

Mr. Compton apologizes first for the late notice about the Open

House but not his late arrival, and then he moves away from the podium and begins speaking in a somewhat off-the-cuff manner to the parents. He tells them that he has eliminated the bells, and "it is so much quieter now in the school."

The truth is that the school is not any less quiet, but the parents do not know enough to dispute this. "You know," Mr. Compton goes on, "they did a study years ago and these animals learned to move to a bell." He quickly claps his hands several times, trying to imitate, I think, either the bell or the animals' sudden movement. "So the animals learned to react, and...the study...." He stops, trying to remember, and math teacher Gordon Davison calls out to him from the side of the gym, "Do you mean the study with Pavlov's dogs to a ringing bell?"

Mr. Compton gets excited. "That's right, Pavlov's dogs!" His face goes frog-like. "Those dogs would move when they heard a bell. We don't have bells anymore, so students only move when the teachers tell them to. The hallways are quieter now." He smiles widely.

The parents stare politely back at him, and many shift uncomfortably in the fold out chairs.

I leave the gym at 6:35 before Mr. Compton is done speaking. The Open House is over at 7:30 P.M. but only three parents show up to my classroom (Each thinks the Open House is designed as a parent/teacher conference opportunity) before I leave at 7:30. They either did not understand Mr. Compton's broadcast phone message or they ignored it.

I get a text from my wife Sheryl: *When are you coming home?*

After the levy meeting maybe by 9 30, I text back.

Her response does not surprise me: *What is wrong with you? You are insane.*

At the levy committee meeting in the board conference room, only five people in total attend this time, but Mr. Zimmerman hides his disappointment with smiles and jokes about how poorly the Cleveland Browns are playing. I read my phone script to the other four, and they sullenly approve of it.

It is only when we walk out after 9:15 P.M. that Mr. Zimmerman reveals his frustration directly. "I don't know why more teachers don't show up," he complains. His face is down, but I know this statement is directed to me. *Do I look at him and hear the rest?*

When he does not continue, I take the bait and say, "I don't know why either." Which is a lie. I do know: They don't come because their personal time is valuable to them, and they'd rather not spend it with him and this committee. In most teachers' opinions, the Bayview residents are not going to vote for the levy.

"Don't they care about the school?" Mrs. Zimmerman asks, her voice almost whining. Both she and her husband slow their pace to their cars, and I sense they want to talk about this in depth.

So I stop, straighten my posture, and look directly at their faces. I speak evenly. "They definitely care about the school system," I tell them. "But right now, they could be working on lesson plans, grading papers or tests, attending graduate school classes, or simply helping their own children with their homework. There could be a hundred reasons they don't attend these meetings."

"*You* do." Mr. Zimmerman says this, and I hear it more like a question, as in, if you're here, why aren't they?

When I don't respond, he stops a few feet away from his Mazda, and I hear small stones crunch beneath his boots. "Some people are probably still holding grudges." Mr. Zimmerman smiles after he says this, trying in some way to be friendly.

Grudges?

I resent myself for asking, but I ask anyway, "What do you mean?"

"You know...the strike."

"The strike was five years ago," I clarify for him.

Mr. Zimmerman is ready. "Yeah, but a lot of staff still remember it."

I make myself stay quiet this time.

As I drive home I recall the strike: The useless picketing. Holding a sign that demanded, "We Want a Fair Contract." My colleagues grumbling about the anti-Christ superintendent. Our fear the strike would never end. Mrs. Zimmerman was on the school board then, and I remember, pulling now into my driveway, that she voted after the strike ended to terminate the superintendent's contract when the board voted that summer.

I put a plate of spaghetti and meatballs in the microwave, and as it warms up I tell my wife Sheryl about the unproductive levy meeting.

She joins me in the kitchen, shakes her head, and glares at me. "Why do you bother? You're *retiring*. And besides, Ethan, I really don't want to hear about that Bayview stuff anymore. It's too depressing." Her eyes are hard, and I interpret that to mean I'm spending too much time at Bayview away from the family.

I consider her comment for a moment. I want my answer to the *why do you bother* to sound logical and to provide a clarity and relevance that will diffuse her argument. However, all I say is, "I guess I bother because I just do. I'm still a teacher there."

Sheryl swipes strands of her auburn hair off her cheeks and tucks them behind her ears. Her pretty face scrunches into a grimace. "It doesn't make sense. Even if the levy does pass, you won't benefit from it."

She's right. I had buried the fact that the Bayview School District would not receive the funds from the levy tax until January 2014, six months after I've retired. Nevertheless, I search my brain again for a response that will make sense to both of us. Here's what I say: "I guess I just want to experience *everything* my last year."

Sheryl shakes her head again. "Yeah! Too much." Then she leaves the kitchen, and I pull my plate of spaghetti out of the microwave. I'm starving.

I go on-line as I eat my dinner, swirling the spaghetti around my fork, and read on my NEA newsletter that Secretary of Education Arne Duncan is quoted in an Associated Press article calling "for the nation to move as fast as possible away from printed textbooks and toward digital ones...Over the next few years, textbooks should be obsolete." He references South Korean students, who have outperformed U.S. students in the past, and the need to be more globally competitive. "The world is changing," Duncan says. "This has to be where we go as a country."

I read in my newspaper that in Warrensville Heights, a community that is a twenty-five minute drive south of Bayview, Shaakira Dorsey, a sixteen old girl, was beaten to death by another sixteen year old after school for criticizing that student's flatulence in class earlier in the day. A group of adults, including Shaakira's stepfather watched the fight. An editorial in the Cleveland *Plain Dealer* comments, "She died for what? Sometimes this world makes absolutely no sense."

FRIDAY, OCTOBER 5

All the girls who had been suspended for fighting are back, albeit in different classrooms, and I am definitely grateful that Mr. Morgan changed two of the girls' schedules to move them away from their boxing ring opponents. Tina Wills remains in my first period and after she keeps getting out of her seat, I approach her and whisper, "Tina, it makes me nervous when you get out of your seat."

She peers up at me with almond-shaped eyes. "Why?"

I struggle somewhat to say this. "I keep thinking...you are getting up to fight again."

"Oh, Mr. Miller," Tina whispers back, "I'm not going to do *that* again."

The day ends with our Homecoming Pep Rally – forty minutes of rah, rah, rah put on by Gretchen Suchs and her student council officers.

The football team is introduced. At least I think I am supposed to hear their introductions, but the sound system in the high school gym is not working properly. The boys – only half of them are wearing their jerseys – stand in a line in front of the other students in the bleachers and jostle and tease each other while one of the senior captains, a thickly built defensive lineman who was ejected from a recent game for fighting an opposing player on the field, tries to introduce each one. We cannot hear their names, so John Garfield, one of the custodians, comes over and taps the head of the microphone several times and decides it is working properly. He hands it back to the football captain and leaves. We still cannot hear the all the introductions. Most of the names sound like "Mimm, Jith, Shhhrrr..." I do hear, however, the team captain say, "Here's Jay D...Here's T-bone...." As each boy is introduced, a nearby teammate pushes him or laughs. Is this why our football team has only three wins in three years?

Then Student Council advisor Gretchen Suchs takes the microphone and tries to tell the students how they must dress for the Homecoming dance on Saturday but again no one can really hear her because she talks so quietly and the microphone still isn't working properly. This makes Mr. Compton request the microphone from her and then stand straight in his dark brown suit, his eyes staring at the students in the bleachers, a posture demanding they get quiet. This prompts students to start shushing each other. When they finally quiet down, Mr. Compton tells them they must stay quiet at the pep rally and listen to the speakers.

Stay quiet?

At a pep rally?

Irony?

But before he can finish, Oscar, the security monitor, suddenly screams at a student in the stands. "Raymond, shut your mouth!" This is followed by a chorus of laughter.

Mr. Compton is momentarily stunned by the Oscar's admonition of Raymond but repeats his demand that students stay quiet, which they do for only two minutes before they start catcalling the cheerleaders who are now moving onto the gym floor, the bright gym lights shining off the sparkles they have on their faces, to do a dance.

As the cheerleaders position themselves in the center of the gym, on the other side of the gym sparkplug Suzanne Smith runs up and down waving her hands, inciting the 6th through 8th graders to do the wave. Her face is painted royal blue and white. She does a cartwheel. Some middle school students cheer for her.

Afterwards I return to my empty and quiet classroom and suddenly hear two girls screaming at each other in the hallway. My pulse races. I stand, lean a hand on my desk, and realize I am totally nervous about this. Nevertheless, I step into the hallway and the two girls are right there. I check out the perimeter, quickly glancing left and right down the dim, near-empty hallway, and start to decide which girl I will grab first.

But they are only arguing. They're not angry. I sense my pulse lessening and feel relief wash over me.

I return to my classroom and think back to my first years – the early 1980s – at Bayview High School. In truth, coming to Bayview changed my life. I was the head wrestling coach for twenty years and had ten state champions. I was even honored as Ohio's Wrestling Coach of the Year in 1990. My framed picture hangs on the wall down by the gym corridor, just above eye level so the kids can't easily spit on it.

And to make it even better, I went out to a local tavern one Saturday night in 1987 with an assistant coach and met Sheryl. We started dating, and on Christmas Eve 1988 in front of all her family at her grandmother's house I proposed to her. We married in 1989, and a year later she was pregnant with our daughter.

Back in the day, I could bring my infant daughter to a wrestling tournament and all the moms would take care of her while I coached and my wife worked the hospitality room. The superintendent and principal back then came to the tournaments and sat with the parents and cheered all out for the boys.

I had a great job at Bayview, a wonderful wife, and a beautiful daughter. Indeed, I started to feel complete. Then everything crashed.

Money problems hit the school district in 2000, and the wrestling program (along with cheerleading, baseball, band, etc., etc.) was eliminated. Bayview went with only two sports each season and, of course, the winter season meant only boys and girls basketball. These sports maintained their funding because two school board members had children on the teams. After that, we lost six levies in a row over five years.

In 2002, when I sat across the school board president at a public meeting and appealed to him to re-install the wrestling program, he said, "Rasslin'? You talkin' 'bout rasslin'? This school ain't got no money, and you want to save rasslin'?"

In 2004, the next school board president, who was an attorney, announced at a public forum that the school could solve all its money problems if 400 people – teachers, parents, administrators – each went out and fund-raised $1000 each, asking friends and neighbors for the money. Later, it was discovered that this school board president didn't even live in the school district, and he was forced to resign.

Now on October 5, 2012, I am the old man at our school, and no one really knows or cares about our school's history or traditions. Maybe Allison does.

This is only October, and I think I am experiencing teacher burnout. I am trying very hard not to count the days.

SATURDAY, OCTOBER 6

Our Homecoming football game was yesterday, and according to my NEA newsletter we differ dramatically from a high school in Kountze, Texas. We played in a pouring rain; they had a warm, hazy sky. We had a sparse crowd while their bleachers were nearly full. Our team lost, theirs won.

A *New York Times* article today reports on a controversy in Kountze over hand-made banners with scriptural passages being waved by cheerleaders at football games, which has "embroiled this East Texas town in a heated debate over God, football and cheerleaders' rights." The article notes school authorities had banned the banners "because they believed [they] violated the law on religious expression at public school events. In response, a group of 15 cheerleaders and their parents sued the Kountze Independent School District and its superintendent, Karl Weldon, claiming that prohibiting the students from writing Christian banner messages violated their religious liberties and free-speech rights."

WEDNESDAY, OCTOBER 10

A new school board member who had been appointed to the Bayview school board at their Monday meeting two days ago submits his resignation. A rumor is floated among the teaching staff that he was nervous about the FBI background check that is mandatory for both school personnel and board members, so he chose to quit instead. True or not, this does not surprise me. Who really would want to serve on this school board anyway?

Just yesterday in church, one of the readings was from James, the third chapter: "Not many of you should become teachers...for you know that we who teach will be judged with great strictness. For all of us make many mistakes."

How true.

Personal letters are the focus today in my English 10 class. I tell a story because a best practice teaching technique is using stories that have a conflict or a complication related to the subject matter. Since today's lesson is about emails and personal letters, my story is about a Dear John letter I received from a girl whose name I have forgotten but for today I call Veronica.

Here's the story I tell my students: I met Veronica in the summer before my senior year of college and we dated for about six weeks. She was pretty, lively, and fun. We enjoyed spending time with each other and promised to write (no emailing or texting in 1977) after I returned to Miami University. Write we did, until I received her Dear John letter three weeks before I was to return to Cleveland for Thanksgiving vacation. She had met another guy and was not interested in seeing me anymore.

I was upset and depressed, so my buddies decided to take me out the Friday night after Thanksgiving to help me forget about Veronica and the break up. Unfortunately, we ran into her and her new boyfriend, and the remainder of the evening did not go well.

"Did you get into a fight with him?" one student asks.

Another calls out: "Did you knock him out?"

I refuse to tell them the specifics and go on with my story, pleased that they are listening and engaged. I tell them that Veronica did write me once more after I returned to Miami University. She criticized my "immature" behavior and called me a jerk along with some other profane terms. This makes some students laugh.

Then I tell them how I responded to her letter: I marked the errors in punctuation and spelling, suggested some better diction than the profanity she offered in her letter, and wrote a summary comment at the end which was, "I may be immature but at least I know how to write a competent and coherent letter." Then I stuffed the corrected letter into an envelope and mailed it back to her. The students laugh at this and want to know if my story is really true.

"Absolutely," I tell them. "Absolutely."

THURSDAY, OCTOBER 11

The day is chilly but sunny, and the sunshine lifts my spirits as each class period transitions into the next one. On television, the news stations' meteorologists have informed us the weather is broken and we should not hope for any more warm days. Regardless, I look out the classroom windows at the leaves changing color and a green lawn on the other side of the school driveway and imagine myself at a mountain cabin in the Ozarks and I'm rich and I can even afford the tuition at Ivy League schools for my sons.

One of my sophomore students, Jamie, tells me she is tired of looking at the same pictures (famous individuals like Nelson Mendala, George Patton, Bill Clinton, Michael Jordan, and Maya Angelou and the words "Read a Biography" on one bulletin board. Would I let her make the next bulletin board? I do not let more than two seconds pass before I tell her of course she can. "Absolutely, Jamie. It's all yours." I want to kick myself for not thinking of this sooner.

Jamie's eyes are on the other bulletin board that is a collage of letters and posters about the mail service through history. "I want to do a winter theme," she says.

"Sounds very timely," I say. "It's all yours."

I receive another highlight during the day when Angie Owens, who graduated last school year, visits my classroom at the end of the school day. A year ago, after I asked Angie why she wore so much jewelry, she told me feared her mother would sell her necklaces and rings at a pawnshop if she didn't.

Today, Angie says, "I just want to thank you."

Thank me? The last time I saw Angie was at her graduation in 2012. "For what?" I ask.

"Thanks to you, I am so far ahead of my classmates with my writing. One of my professors even wants to publish one of my papers."

"That's awesome," I tell her. "I am so pleased to get news like this. I want to thank *you!*"

Angie tells me her paper will be published in a school literary magazine and she just knows so much more about writing engaging sentences than her classmates at Central State University in Ohio. I love hearing news like this because it convinces me I am doing the right thing in my classroom.

Later that evening, I attend a Community Forum event hosted at the school by our superintendent, who first introduces school board president Mrs. Gerta Zimmerman whose rambling talk includes the school levy signs, the need for poll workers, the booster club spaghetti dinner on Saturday, improving school programs, the Friday football game, callers needed for the Wednesday phone banks, then back to levy signs, and finally her "vision."

Our school district has about 950 students in grades K-12, but only nine parents are in attendance for this Community Forum. I am one of only three staff members who attend this evening event. We hear Mrs. Zimmerman's vision: She wants Bayview to be a "positive school where the students learn Chinese and know their math equations. We should put on a Broadway musical, and our teams should win a state championship in something. Bayview could be a really good school. We have to get the kids off video games and learn Chinese." She also declares students need to learn engineering and technology so they can travel into space. She refers a couple of times to the NASA technicians and the astronauts involved with Apollo 13, and it occurs to me that she must have recently seen the 1995 movie starring Tom Hanks. Then she smiles, waves at the twelve of us in attendance, and walks back to her chair.

Even with the small number of parents there, several issues emerge. Parents are concerned that we have no yearbook, that budget cuts by the state government have gutted public education making residents pay more in taxes, that a middle school teacher did not return a phone call, that the students' schedules kept changing, and that not enough teachers were in their classrooms at the Open House event. One parent even declares that her daughter was enrolled in the wrong grade. Dr. Andrews addresses each complaint in turn, and I sense his exhaustion growing as the evening and the criticism continue.

One mother protests, "The middle school hallways stink. I was there picking up my daughter. I think some kids are leaving old lunches in their lockers. It makes you want to run to another school district."

"Don't do that," Dr. Andrews says to her gravely. "Don't run away. Stay." He then tries to encourage all the parents. "We're not only monitoring the kids, we're also monitoring the teachers...and that's how they will be evaluated."

I sympathize with our superintendent this evening. I truly do. He is not dismissing any complaint; nor is he skirting their questions. Unfortunately, the Community Forum ends without any real resolutions or commitments, and as I leave I notice that the superintendent standing near the podium, his arms crossed, listening earnestly to the woman who was upset she did not receive a return phone call from her middle school teacher.

FRIDAY, OCTOBER 12

Today is an in-service day. We are mandated to receive training in cultural diversity because Ohio's Office of Civil Rights received objections about our school district. Last year a mom complained several middle school teachers discriminated against her transsexual son, and a previous principal supposedly told some students they behaved like they lived in a third world country. Soon thereafter, he was fired.

We begin with an icebreaker where the superintendent tells us to line up around the gym according to our years of service in the Bayview School District, but we must do this without talking. My colleagues start waving their fingers, showing three, twelve, twenty fingers to indicate their individual number of years. I do not have to do this. I go immediately to the end of the line. No one has worked in the Bayview School District longer than I have: 32 years (I taught for three years at another high school before coming to Bayview).

We then count off from one to eight, split up into ten groups with our counterparts with the same number, and sit at tables around the gym's perimeter. My assumption is this in-service is to help a mostly white staff learn to work better with minority students. Dr. Andrews, in fact, announces that the OCR, after conducting interviews, has labeled our school as "a racially hostile school district" which has "a history of racial discrimination." Therefore, we must receive this training and then be monitored for the next 3-5 years to make sure we are in compliance.

This prompts some questions from my colleagues. What racist acts did we commit? Who accused us of this? What staff members were interviewed? When did all this happen?

Dr. Andrews either ignores or deflects the questions. He will not identify the accusers, nor does he tell us who was interviewed.

Peculiarly, the opening discussion shifts to fights in our school and middle school intervention specialist Julie Hanson tells a story about a recent fight between two boys that happened in her classroom. She wants advice about what she should do when there is a fight. Dr. Andrews suggests she needs to be more observant in her classroom, that fights typically have precipitating factors. Students always say something first.

"Not always," Julie says, her face showing disbelief that her story would be doubted. "This fight, they just went at it. They didn't say anything to each other."

"There is always *something* before they fight," Dr. Andrews asserts from the portable podium.

"No, there wasn't," Julie argues, her face still a look of surprise. "They just started fighting. What should we do?"

Some other colleagues steal glances at me. They know about the two girl fights that happened spontaneously in my classroom.

Dr. Andrews gets upset with Julie. "I don't appreciate what you said...that sarcasm."

Although the rest of us are somewhat stunned by this, Connie, an elementary school teacher, tries to help Julie and says as a female she too personally feels uncomfortable breaking up a fight.

Dr. Andrews advises her, "Ask some young men in the room to help you."

Connie teaches first grade. She trades wide-eyed looks with some of her elementary school colleagues and then gets quiet.

Dr. Andrew's face gets stern and lets us know he wants to make stopping students' fights a priority. Waving a finger toward the ceiling, he declares that from now on, security personnel will not just be sitting down in the hallway during the day, they will be walking the hallways on patrol. Dr. Andrews then laments that the real problem with school fights is that kids "are videotaping these things, putting them on YouTube. We need to take control of our classroom, we need to take control of our lives, we need to take control of the direction of this school."

Table groups are then assigned to discuss the issue of stereotypes: When did we ever experience this personally and when have we observed it? I go first and tell the colleagues at my table that when my brother and I were traveling in Greece in 1978 and a taxi driver stereotyped us as being "epithetikos" when he learned that our ancestry was Spartan. His stereotype was that males of Spartan ancestry are often tough and violent. These days, stereotyping can be seen daily on Disney's kid shows where smart teenagers are nerds and teachers are fools.

Gretchen Suchs refers to the stereotypical portrayals of black youth as thugs on rap videos and explains to our group that she has told her black students she is offended when they use the n-word. Nancy Johnson chimes in and wants to know why a white student is punished for using the n-word but a black student is not. Ander Klyszewski, who is of Croatian descent, tells us how a black student in his class told another black student, "You quit acting white." Gail, an elementary school teacher at our table, chimes in and suggests that their use of the n-word is "a cultural thing."

I suddenly feel a great melancholy and ask, "Gail, do you think Dr. Martin Luther King, Jr. would accept the n-word as part of his culture?"

She looks at me for a moment and then re-groups. "No, I don't really mean it's cultural like that, I mean it's a socio-economic thing."

Nancy Johnson joins her. "That's what I mean, too; when I say cultural I mean socio-economic. They're the same thing."

I feel compelled to respond but I find myself stuttering, like I can't control my lips anymore. Third grade teacher Loretta Billings, who is black, plants her hands on the table, stands, and says, "This whole conversation is irritating me." Then she stands and walks away.

After Dr. Andrews calls out on the microphone to end our table discussions on stereotypes, Loretta returns to the table but sits staring away from the rest of us. Next, we hear from Dr. Andrews an unrelated story about a student he knew twenty years ago who failed math but grew up to become a preacher.

Dr. Andrews then directs his secretary to walk around with a cordless microphone for any more stories or comments, and Allison Means, who can never remain quiet in a group setting, grabs the microphone hard and almost shouts, "If I'm being called a racist, I still want to know who is saying that? What's going on here?"

No one wants to follow her, so the morning in-service ends with Dr. Andrews, still on his Kumbaya approach, referring to Michael Jackson and the other performers who participated in the "We are the World" song. We should follow their lead, he asserts. He wonders if anyone wants to join him in singing.

No one does.

I think I am supposed to leave the in-service today feeling inspired and more knowledgeable about minority culture, but I do not. *What is wrong with me?*

SATURDAY, OCTOBER 13

The levy committee has a "Hot Spot" rally to promote the school levy. This rally takes place actually at the intersection of Chardon and Richmond Road, which is a main intersection in Bayview, where we hope our signs and shouts will reach a maximum amount of drivers on this chilly and overcast day. Fifteen kids, three parents, and I (no other teachers) are at this rally, and we split up at the intersection and branch out at each corner. None of these individuals represents the elementary or middle schools. This makes me wonder why more elementary school parents are not involved when they have more at stake since their children are just starting their long march through the Bayview school system.

Jordan Wilcox, one of our school board members, a heavy-set man with bushy eyebrows beneath a blue stocking cap, stands next to me on Richmond Road. Actually, we stand side by side on the gravel berm, watching the traffic go by and holding our signs dutifully at chest level, and with his 6' 4" height and heavy bulk he towers over me. Although I had his daughter in class last year he asks me, "What do you teach?"

"English," I answer.

He nods, but I don't think it really matters to him what I teach. "We gotta keep the energy going," he proclaims. "The synergy."

Even though I do not know what he means, I do not ask him to clarify. When he turns to check out the on-coming traffic, I study him for a moment, as if I can learn his biography by staring at his face. I imagine him as a high school student and wonder, What grades did he get? Did he play football? How did he end up in Bayview? My pondering stops when he turns back, and I pretend to look down the road for the next car.

Mr. Wilcox shakes his head and drops his sign for a moment. "Everybody likes to go to a meeting," he says, "but we need people to do the grunt work." He then lifts his sign again, waves it a little, and glances up and down Richmond Road, which is momentarily empty of cars. "This here, this is the grunt work."

"Every effort counts… I'm certain it will all pay off." I say this with some enthusiasm and hope he cannot detect that I doubt my own words.

"Yeah, I get it," Mr. Wilcox adds. "We got to put the work in. But this levy means more money out of our pockets. I get it that you want yours, but what about me? When do I get mine? Huh? When do I get mine?"

Later, I meet my brother for a beer and, although he is a surgeon at the Cleveland Clinic, he summarizes the teaching profession for me. He says, "Performance counts at my job; endurance counts at yours."

MONDAY, OCTOBER 15

I put this sign up in my classroom:

"There is no one who has lived or who will ever live who has your special talents, skills, or personality. You are obligated to develop the best about yourself."

In each class I point it out to the students and ask for reactions. Most say they like it. Some say the statement is "deep." But unfortunately no one expresses any interest in delving into the statement beyond that. Nevertheless, I tell myself not to be discouraged. I still want to be that inspirational teacher and, although this quote failed, maybe another one will work. I guess I just have to keep looking.

Mr. Compton sends this email to the staff: "I want to express my sincere THANKS to all the Staff here at Bayview High that attended the Diversity Training on Friday. I believe it was a GIANT step for us in moving this district in a GREAT upward direction. A special Thanks to Dr. Andrews for leading us in this endeavor. My hope is that we can take from that day and build upon it into greater and newer HEIGHTS."

I read this email around 5:00 P.M. as I watch Devin Jones, the football player wannabe, the kid who dances at his desk, try to complete all the assignments he neglected through the first quarter. I gave him this opportunity after he pleaded with me last week to let him make up his missing work, so I said I would work with him after school.

"How do you spell course?" Devin suddenly asks me.

"Which one?"

"Whatchu mean 'which one'?" He closes his literature textbook.

"Well, there's c-o-A-r-s-e, which means rough, and there's c-o-U-r-s-e, which has several meanings like a class or a program, a direction, a route...even the way, let's say, blood can flow through your veins."

"No, I don't mean those definitions. I mean the one for a dead person."

I pause for a moment, then: "You mean *corpse*, as in c-o-r-p-s-e."

He keeps his eyes on his paper. "But it doesn't sound like that."

"It doesn't?"

"I don't know," Devin says and starts writing big looping letters on his paper.

I think he's working on my assignment to explain the characters who died in a short story we read earlier in the year. I have promised to give him full credit for this late work if he was willing to come in after school and complete his missing assignments. At about 5:30 P.M. he stands, saunters over to me, and plops all his papers on my desk

I wait until he has returned to his desk and gathered up his textbook and notebook. "How sad is this," I say to Devin, "that you neglected this work when it was assigned and now had to spend about three hours after school today and who knows how many more hours tomorrow after school just before the quarter ends to do it."

This time, it's his turn to pause and then say: "I don't know." His eyes stay on the papers on my desk. They form a mini-hyphen between us.

"Why can't you get your work done when it's due? Is anything getting in the way of you completing assignments by their deadlines?"

His face is unreadable, a mask of indifference. "No. I don't know."

We study each other for ten seconds, and then he moves to the open doorway.

I call out to his back. "Please, Devin, don't make this mistake again."

WEDNESDAY, OCTOBER 17

When the staff meets in the library at the end of the school day for the weekly PLC, I lead a brief in-service, originally requested by Mr. Compton, about expanding our students' skills as readers. First, I do survey and ask my colleagues how many books they have in their homes. Fellow English teacher Gretchen Suchs estimates she has around two hundred, not counting the picture books she has for her toddler daughter. Military veteran and 6th grade teacher Ander Klyszewski claims he has around 1000. I inform them that research says that children in homes with over 100 books in them achieve higher math scores on standardized tests regardless of their parents' education. Moreover, I say, students who read 15-40 minutes in class have higher test scores. I distribute a paper with bullet points clarifying this research on reading.

"I can't get them to read more than two minutes in class," high school science teacher Jim Simmons complains.

In an I-can-top-that sequence, my colleagues call out the minutes of their students' reading endurance: a minute and a half, one minute, then thirty seconds until sixth grade teacher Ander Klyszewski wins by declaring his 6th graders can read no longer than fifteen consecutive seconds. Jennifer Stimson draws triangles and circles on the paper I handed out. Several others, I see, join her and doodle circles or boxes on their own papers.

Several other colleagues nod their heads, and Ander crosses his arms over his chest and stares at me, his bald head glistening under the bright lights in the library.

I ask my colleagues if they think our school has "a culture of reading." In other words, do we promote reading on a daily basis? Do we encourage reading as a means of learning? How many of our students do leisure reading along with their academic reading? We debate the answers to these questions for five minutes. Most think we try to promote reading; too many think we don't do enough.

Then I tell them to tell their students (like I tell mine) that part of our job as teachers is to train them to read material they will more than likely find boring (i.e., textbooks, training and repair manuals) in college or their careers. We can complain that students neglect reading today because of digital diversions and television, but we still need to promote, if not demand, more reading in our classes. Part of that is getting students to interact critically with their textbooks, to read, for example, a history textbook like a historian, a science text like a scientist, a math book like Pythagoras.

I monitor the attentiveness of my colleagues throughout my presentation and feel a slight sense of disappointment when I note that too many have glazed looks or their heads bowed as they manipulate the cellphones in their laps. Ander, however, stays focused on me and slowly shakes his head in silent resistance as I finish by emphasizing the need to demand students do close reading.

THURSDAY, OCTOBER 18

Only five people attend the levy committee meeting, which tonight is at the Bayview City Hall building. One of them is Margaret Craft, the principal at the elementary school. When we are finally settled in the conference room around a large table, Margaret starts rocking in her chair. In fact, she is fascinated that she can lean so far back in her chair and then rock forward again, as if she was sitting in a rocking chair. For several minutes she rocks back and forth, grinning and chuckling as she shares her amusement with the rest of us.

"Look at me," she exclaims, rocking back and forth. "Look at me. Oh my goodness. Who sits in this chair when they have meetings here?"

No one answers her because none of us know. When we discuss the upcoming schedule of levy events, Margaret declares she has been unable to attend previous levy meetings and any weekend events because there have been multiple deaths in her family and she has had to attend funerals each weekend in September and October. I almost ask her to list the seven dead family members, but of course I do not.

The conversation drifts to state-mandated guidelines that levy committees must follow, and for some odd reason Margaret announces she has four Masters' degrees. One of them, she declares, is a law degree although she has yet to pass the second part of the BAR exam.

Mr. Zimmerman solicits me to talk to Dr. Andrews on Friday about using the school phones to make the levy calls, and I turn to Margaret to ask her as a fellow administrator if she knows his schedule for that day.

"He'll be out the office between eleven A.M. and one P.M.," she says.

"Okay, but do you know his schedule...when he might be available?"

She rocks in her chair. "He'll be out the office between eleven A.M. and one P.M.," she repeats.

"I got it," I say calmly. "He's not available between eleven and one. What I need to know is if you know his schedule the rest of the day."

This makes her stop rocking and glare at me. "I'm sorry! I didn't mean to offend you."

I process this briefly: *Offended? No, I'm frustrated.* "I'm not offended," I tell her. "I just needed to know if Dr. Andrews will be in his office in the early morning. I get it that he won't be there between eleven and one."

"I don't know that," she says. "All I know is he will be gone between eleven and one."

I don't talk to her again.

As the meeting nears its conclusion, Mrs. Zimmerman complains that not enough teachers and parents are involved. Mr. Zimmerman nods his head as his wife talks and then says, "They've lost the enthusiasm for the district." He goes on to criticize Ohio's legislators, who "don't want public schools anymore." He probably would be interested to know that there were 248,000 public schools in America in 1929, according to NCES. Now there are 99,000. This makes me wonder about the future of the Bayview School District if the levy fails.

FRIDAY, OCTOBER 19

During my free period today I meet with Mr. Morgan to discuss his evaluation of me. Administrators are required to evaluate teachers for an entire class period at least once before November, but Mr. Morgan observed me teach for only five minutes at the very end of my first period the day before.

Now in his office, he spends the first twenty minutes telling me about *his* first job teaching at a correctional facility in Indiana, his trying experiences with the former superintendent of the Cleveland Municipal School District, and finally, during the last five minutes of our meeting, his observations of me and my lesson on characterization in works of fiction. He hands me my copy of the "Certified Employee Classroom Observation Form" that he has completed with a green pen. I receive all Excellents and a couple of Satisfactorys. I examine the paper and realize sadly that this is my final evaluation as a teacher, and I still have not achieved all Excellents.

I read Mr. Morgan's comments: "Classroom atmosphere was conducive to learning process with neat-looking posters and student work on walls. Neat bulletin boards. Well-prepared lesson. Something about story characters. Students were engaged in the learning process. They asked some questions. Holds students to high standards. Vocabulary. Students know what to expect from teacher and how they will be evaluated."

Mr. Morgan's smile looks more like a grimace. "Those kids at the kids' prison could really learn something from you," he says to close out our meeting.

SATURDAY, OCTOBER 27

Hurricane Sandy has hit the East Coast, and here in northeast Ohio we get Sandy's western fringe of rainy weather. Although a cold, drenching rain falls, about eight of us (five teachers) gather in the lobby of the administration office to do another "Hot Spot" rally and canvas eight neighborhoods to pass out levy literature door to door. Mr. Zimmerman asks who wants to hold signs at an intersection and who wants to walk door to door. Middle school teacher Julie Hanson and I volunteer to canvas door to door, while the others choose to stand at the Chardon and Richmond Road intersection again.

So I drive Julie from one street to another for the next two hours where she takes one side and I the other to stick levy literature in door handles or rubber band them to door knobs. In a short time I am drenched (no umbrella), but I keep the brochures dry inside my jacket. I probably drop off about 400 brochures today but not once do I see a Bayview resident.

MONDAY, OCTOBER 29

Mr. Compton sends the staff this email:

Greetings Staff:

As we wind down the month of October, I would like to THANK all of you for a super first quarter. As we begin the 2nd Quarter of Educating our Students, our goal will be to move our students to even greater heights in their studies and their work habits.

As our students enhance their sense of personal efficacy and adopt the philosophy that they are capable learners and that their actions have direct and positive consequences, they will become more productive and positive participants.

When our students perceive themselves as having an autonomous control of their own learning in the academic setting, your classroom management problems will diminish and the culture of the classroom will improve remarkably. And, when this transformation occurs, we will serve as true coaches and guides in our increasingly joyous classrooms.

So, in this 2nd grading period, let's help our students to become effective and independent planners, which will allow them to perform at high levels and achieve both curricular and societal goals. In turn, this will allow you as the teacher to enhance your instruction to emphasize creativity, innovation, and independent performance on tasks and projects within our students.

Have a Wonderful Week!!!!!!!!!!!!!!!

Also CONGRATULATIONS to the football team for a GREAT season!!!!!!!!!!!

Although I do not have the time to research it, I suspect he copied this from some other source. Our football team won two games and lost eight; they are 3-27 over the last three seasons. If that is a great season, what, in fact, is excellence at Bayview High?

WEDNESDAY, OCTOBER 31

Hurricane Sandy canceled both school yesterday and Halloween trick or treating tonight. The severe flooding, power outages, and dangerous road conditions prompted superintendents across the Cleveland area to cancel school the day before. This is a first for me: school being shut down due to rain (instead of snow). I admit I enjoyed sleeping in to 8:30 A.M. on Tuesday.

Today at our usual Wednesday staff meeting Mr. Compton tells us at the end that male teachers should wear a tie for the parent-teacher conferences that will be held on Thursday. When he acknowledges the female staff members and how they should dress, he stumbles and tells them to wear a "dress suit." When several female colleagues ask him to clarify the expected apparel for them – to define what he means by a "dress suit" – he gives up and simply tells them to "dress nice."

THURSDAY, NOVEMBER 1

Even though the day begins with more clouds, a cold drizzle, and the prospect of being at Bayview High from 6:30 A.M. to 9:00 P.M., I start the day by amusing Gretchen Suchs who teaches freshmen English next door to me. I place in her mailbox a card that shows a bunch of pigs at a trough and my written message that reads: "Which one is Snowball, which is Napoleon, and which is Squealer?" These are all animal characters in George Orwell's classic fable/novella *Animal Farm*. Before first period, she comes to my door and laughs. "Very cute, Ethan," she says, waving the card in her left hand. "I got a kick out of this."

I also wrote that she should hang in there during conferences, which take place from three to nine o'clock in the gymnasium after the school day has ended. I hope to follow my own advice after my Honors students exit class at 2:30. I have just enough time to gather the papers I want to take to the gym, use the bathroom, and get set up with my grade book and laptop at my assigned table.

Then from 3 P.M. on I greet and talk to one parent after another, and when I look into their faces I often see an older version of their son or daughter. Mr. Karl Horrigan, in fact, says his son, who is Karl Horrigan, Jr., is hyper and often unfocused. He admits, "I'm kind of hyper, too...but I've learned to channel it."

I am convinced of this because as we talk he continuously folds and unfolds his son's report card in his hand. Next to him, Karl, Jr., sits quietly and still.

Other parents use the conference time to berate their son or daughter who attends with them or to complain about their child's laziness or to tell me their child has been a poor student for years, even back to second grade. I listen, nod a lot, and express sympathy before offering suggestions. For instance, I suggest they not ask what their son or daughter has for homework; rather their question should be "Why did the teacher assign this to you?" as a way to open up a dialogue about the homework's intent or importance. I show parents their child's Writing Chart, explain its value, and offer suggestions about helping their child proofread their compositions. Finally, I explain over and over the stories and novels we will be reading next in class. Then it is their turn to nod, but that is all they do.

THURSDAY, NOVEMBER 1

During the school day Mr. Morgan goes from teacher to teacher during the day to ask if someone will "facilitate" the awards assembly that is supposed to take place at the end of the school day. At this first quarter awards assembly students receive certificates for Merit Roll, Honor Roll, and Perfect Attendance. When he barges into my classroom during second period and asks me, I decline.

At lunch, I find out every teacher turned him down. How can we facilitate an awards assembly without any preparation? We have had no previous involvement in the organization of the students' awards or the assembly format. Nevertheless, according to Mr. Morgan, Mr. Compton wants one of us to run the awards program, and he even cuts the regular school day an hour and a half so that the end of the day can be devoted entirely to the assembly, which takes place in the gymnasium.

Since no teacher volunteered, the assembly begins with Mr. Compton announcing from a portable wooden podium the Merit Roll winners, and as he calls the very first student's name, a small crowd of kids in the bleachers point at the boy and start laughing. *How could he be on the Merit Roll?* they are implying. Someone even yells, "No way!" For other students, after Mr. Compton calls them forward, their friends echo the name, as in "Savanah, Savanah, Savanah!"

At times, Mr. Compton struggles to pronounce a student's name, which prompts momentary confusion at the microphone and more laughter from students in the bleachers. Once he recovers from this, he starts calling out students' names and their GPAs in a quick, staccato voice, emphasizing each number of the GPA:

"And Angelita Murphy has a..."

"Three.

"Point.

"Eight.

"One.

"G.

"P.

"A."

The students, in turn, walk down the bleacher steps, step to the podium, receive their certificate, and then line up by grade level on the gym floor facing the bleachers. Some high five each other. Between calling out names, he pauses and waits for the students in the bleachers to quiet down, reminding them parents are in attendance. Actually, only three are in attendance, and one is science teacher Jim Simmons whose son Joe stands holding his Honor Roll certificate.

In the bleachers, many students are not really being loud; in fact, most are examining their cell phones – texting, playing a game, maybe checking emails. I hear others debate how a certain classmate earned Honor Roll status. Most of them though just stare ahead, glancing at the award winners, waiting for the next name to be called and soon realizing it won't be theirs.

After Mr. Compton finishes announcing the Honor Roll students, he transforms this serious awards assembly into a semi-pep rally: "Let's give it up for our Honor Roll students!" he yells into the microphone. There is only mild applause, even from the teachers.

Now Mr. Compton's voice gets soft into the microphone: "I know some of you didn't get certificates, but I know you're trying. You just have to put forth more effort." He follows this by oddly thanking the students for coming to school and passing their quizzes but suddenly becomes annoyed with a group of students who are sitting directly in front of him and down below me. I do not know what they are doing or saying to make him angry, but he orders Oscar to sit with them and quiet them down. Actually, he says, "Mr. Smith, make them shut their mouths."

The assembly winds down, and I notice more than several students take their certificates, fold them up into little squares, and shove the paper into a back pocket. Mr. Compton tells us all to return to class since there are still thirty minutes left in the school day, so all the students and faculty exit the gym. I admit I am unprepared for this. I thought the assembly would last to the end of the school day, but I return quickly to my classroom, weaving between slower-moving students who are in no hurry to return to their academic classes. I need to get something on the white board.

I unlock my classroom door and wonder how I'm going to keep twenty-five Honors students busy for thirty minutes. I'm disappointed that I failed to plan ahead or to realize that Mr. Compton's awards program would not last the entire time. For a brief moment I feel encouraged when I peer out the window and see the sun come out. Students begin to drift in and ask if they need their books. I tell them no and, a lesson plan forming in my mind, write one word on the white board: achievement.

After they're all settled and almost quiet, I give my students the directions: "You have just witnessed an awards program dedicated to honoring academic achievement here at Bayview High School. Many of you here, in fact, received certificates for either Merit Roll or Honor Roll status. Congratulations!

"But what exactly does achievement mean. Certainly, there are probably several dictionary definitions and many more personal definitions. Here's what I want you to do...Write a one page essay about the word achievement where you explain this word with both a dictionary and personal definition, along with either an anecdotal or metaphorical reference. You now have a little less than twenty-five minutes to complete this to a final copy.

"I will move around the room and help as needed."

There is a momentary rustling of paper being pulled from spiral notebooks and the clicks of three-ring binders being opened and then snapped closed as students start their work. They lift their heads, check out the word achievement on the white board, and then lower their heads to start their writing. Some move to get dictionaries from the bookshelf. After a several minutes I start my slow pace up and down the aisles to glance over their shoulders at their essays and offer suggestions on word choice and punctuation.

Tonight at the dinner table my wife and I silently eat baked chicken and mashed potatoes, my favorite meal. Actually, she bakes chicken, vegetables, stuffing, and chicken broth into a casserole – like an open chicken potpie without the crust – and serves it with a pot of mashed potatoes. Sheryl calls it chicken goop, and after I douse it with ketchup I greedily shove spoonfuls into my mouth.

Sheryl has demanded I not talk at home about Bayview stuff – she doesn't want to hear me vent anymore – so I just scoop chicken goop on my plate and eat as I read my newspaper. The Associated Press reports that a "former treasurer to more than a dozen Ohio charter schools was sentenced Wednesday to two years in federal prison for embezzling more than $470,000 in federal education funds from four schools over six years. Carl W. Shye Jr., 57, of New Albany, tearfully apologized and...U.S. District Court Judge Gregory Frost said his sentence was designed to send a strong message to others contemplating stealing money from public schools and their students."

This makes me wonder if Carl W. Shye, Jr. was a Merit or Honor Roll student in high school.

MONDAY, NOVEMBER 5

Tomorrow is Election Day, and I plan to vote for President Obama because I feel he is more an advocate for public education than Mitt Romney. Recently, I read that between April 10 and September 24 of this year, an estimated $72.5 million has been spent in Ohio to air 132,469 political campaign commercials, which is way more than any other state. The article claimed that if you were to watch the commercials consecutively, it would take a month and a half – and that was just through September 24. That figure could probably be near $100 million by today. This fascinates me and makes me think these facts could possibly interest my students. We teachers call this the "teachable moment" where an event, significant or not, can be used to make a meaningful point to students, so I suppose the ways campaign groups attempt to persuade voters to elect one candidate over another could be considered one of those moments.

I need to find out in each class, therefore, what my students really know about this election and how they feel about the candidates and the issues. First, I begin class by checking to see if they can recognize a statement of fact vs. a statement of opinion by having them examine two sentences about our school ("Bayview is an eastern suburb of Cleveland" and "Our school has the best students in the nation") on the white board, and almost all students easily identify the first statement as fact and the second as opinion. Then I have two students read the dictionary definitions of fact and opinion and follow this with a survey: "Which type of statement do you hear more during your school day – facts or opinions?" Most say opinions.

Next, I show YouTube video clips of candidates' commercials, and I ask students to identify the facts and opinions presented on these commercials. The lesson that began with promise immediately weakens as students complain the commercials go too fast, and instead of critiquing the candidates' use of language, they criticize their appearance, as in "He's ugly. I wouldn't vote for him."

Nevertheless, I plug away and challenge them to write two to four sentences that can only include facts promoting any candidate. Most choose Barack Obama, but as I move up and down the aisles and peer at their papers I read statements like, "Obama is cool" or "People should vote for O'Bama because he's done a lot for our country" or "I don't like Rommey."

Another teachable moment? No, I decide. Do not correct them yet.

When they finish I direct students to exchange papers with a classmate who must then evaluate the sentences – Are they facts or opinions? This is my first formative assessment. Unfortunately, since they agree with each other so often, they fail to see these sentences as mostly opinions.

So I explain again the differences, provide some more examples, and have them read pages in their textbook that explain the context of opinions. I re-play the videos of the candidates' commercials to see if they can now recognize the opinion-oriented rhetoric, and I am encouraged when a few students can.

I finish class by having them work with a classmate again to examine and mark the opinions they find in a collection of candidates' campaign flyers I have received in the mail and saved over the recent weeks. I remember reading somewhere that a teacher's challenge is to help students who might vary in their socio-economic and academic backgrounds decode the language used by politicians and become knowledgeable citizens. At least, I think that is what I am supposed to do.

WEDNESDAY, NOVEMBER 7

The pro-public school candidate Barack Obama is re-elected President, and miracles happen: Ebony Burrell has withdrawn from Bayview High (true to her word, Ms. Jackson has moved to Cleveland Heights) and the Bayview voters passed the school levy. We teachers all feel relieved because the state will not take over the school district's finances and we can pay hopefully off our deficit.

The bottom line: Bayview now has some extra years before it could be annexed by another school district, before we have to go to the voters again for more tax money, or before we have to walk Bayview neighborhoods again in the rain to pass out the next brochure supporting another school levy. Most importantly, we can get on with our teaching lives.

Maybe the school can also purchase some new defibrillators since the ones in the school now don't work, and the batteries are so outdated they cannot be replaced. The school nurse tells us this at our staff meeting and that if a CPR emergency presents itself we should just remember the "Staying Alive" beat and compress the chest 100 beats her minute.

By the way, when I address the election results in class, only two or three students in each class know that Joe Biden is the Vice-President, half are not familiar with Mitt Romney's first name (Most call him Milt), and none can cite any of the issues that were on the ballot other than the school levy. Indeed, they are indifferent. "Why bother?" one student argues. "We can't vote."

FRIDAY, NOVEMBER 9

I read on the Internet this morning before classes begin that 70-90% of California students who attend community colleges there need remediation in reading and writing. I do not want the students at Bayview to be part of the group that requires remediation when they attend college. I want my students to be prepared for college level writing; I especially want them to improve their skills at writing essays that demonstrate literary analysis and persuasive language.

I discover today in the teacher's lounge at lunch that Big Brother is watching us. A colleague in the elementary school was reprimanded by the superintendent for eating an apple in the hallway at her school. He saw this on a video from one of the elementary school's hallway cameras. She was told this was unacceptable, and the reprimand was put in her personnel file.

I also learn that the elementary school principal, Margaret Craft, conducted an emergency lockdown without informing the staff that it was only a drill. The alarm sounded, teachers closed and locked their doors, and all the students huddled in their dark rooms in a corner away from the door. Minutes later, Margaret pounded on several teachers' doors and yelled to be let in. One by one, each teacher in turn recognized her voice, opened the door, and confronted the principal's right hand formed into a pistol pointed at the teacher's face. Martha then exclaimed, "Bang, you're dead!" This was her test to see if they would actually open their doors during a lockdown. Pointing an imaginary pistol at their faces was her way of emphasizing that they failed her test. She followed this with a verbal reprimand for violating the lockdown procedure.

MONDAY, NOVEMBER 12

I listen at 7:40 A.M. for the PA announcements but again there are none. Nearly three weeks have passed since we have heard any announcements. I wonder, what happens if there is an emergency? How can we learn the important school events? Why hasn't the PA been repaired?

I consider doing something weird today, like making any student who participates in a class discussion talk like a pirate as in, "I aren't straight 'bout the answer, Captain Miller, aaargh!" I do not do this, however. Instead, I conduct my lesson with a normal voice until we read the story "Two Friends" that is in their literature textbook. The story involves two older French gentlemen who decide to fish near the front lines during the Franco-Prussian war of 1870 so I use a French accent when I read their dialogue. The students like it when I read orally and get disappointed when I direct them to finish reading the story silently.

During the silent reading of "Two Friends" during period 1, Marcus asks to use the restroom. He gives me his passbook which students are to have with them in the hallway and teachers are to initial next to the date of the pass to indicate our approval of the student being outside the classroom unsupervised. I look at the page where I am to initial and see that someone has drawn a giant penis. Martin follows my eyes onto the page and says, "I didn't do that. I didn't draw that, Mr. Miller."

"Okay," I say. "Okay." I sign his passbook and watch him exit the classroom. Pick your battles, right?

Later at home, I check my NEA newsletter that references a

Chicago Tribune report that after analyzing data from the Chicago Public Schools, "nearly 32,000 Chicago students in public elementary schools – or roughly 1 in 8 – missed four weeks or more of class during the 2010-11 year, as the cash-strapped district does little to stem a devastating problem." A reporter opines that "truancy and absenteeism in the elementary grades are crippling the education of tens of thousands of children." The Associated Press adds that in Chicago "about 19 percent of kindergartners were listed as chronic truants. Educators say students are missing class for reasons like having to take care of younger siblings."

WEDNESDAY, NOVEMBER 14

Word quickly spreads at the high school that third grade teacher Tracy Thomas was so traumatized by Margaret Craft's fake lockdown and the hand pistol pointed toward her forehead she has not returned to school. Rebecca Leevers whispers to me between class periods, "Tracy's brother was shot in the face and killed, I think, about ten years ago."

"Is Tracy alright?" I ask.

"I don't know," Rebecca says, her face tightening. "I heard she's going on medical leave...and maybe stay out until winter vacation."

We return to our classrooms.

Today's lesson is on story structure – exposition to resolution – and I enjoy pointing out to students that they can find this same structure in other genres. I play a video collage on the VCR of amusing television commercials that follow a typical plot structure; then we listen to and note the plot, characterization, climax, and resolution in Jimmy Dean's ballad "Big John;" and finish by reading the narrative poem "Casey at the Bat" where Casey's strikeout is the climax.

I mentally step outside myself again and observe my students to see if they are engaged. They are. They want to listen to "Big John" twice and their eyes follow line by line on the handout during my oral reading of "Casey at the Bat." I step back inside myself and deal with the issue of how to identify a story's climax since my experience tells me many students often confuse a story's climax and resolution.

I continue this exploration of plot structure by having them work with a partner to provide the next logical and sequential event on a handout "What happens next?" as in, for example, "Glass is heard shattering, a dog barks, and Mr. Gomez turns on his bedroom light.

What happens next?" I subsequently address the reading strategies of previewing *before* we read and making predictions *as* we read.

After we discuss flashbacks and foreshadowing, I conclude the lesson by directing students to read a short story in their textbook and identify, if they can, the story's flashbacks. Most can. When they finish reading I ask the students if they can now look back at the story and point out the foreshadowing. Unfortunately only a few can.

Marcus interrupts this discussion to ask me privately if he can go to the door to pass gas. I allow this because I know his classmates do not want to smell his fart. At the door, Marcus turns his back to the hallway and scrunches up his face. In fact, two or three times a week, at least one male student asks to go fart at the door. I recall years ago when one male student did not even bother going to the door. That was Bobby, and every day second period, Bobby would let one rip. The first time this happened his classmates and I were both surprised and disgusted. They laughed, put their hands to their noses, and complained to him for being so rude, but by week four, we were used to Bobby's loud flatulence. He would fart, his classmates would shake their heads, and I would even try to guess the origin – "What was it today, Bobby? An egg mcmuffin?" – and then go on with the lesson.

Later, at the end of class today I pass back their homework papers on inner and outer conflicts, and Marcus complains when he gets his paper. He plants the paper on his desk, looks at it up and down, and then leans back in his chair grimacing. "Why didn't I get credit for this?" he asks plaintively.

I go to his desk and re-examine the paper. "You didn't follow directions," I tell him. "You were supposed to write only about either an inner or an outer conflict. Instead, you wrote about both, and instead of an entire page, you wrote only four sentences. One about inner conflicts, one about outer conflicts, one that I could not figure out, and a final sentence that actually is a question although you did not apply a question mark. That is why I didn't give you credit. You can try again and re-submit it to me, if you like." I say all this in front of the entire class. I know I am violating Marcus's privacy, but I want to address his complaint head on. In fact, I want the whole class to witness this; I want the whole class to realize the importance of following directions and being thorough with their writing. Marcus never takes his eyes off his paper, as if the more he looks at it, the greater chance there is of a check mark at the top of the paper appearing indicating full credit.

Charkita did not get credit either (She only wrote a paragraph instead of a page). She raises her hand, and after I call on her and hear her ask why she did not get credit, I explain again about the paragraph vs. a page. She asks, however, if she can get at least a half a point. "Sure," I tell her. "I will give you half a point."

"I should get a quarter point then!" Marcus calls out.

I smile. "Okay," I tell him and pretend to write their half and quarter points in my grade book. And the whole time I am thinking about the next two days – my personal days – two days off which were approved by the superintendent back in August.

THURSDAY, NOVEMBER 15

My personal days are for a trip to Las Vegas to meet some friends for a mini-reunion. My mother-in-law drives me to the airport and uses part of our thirty minutes in the car together to ask about my plans after my retirement. Her inquiry, I detect, is motivated by worry. "I hope you're going to do something," she says, "and not just sit around the house."

I will not just sit around the house, I assure her. "I definitely want to keep working," I add, but in truth I have no exact job plans, and I worry if any employer will hire me at my age – I'm almost 60. Nevertheless, after I say this, the rest of the drive to the airport is more pleasant for both of us.

My Delta flight to Minneapolis (my layover stop) with a bunch of strangers does not separate me from fellow educators. By coincidence, sitting behind me are three college teachers who talk nonstop – even during the flight attendant's instructions – for an hour and a half about their colleagues, their college, and their subject area, which I infer to be science because I hear comments about cell structure and research and chemistry. As the landscape slides by beneath us like a giant squares of green and brown on a conveyer belt, I eavesdrop on their conversation as these college instructors talk on and on and on about how their committees are functioning (educators are big on committees), which colleagues have met the standards for tenure, and why some others have filed grievances, and all this makes me wonder if they represent who we are as teachers. Are we just a bunch of talkers?

Maybe we do need to talk. But our talk has to be to neighbors, family members, friends, and especially school boards about the issues affecting our profession; in addition, we should submit letters to newspapers and magazines and articles to blogs to explain the role educators play in shaping our kids' education and the community at large. Indeed, teachers need to examine more closely the problems and possibilities of public education. Maybe my post-retirement plans will involve starting a blog. The afternoon flight continues across the country and I am reminded of Yogi Berra who said, "If you don't know where you are going, you end up somewhere else."

As we near Minneapolis, I peer down at the landscape – a patchwork of farmland, lakes, and then residential streets. Actually I find myself looking for schools, but the only way to find them is to examine the area around homes for football fields. After I find one I look for another, which is typically ten or twenty miles away, suggesting a rivalry established long ago due to geography.

Later, in Las Vegas, I almost regret telling the people I meet for the first time that I'm a teacher because of the responses I hear: Our workday is too short, teaching is easy. Some dealers at blackjack tables think I am just a babysitter. Then pay me like a babysitter, I tell them. If I made just six dollars an hour – most sitters probably make more – and count my school day hours – 7:30 A.M. to 3:30 P.M., that translates to $48 a day for five days a week. That adds up to $240, which when multiplied by 36 weeks a year is $8640. Take that figure and multiply that by the eighty students I teach every day, and my yearly income would be just over $690,000. I would definitely take that.

Others, including my friends, blame the problems in schools on my union. The truth is the National Education Association routinely bargains more for working conditions that benefit *students*, like smaller class size, better school building health and safety, and improved technology and equipment in the classrooms.

I hear comments framed with a hint of jealousy that it must be nice for us to have summers off. The general public does not realize during the summer we re-organize our classrooms, attend professional development seminars, teach summer school, and work part-time jobs to make ends meet. I, for instance, used to be a bartender.

There is a general perception that we work in classrooms where all the desks are arranged in neat rows and all the students raise their hands respectfully during discussions, and the school year ends with hugs and gifts. I make these people consider inviting thirty kids in their living room who are either hungry or tired or angry and then motivate them to clean their house for an hour each day without pay, and that perception crashes in a hurry.

I admit there are some ineffective teachers, but there are incompetent individuals in every profession. I am tired, however, of only teachers being blamed for the problems in education. We confront the real world every day with thousands of students who come to school hungry, who live in poverty, and who may confront violence in their neighborhood. A 2011 Met Life Survey found that the teacher job satisfaction rate dropped twenty percent in one year. How can we feel rewarded as teachers when public officials claim we are either incompetent or lazy?

And, according to my NEA magazine, more than 300,000 educators, teachers, and support staff in the last four years have lost their jobs. I remain grateful that Bayview has money to pay me. I leave several hundred dollars of it on the blackjack tables and slot machines in Las Vegas.

MONDAY, NOVEMBER 19

I need to address this now: I have been wearing the same clothes to school for the last ten years. That is because I am too cheap to buy new garments, and I see no reason to dress stylishly for school. As long as my slacks match my shirt or sweater, I am fine. I observe that most of my male colleagues ignore fashion trends as well.

The Bayview students must agree with me here because most of them just wear jeans and t-shirts. As they pass me in the hallways I like to read the messages on their t-shirts. Over and over, I see Nike t-shirts with innocuous slogans like "JUST DOT IT," and "Don't Suck Just do it" and "Holdin' it down" and "I BE KILLIN' IT." I keep wondering what is *it*? Typically, I observe mostly grammar errors, especially in capitalization or punctuation. To me, this is very frustrating.

TUESDAY, NOVEMBER 20

We are two days away from the Thanksgiving holiday, and I sit alone at my desk during my free period (technically called a Planning Period or Conference Period) typing up the lesson plans I am required to submit to my principal at least by 8:00 A.M. every Monday. I want to get a head start on this and actually submit my lesson plans before I leave for vacation. Outside in the hallway, I hear students' loud voices passing. Someone yells, "Fuck this!" and I ponder for a moment whether to leave my desk and deal with the student who cursed or to let it go.

I look at the door, then at my computer screen where I have typed in so far three days' worth of Subjects, Objectives, the Common Core standards, Teaching Strategies related to the novel *To Kill a Mockingbird*, Guided Practice, Independent Practice, Adjustments for students who are either on IEPs or are Gifted, the Formative Assessment, Technology Element, Final Assessment, and the Closure Activity. My colleagues and I have been submitting lesson plans like this to Mr. Compton as email attachments since the beginning of the school year. Actually, at first we submitted lesson plans under the format we used last year, then he ordered us to provide them under a new format, and now we have been given a third format to use when submitting our weekly lesson plans. When we were first ordered to submit our lesson plans under this new format, Megan Cutler asked Mr. Compton for a model sample so we could duplicate it. He, however, has never provided this.

I have two more days of lesson plans to finish so I decide to ignore the profanity and keep typing at my desk. I rationalize that students probably say "fuck" in the hallways or on the bus or at home every day. My own sons probably use that word with their friends. Plus, I do not know who cursed, so I plant my fingers on the keyboard and let it go. I just let it go.

MONDAY, NOVEMBER 26

On this first day back after the Thanksgiving holiday I sit at my desk in the quiet building. Only Rebecca Leever is there ahead of me. As usual, she has arrived around 6:20 A.M., and I sign in today at 6:24. I pass Rebecca's open classroom door, and she smiles and tells me to check out the new email from Mr. Compton. So in my own classroom I turn on my computer and immediately check my emails. Only a few new ones are there, but the one she wants me to look at is the one all of us received from our principal. Here it is, spelling errors and all:

I hope that all of you had a wonderful and restful Thanksgiving Break and ate a lot of turkey. My hope is that you took the time to reflect on the many things you are 'Thankful for.

Please see below for a list of 'non-negotiable items' that must be completed by November 29, 2012. Please note that Mr. Morgan and I will confirm that each staff member is in complience with each item on November 30, 2012.

CLASSROOM DOOR WINDOWS: All classroom windows must *not* be covered with curtains, decorations, etc. Please remove all items by 4:00 PM today.

CLASSROOM WINDOWS: All blinds should be ½ way down the window.

LESSON PLANS: Lesson plans should be emailed to me by 8

AM every Monday morning. NO Exceptions -- NO Excuses. Any teacher not meeting this deadline will be considered to be insubordnate.

WORD WALL: The words on the *'word wall'* should be at grade level and current. In addition, all word postings should be consistant; use the same font/size for all words, if you are typing the words. Your *'word wall'* must be interactive. If your word wall is behind a desk or a table, you will need to move it to a more interactive spot for students to see and be able to use.

CUSTOMER SERVICE PLAN: Be mindful of our customer service plan, and impliment with fidelity.

ROOF LEAKS: Teachers should email me any time there is a leak in the roof. *DO NOT* contact the custodian, cleaners, or maintnance supervisor.

COPIER: *PLEASE NOTE*: All staff will have a limit of 200 copies per month. Furthermore, each teacher will be given two reams of paper per month.

CLEANLINESS OF BUILDING: Please ask your students to use the door handles when opening doors. Also, have students' pick-up where they may put down (paper, etc.) It is important that we begin to show pride in our building so that it will be filtered down to our students.

AS YOU LEAVE FOR THE DAY: ALL classrooms must be cleaned.

The original font is actually a 16 pt. Georgia Bold, and I do not know how to react. The demands, the misspellings, the threats. Does

Mr. Compton truly know the meaning of *fidelity*? I stroll over to Rebecca's room and tell her I read Mr. Compton's email. "I'm checking your window shades," I tell her, looking past her to the windows.

She laughs and says, "With all the issues we have to deal with here, he's worried about windows? About windows?! Really? *Really?!*"

I shake my head and return to my classroom. Is this simply about power? Is Mr. Compton just trying to demonstrate his authority? Or is he just following orders from Dr. Andrews and channeling this down to the teachers?

I greet other colleagues as we pass each other in the hallways going to our classrooms, and most of them look rested and eager. I wonder, however, if their moods will change once they too see our principal's email.

Either way, to me this is more than any administrator's assertiveness that I have experienced in the past. Maybe Mr. Compton wants us to know he's the alpha dog. Maybe he's hoping one of us will be insubordinate. And maybe one of us will be, but it won't be me.

To me, these are a series of challenges: Covering my door windows – find some poster paper and tape it up – check. Pull down the blinds half way – easy – check. Turn in lesson plans by 8 A.M. Monday morning; I will submit my weekly lesson plans before I leave my classroom on Friday afternoon – check. Update my word wall – no problem, I have a drawer full of literary terms I can staple on the board – check. And clean my classroom? Give me a broom, cleanser, and a rag. I'll get it done – check.

In the past I always began the Monday morning class after the Thanksgiving holiday with a survey question: What is your favorite part of the Thanksgiving meal? *My* answer is always the same: My sister's stuffing. Now, however, I don't ask that question in fear of embarrassing students who either don't celebrate Thanksgiving or whose family cannot afford having a special meal.

Instead, today, I welcome back my first period students and generalize that I hope the holiday was restful and rewarding, that they enjoyed spending more time with family and friends. Then after I ask if they read chapter 2 of *To Kill a Mockingbird*, I discover that only two students in my first class completed their reading over the vacation. Other students reveal shamelessly that they never took the novel out of their lockers.

I lower my face to my desk to hide my frown and then say, "No problem, we'll just do some silent reading to catch up."

"No," someone calls out. "You read to us, Mr. Miller. Please!" Two or three more students join in. "Please...Do that voice you do."

I look up now, and their faces and eyes plead with me.

"Two pages," I respond. "That's it. Then you're on your own." I agree to their request because I fault myself for believing they could read nine pages of chapter 2 over the five days they had off. Plus, I know they like the Southern accent I use to portray Scout Finch's narration.

I need to provide – every teacher should, in fact – sustained silent reading time in class. Therefore, after I've read, as requested, the opening two pages of chapter 2 of *To Kill a Mockingbird*, I watch them read silently on their own. Their heads are tilted forward, their eyes on the novel, their fingers clutching the corners of the pages ready to turn them. I like to watch them to see how long they can do focused reading before they quit, or "break." Most can go over ten minutes, and this, generally, satisfies me.

When I start my period 5-8 block class, Autumn Smith gives me a smile and surprises me a little when she asks how I spent *my* Thanksgiving. For a minute or two the two of us talk about pies and then dark vs. light gravy on mashed potatoes, which prompts Connor Reese, who is eavesdropping, to think we are talking about light vs. dark-skinned people.

"No," Autumn says to him, exasperated. "Gravy...light or dark gravy!"

"You said people, I heard you," he says.

Autumn shakes her head. "You an idiot."

"Okay, that's enough," I order. "Let's get started."

After several minutes of reading *To Kill a Mockingbird*, Jenny Wilson, who is now in this class, calls out, "This book is boring. I don't want to read it no more." Then for some unknown reason, she spends the next ten minutes laughing uncontrollably and the last half of class with her head down on her desk. She is not alone. So does Connor, even after I lightly tap his shoulder to get him to pick his head up. He simply shrugs off my hand and mumbles something I cannot understand. I return to the front of the room and return to watching their classmates read *To Kill a Mockingbird*.

Harper Lee's only book is a classic of American literature, and I believe in teaching the classics. One of my father's friends, a man in his seventies, complains to me every time we see each other: "Ethan, why don't they teach the classics anymore?" He is not talking about *To Kill a Mockingbird*; he means the works of Plato and Sophocles and Milton and Shakespeare. I tell him we do have students read some of Shakespeare's plays but not the other authors' works he views as classics. I believe in rigor but not rigor mortis in my classroom.

In contrast, I know colleagues who have students read job applications, cookbook recipes, appliance manuals, and cell phone contracts instead of classic literature. Nevertheless, my students have been reading *To Kill a Mockingbird* for thirty years, along with *Lord of the Flies*, *Animal Farm*, *The Tragedy of Romeo and Juliet*, *Of Mice and Men*, and *A Raisin in the Sun*, and I always hope my students both enjoy and appreciate them. I agree in part with Albert Einstein who said, "The only thing that interferes with my learning is my education."

FRIDAY, NOVEMBER 30

We are eight chapters into *To Kill a Mockingbird,* and I am still using a Southern accent when I read Scout's narration out loud. I know there has been some debate about reading orally to students. One side says that oral readers worry more about the pronunciation of words while silent readers focus on the meaning of those words. Vocal reading typically takes longer than silent reading, but some studies suggest that oral reading produces better comprehension for many elementary school students. Oral reading seems to generate greater interest in the literature than silent reading, but the ultimate goal is literacy regardless of the approach. I use both methods. Oral to start, and silent to finish.

I allow them to read "popcorn" style at times where one student begins to read orally, stops, and then calls on a classmate to continue. I challenge them to agree or disagree with each other about the issues presented by *To Kill a Mockingbird* (Are the children foolish for believing the urban legends related to Boo Radley?), and I clarify to them each day how I plan to evaluate their work before they exit class. At times I even use games (I call them contests, however) to keep their attention and interest on the material, as in "Can you stump me about any character or event in the novel?"

I usually show students at the beginning of class the quiz they will take at the end of the period or chapter, or I explain the exact form of the assessment they should expect. Then we read and discuss the chapter with me using "cold calls;" that is, they do not need to raise a hand to answer my open-ended question. I just call on a student randomly.

We debate about Boo Radley – Is he a victim? – to help reinforce an understanding of this character. I praise students and remind them as we continue our discussion, "Here comes a quiz question." Then they take the quiz at the end of the period.

Before she leaves my classroom at the end of my last class, Honors student Monique, the five foot tall basketball guard who I worried would fail the class, waits while I erase my white board. Since our hallway conversation where I tried to scare her about being ineligible, Monique has thankfully resisted the urge to talk and socialize. When I turn away from the board, Monique tells me, "You are really a good teacher, Mr. Miller. I like the way you teach. If I don't do well, I know it's on me."

I gaze at her for a moment, processing the compliment. "I appreciate you saying that, Monique. What a great way to end the day. And I want you to know, I'm pleased with the progress you're making with the novel."

She smiles once. "Well, I just wanted you to know." Then she smiles a second time before exiting my classroom into the noisy hallway. This is the same girl who catcalls her opponents on the basketball court when they are at the free throw line.

I watch her go and smile, unfortunately too late for her to see.

Today is payday, Christmas is coming, and my wife and I tonight have a serious conversation about our lack of money to use for presents. She says this although she wants to quit her job as a director of a day care, and the loss of her $1400 per month take home income worries me. Even with her salary we do not make enough money. Public education is a $500 to $600 billion institution and I wish I had just a little more of that money in my pocket.

MONDAY, DECEMBER 3

I check my emails this morning, and I notice another one from Mr. Horrigan. Since September this is his eleventh email to me about his son Karl, Jr. Here is what his email says:

In looking over Karl's on-line grade for 2nd Quarter, I see many assignments/ papers below a "C" grade. Karl says you took off points because he used the word scrumptious in his essay. Is this correct? I think scrumptious is a great word. We need to talk. Let me know if you're available Tues, Dec 4th to talk at 2:30 pm.

I respond immediately and agree, of course, to meet with him, but I am getting weary of these meetings. This will be our fourth face-to-face meeting about Karl, who is getting a D in my English 10 Honors class. During our previous conferences, I talked only at brief intervals as Mr. Horrigan used the majority of time to lecture his son about the importance of getting an education and rejecting the notion that he could achieve a career in the NBA.

I have a strong anxiety now, however, that Mr. Horrigan has a complaint with *me* about how I have assessed his son on his papers. I plan to show him the Writing Chart I use to document all students' papers, Karl's writing portfolio, and then samples of his work. This is a conference I have had a hundred times during my life as a teacher – where I have to justify a score or a grade on a paper. I have no problem being accountable.

According to the latest round of NAEP testing, "U.S. teenagers' texting, tweeting and posting on Facebook hasn't improved their writing, even when students have laptops with a spell-checking program. Nearly three-quarters of the eighth and 12th graders failed to achieve proficiency on a national writing test, according to a U.S. government report released today." The piece quotes Susan Pimentel of the National Assessment Governing Board saying that most students' writing "falls far short of the well-organized, well-developed prose that connects with those they are trying to reach."

My approach to writing is pretty systematic. I begin my composition work previewing the assignment by using a video clip, a debate, or a freewrite related to the topic. After I announce the assignment requirements, the students and I collaborate on the assessment criteria ("How should this paper be evaluated?" I ask, and we brainstorm the evaluation criteria). We do some prewriting (a cluster, a list, a chart), complete, if needed, a graphic organizer, and then write a first draft. After they have written their drafts, we engage in peer editing.

Students need my input, too, so I collect the second drafts and comment on them in detail. We complete the process by publishing. In the past, for instance, students have mailed letters; we have sent Veterans Day essays to local veterans; we have produced class literary magazines; and we have created poems with third graders to post in their classroom.

I think I know how to teach effective composition skills. I'm ready at any time to talk to Mr. Horrigan about the word "scrumptious."

TUESDAY, DECEMBER 4

I have arranged a triangle of student desks for Mr. Horrigan, Karl, Jr., and me to sit at our conference today. Mr. Horrigan arrives promptly at 2:30 P.M., joined by Karl, Jr., who slumps in at a desk and looks at neither of us. I shake hands with the both of them and sit down myself.

"Karl has this foolish idea," Mr. Horrigan begins, his hands flat on the desktop, "that he's going to be a professional basketball player. I want him more focused on his academics." Mr. Horrigan is dressed formally – a dark suit, white shirt, plaid tie – which makes me suspect he's just come from his job as an office manager at a local insurance company,

I nod and say, "That seems reasonable."

"I'm demanding he report to the library from 2:30 to 3 P.M. every day to study and then receive a written notice from the librarian that he was in the library during that time. Then Karl must report to the athletic director's office and continue working on homework until 4 P.M. when the basketball players are to begin getting ready for practice. Karl must receive a written notice from the athletic director that he was in the office studying or doing work." Mr. Horrigan turns, gives a sideways glance at Karl, Jr. who keeps his eyes on his desktop.

When Mr. Horrigan stares at me, I realize it's my turn to talk. "Again, that seems reasonable."

Mr. Horrigan smiles, apparently pleased. "I also want Karl to get a zero on any late assignment." He leans towards me. "Plus, email me whenever he turns in something late."

"Okay," I say, desperately hoping now that Karl, Jr., never neglects a deadline. I'm also wondering when Mr. Horrigan is going to ask about the word scrumptious, which Karl, Jr., used in his descriptive restaurant review. Karl, Jr., in fact, stays slouched in his seat, nearly forgotten so far, and I suspect he has heard these comments from his father before.

Mr. Horrigan leans back, and I can tell he's uncomfortable having to squeeze his bulk into a student's desk. "Everyone, including Karl, especially Karl, has to be accountable."

I nod and fold my arms across my chest. "I have no problem with being accountable." It's true, I don't.

"I've told Karl all this." He turns again to peer at Karl, Jr. "Haven't I?"

Karl, Jr., nods and finally speaks, "Are we done yet?"

Mr. Horrigan straightens his back. "No, we're not done, are we, Mr. Miller?"

I pause. I'm with Karl, Jr. It feels like we're done. I think this is the right answer, so I say, "I guess not."

His face serious, his eyes narrowed, his voice philosophical, Mr. Horrigan says, "These boys, especially my son, they're student athletes. They should care more about school than just getting Ds to be eligible, but that's all they care about. It's the culture. The culture has to change. Right now, all they care about – and that includes the coaches – is winning games. The environment has to change.

"I got two other kids in the Bayview system, I'm a homeowner, I do my shopping in this town. They should put signs up in stores with names of kids going to college, not just posters of the sports' schedules."

I look at him. We should both know that's never going to happen, but I say anyway, "I agree."

Mr. Horrigan's eyes sweep the room, but in actuality, he's looking through the walls at all of Bayview High School. "I want to change the culture at Bayview," he declares. "You know, half the basketball players don't attend mandatory study table. I know these boys. They don't do their homework, their parents don't come to parent-teacher conferences, and I don't think their coaches ever talk about their academics."

Okay, I realize now, this conference is not about Karl Jr.'s writing. Mr. Horrigan simply needs to pontificate to someone, and he chose me. I put a concerned look on my face, nod a little, and lean forward, my hands gripping the sides of the desk. "I wouldn't know all that, but you're right, there should be more of a focus on academics."

At Bayview, the players on the varsity basketball team, which is in first place in the conference, often strut down the hallways as if they were Roman generals in front of their legions. I've seen them. They never show an interest in getting to class on time, and when I have urged them to get what they need from their lockers and hurry up – "You don't want to be late, do you?" – they roll their eyes at me and take even longer to get their books and close their locker doors. Their homework is sloppy, the papers usually crinkled and folded about six times. And I'm not surprised the coaches, who are not Bayview teachers – they're AAU coaches from outside the school district who typically show up late themselves for their 4 P.M. practices and call each other "bra" – don't stress academics.

Mr. Horrigan points at me. "You know, people don't buy homes in a city because of the basketball team. They want to know the school system is good. I'm not trying to throw anyone under the bus, but I'm wondering who in this school cares about these boys' schoolwork, their academics."

"I do," I say immediately and look him in the face.

"I know you do, Mr. Miller. You always respond to my emails. Like I said, I'm not trying to throw the other teachers, the athletic director, or the principal under the bus, but I just think the culture has to change."

"I understand completely, Mr. Horrigan...but is there something else you want me to do other than emailing you when Karl neglects an assignment deadline?"

Mr. Horrigan pauses, his eyes shifting in his head, as if my question has caught him off guard. "No, I guess not."

"Do you want to discuss Karl's writing?"

"No, I'm okay with what you're doing. Karl tells me he's learning a lot." He turns to Karl, Jr., and adds, "You gotta do better. You should do what Mr. Miller suggested in that email a while back and do more than one draft. Let him see it and tell you what needs to be fixed."

"I have been," Karl declares.

"No, you haven't, Karl," I reveal.

"Well, I wanted to...."

Mr. Horrigan shakes his head. "See what I mean...it's the culture. I don't want to give up and move out of Bayview, like so many other parents before me have. My kid – probably all these kids – needs a more structured culture. At the end of the day, it's about the academics." He's right. It is about the academics, and it is the end of the day.

WEDNESDAY, DECEMBER 5

We have our weekly staff meeting in the library where Mr. Compton distributes the agenda and advises us to take notes. Oddly, he begins with the third item on his list: "Classroom Cleanliness." Mr. Compton stands tall in his gray suit and pale crimson tie and tells us he has inspected some classrooms during the previous week after school and found food scraps, candy wrappers, and other trash on the floors. He's disturbed about this. "There is trash up and down the walls. We've gotta pick up the paper," he exclaims. "We've gotta pick up the trash." And like the weather outside, the mood in the brightly lit library becomes immediately chilly.

Trash is up and down the walls?

I look past Mr. Compton and see intervention specialist Julie Hanson standing just outside the library door in the hallway. I do not know why she does not come into the library. Julie begins waving a hand and gesturing to someone at a table to my left. Several of my colleagues sitting at that table notice her gestures, make eye contact, and begin pointing fingers at their chests. "*Who? Me?*" they mean. They finally figure out she wants Suzanne Smith. Julie keeps waving her hand even as Suzanne leaves her seat, walks past Mr. Compton and goes into the hallway. Mr. Compton ignores all of this.

After some whispering for a minute or two outside, Julie and Suzanne nod at each other, obviously agreeing on some plan. They enter the library together and walk past Mr. Compton, who continues to ignore them as he finishes his complaints about the trash he saw in the middle school hallway last week. "I'm asking you, Mr. and Mrs., Miss, ladies and gentlemen...in the middle school hallway, that second floor is trash city." He then introduces our new maintenance director Mr. Ted Buchman, a short but hefty man with leathery-looking skin who was hired less than a month ago. Typically, all new custodians are put on a four-month probationary period, but Ted was named maintenance supervisor after just over three weeks on the job.

Mr. Buchman smiles, he spreads his arms, he looks around the room. "I'm not asking you to clean your rooms," he says, sounding almost apologetic. "My guys will do that. I'm just asking you to look out for the trash." He, too, tells us about the trash he has observed in some classrooms, but then a call from the superintendent comes in on the walkie-talkie on his belt and he exits the library in a hurry. I do not know about my colleagues, but I am confused. I had the impression Mr. Compton wants us to pick up the paper left on the floor in our classrooms and outside in the hallways. Mr. Buckman, however, seems to contradict that.

Mr. Compton then explains we teachers do not have to pick up this trash; he advises us instead to make the kids pick up the papers they drop in the rooms and hallways.

This makes Julie Hanson shake her head and call out, "I can't get them to pick their trash up without them calling me a bitch."

"I don't want to..." Mr. Compton responds quickly, "I, uh, well, you can..." But that is it. He looks again at his paper with the agenda items for the meeting. "Next topic."

This next topic is lesson plans. He demands we follow the format he wants – I interpret this to mean some of my colleagues must not be – and repeats verbally what we have read in his emails: "No exceptions, no excuses!" He also wants to see more Word Walls. This, too, is required. He wags a finger at us. "No exceptions, no excuses!" In fact, he tells us, our Word Walls need to be updated every time we start a new lesson, and if we neglect to follow the format he wants for submitting lesson plans or to create "an interactive word wall," we could be considered to be insubordinate. "I'm coming to that person, and I'm going to write that person up," he announces sternly.

Seventh grade teacher and a 2004 graduate from Bayview High School herself, Cindy Greenlee's face is tense. She stares at Mr. Compton, her face framed by curly brown hair. Her voice is on edge. "When are we going to get the time to do all this? Are we supposed to stop *teaching*?"

"Absolutely not," he answers loudly. "Absolutely not."

Cindy cannot let go of this. She matches Mr. Compton's angry tone word for word. "These demands, demands, demands...This is my best year with my students, and I'm going to get written up?"

Mr. Compton has the last word. "This is the first time this year that I said I will write someone up...Moving on."

No one else wants to say anything. No one, I think, even wants to be in this room anymore.

Gretchen Suchs, however, isn't intimidated. She raises her hand cautiously and explains in an almost-apologetic voice the word wall demand could be a problem. Her students are currently reading *Roll of Thunder, Hear My Cry*, she explains, and she is unclear how she can put a hundred vocabulary words from the novel on her bulletin board.

"Let's talk," Mr. Compton says and waves his hand dismissively. He is getting frustrated with us. Even upset. His voice gets louder and goes on to the next item: "Week in Review." From now on, each department must submit, albeit voluntarily, by the end of every week a summary of the events happening in our classrooms. He approaches several teachers individually with a paper displaying the Week in Review format. "Mrs. Suchs, would you complete this for the high school English Department?" She nods her head and takes the paper. "Mr. Grasser, for social studies?"

"Sure," David responds indifferently and reaches for the paper. Mr. Compton, smiling pleasantly the whole time, continues moving around the library, table to table.

I peek over Gretchen's shoulder and examine the form; the top of the paper says "Week in Review" and directly beneath it the days Monday, Tuesday, Wednesday, Thursday, and Friday are listed. This prompts Gretchen to wave a hand and ask: "Are we supposed to write a summary of what we're doing *each day?*"

"No, for *the week*," Mr. Compton answers quickly. He stops handing out papers and tells her to ignore the days individually and just give a summary of the week.

Then why does the form list…oh, never mind.

Mr. Compton moves to the next table to hand out the "Week in Review" paper. "Mrs. Greenlee, would you complete it for the seventh grade?"

"No," she says flatly.

I can immediately tell Mr. Compton is not prepared for this. Nevertheless, he smiles and turns to Tom Black, the math teacher, and asks him to write the Week in Review summary for the seventh grade. He, too, refuses. Teresa Duncan, the seventh grader teacher who teaches social studies and has only been teaching a month and a half, sees him coming toward her and even before Mr. Compton can ask, she says, "I don't think I can do it either. I'm new here, and I feel a little overwhelmed with what I have to do already."

Mr. Compton somehow maintains his smile, hiding either his anger or frustration, and says, "Well, I will leave the paper on the table here and hope that one seventh grade teacher will take it."

Our next obligation is to create a Holiday Homework Packet. This is a packet of 20-25 multiple choice and short answer questions that all students must complete over the vacation period. We are to ignore the restrictions on using paper (to save money) he announced in his previous email and demand students do this. Then we must grade it after they turn it in upon their return in January. Plus, he wants a copy of our Holiday Homework Packet with the answer key by December 14.

The Holiday Homework Packet takes me by surprise because I was not intending to give *any* homework over the vacation other than to assign students to finish reading *To Kill a Mockingbird*. Someone suggests we should be politically correct and call this the Vacation

Homework Packet. Some students' families may not be celebrating *any* holiday. Mr. Compton agrees that that is a good idea and adds that we all must use Vacation Homework Packet as title on the cover page for our packets.

"Why vacation?" Rebecca Leever asks. "For some students, it may not be a vacation. Maybe we should call it Winter Homework Packet."

"No," says Mr. Compton. "I like Vacation Homework Packet."

I raise my hand for the first time. "Don't misunderstand," I say as the room gets quiet, "I am going to create the *Vacation* Homework Packet as directed, but I wonder, first, if the students will actually complete it. I am having difficulty getting students to complete the Monday, Tuesday, Wednesday, Thursday homework. Second, I worry that the students who do turn it in will just copy from a classmate, especially since multiple choice and short answer questions are involved." I pause and then tell a white lie, "I was considering having students write a paper over the holiday. That would be an individual assignment and one they couldn't copy from a classmate. It reduces the risk of plagiarism."

There is a long pause, and the room stays quiet. Mr. Compton looks at me, then at the paper in his hand listing the agenda items for the meeting. He breaks the silence with, "Moving on. Next topic."

Mr. Morgan takes a turn and announces that as the scheduler, he is already making plans for the next school year. In fact, we should anticipate some changes. "We're not going to offer all the same things we are offering this year...and you may not be teaching the same things next year. The schedule is not built on the staff, you know, it's built on the students." There is more: "Courses will be based on data, not who will be teaching them."

Data?

Some of my colleagues hear this as a warning, and the tension in the library is almost palpable. A dozen teachers squirm in their seats, and some of us sneak peeks at the clock and then at each other. Mr. Compton, however, has more to say. He lowers his voice and slowly buttons his suit coat. "If you ever feel I've disrespected you, come talk to me." The real issue, he admits almost angrily, is that *he* does not feel respected. Especially at these staff meetings. "I hear people talking, whispering, saying little jokes. I know you all are whispering about me."

He puts his hands on his chest near his heart. He softens his voice. "I love what I do…I wish I knew what you say about me." He glances quickly at the paper in his hand. "Moving on."

His comments shift again when he complains that not enough of us attend the athletic competitions or school plays. He pleads with us, "It would be so nice out there to see more than one face supporting our kids."

Mr. Compton's jumbled tirade continues. We need to be more careful with how we post paper on our walls. Too many teachers, he stresses, have sloppy looking walls. He narrates what he thinks is an amusing story about his father who used ugly black electrical tape to repair appliances and even clothing. In contrast, we need to be more selective about using masking or scotch tape, "to take more pride in our stuff." A vague discussion follows with my colleagues wondering how to post paper on the walls – what should we use? *Tape? Glue? What else is there?*

The meeting nears its conclusion with a complaint from Melissa Fleck about the women's bathroom on the second floor. "The floor is filthy in there. It stinks. And there isn't any toilet paper." She explains she has asked for cleanser from the custodians since the beginning of the school year but has never received any. "It's so frustrating," she says. "I've been in my son's school, and unlike Bayview, it's spotless."

Mr. Compton tells Melissa to email him about the bathroom, and she sighs that she has. Three times! "Again, please," he smiles at her, and she sinks back onto her wooden chair.

More squirming. More glances at the clock. Papers are shuffled on the tabletops. But Mr. Compton is not done. Now he thinks we should have a holiday party. "Let's do something together. I tried to do something last time at Thanksgiving and no one stepped up to take charge." He pauses and looks around the library.

We, however, do not look back. No one, to be sure, wants to put all the effort in to organize a holiday party.

Thankfully, a minute later, the uncomfortable silence is broken by the new physical education teacher, Jeff Jones, who proclaims, "I'll organize the party."

A lot of us smile at Jeff, and a few of the faculty even clap. Jeff has been working at Bayview less than a month after replacing the previous physical education teacher, an older man who weighed over three hundred and twenty pounds and walked with a cane. He quit, the rumor claims, because students kept parking in his handicapped space.

Mr. Compton claps his hands and thanks him. Jeff's offer seems to inspire him. "We gotta pull the ship together," he exclaims. "We're all in this together. Let's keep rowing."

The meeting now over, I am one of the last teachers to leave the library, and when I look back to see if any chairs need to be pushed in, I notice the "Week in Review" paper for the seventh grade is still on the table.

WEDNESDAY, DECEMBER 12

Mr. Compton's email today congratulates us. Today the staff has perfect attendance and his email also tells us to "Have a great day!" Actually, this statement is followed by eleven exclamation points.

Another email, this one from the superintendent's secretary, tells us two custodians, Walt and Stan, are retiring, and we are all invited to attend a retirement celebration for them at the board office next week between noon and 1 P.M. But who can attend? Almost all of us are in the classroom teaching students at that time.

Eddie Collins, one of my sophomores, walks tentatively into my room around 7:25 A.M. and wants another update on his grade in English 10. This is the third day in a row he has asked for an update. And each day my response has been the same: a D because of some below average quiz scores related to *To Kill a Mockingbird.*

Eddie becomes visibly shaken. "How can that be?" he demands. "I've done extra credit."

"True," I tell him, "but I don't tabulate the extra credit until the end of the quarter. You are certainly welcome to do more extra credit if you like."

Eddie says his mom wants to know his grade and asks if I would I write it down for him. I suggest a better option: "How about I call her?"

He considers this briefly and then agrees, so I dial the number. When she answers, I explain to Ms. Jones, his guardian, all about Eddie's recent performance: He is completing more of his work, but he still is inattentive in class and doesn't follow directions. Ms. Jones tells

190

me she has plans for Eddie to go to college and he better learn now rather than later that he has to pay attention in class.

"That's the key," I say into the receiver. "His college teachers may not repeat information like we high school teachers do."

"I used to be a troublemaker," Ms. Jones admits to me. "But I was an honors student by the time I graduated."

I hope she doesn't think I'm patronizing her when I say, "You sound like a good role model for Eddie. There's much he can learn from your story."

"And I'm strict!"

I'm thinking she is going to say more, but when several seconds pass in silence, I realize it's my turn to talk again. "You're doing the right thing for him." Next to me, Eddie uses the fingernails of his right hand to scratch the fingers of his left hand.

"He hates my guts," Ms. Jones tells me next.

I tell her I have teenage sons, too, and they might dislike me at times for the way I parent them.

"They have to learn," she says in a Dr. Phil voice, and I sense our conversation has not really been about Eddie. Instead, Ms. Jones is giving me parenting advice.

"Yes," I respond. "Yes, they do."

After we hang up, Eddie asks for more extra credit, which I give to him before he leaves to get to his first period classroom.

I have a new student, Jeremiah Jackson in my first period class. His first day was Friday of last week and since then he cut class once and missed the first half of class the other two times, including today. When he strolls into class empty-handed, I remind him to return to his locker to get his notebook and the novel *To Kill a Mockingbird*, which I gave to him the first day. He rolls his eyes and leaves the room. This makes me wonder what prompted him to leave his previous school. A divorce? His mom running from an abusive father? An expulsion? Whatever the reason, when Jeremiah returns, still without a notebook or the novel, he plops down grudgingly at his seat, and I cannot escape the notion that Jeremiah is a very unhappy young man.

Our regular staff meeting at the end of the day begins with Phil Oster, our director of security, announcing that on Friday we are going to have a lockdown drill. It will be at one o'clock. Doors must be locked. Lights turned off. Students must not be visible from the doorway windows.

Almost immediately several colleagues raise their hands. What about the outside windows on the other wall? What exactly is the lockdown signal? What about those students using the bathroom or those out in the hallways? What about them? Who should we call if there is a problem?

Phil tells us the first thing we should do is "go outside and lock your door." This confuses some colleagues who ask if they should then stay outside the classroom. No, Phil clarifies, just make sure the door is locked and go back inside your classroom.

He tells us about ALICE which stands for Alert, Lockdown, Inform, Counter, Evacuate. He defines each of the terms and elaborates on Counter. Here, we are to attack the perpetrator or charge him, even if he has a gun. Some teachers want to know how we are supposed to do this. Phil tells us to throw books, pens, and pencils, whatever we have at him. Then charge him.

"Charge him?"

"Even if he has a gun?"

Yes, Phil advises, because that way he might panic and run away.

Ander Klyszewski, who served in Iraq as a member of the Army Reserves, says, "Take it from someone who's been shot at, you need a weapon." He then recommends we use a fire extinguisher.

"But Ander," I say, "my classroom doesn't have a fire extinguisher." I glance around at my colleagues. "Does anyone have one in their classrooms?"

All my colleagues shake their heads.

Phil concludes by informing us that someone will come on the PA and announce when the lockdown is over. In short, we will be told, "All clear." Math teacher Jennifer Stimson says in her previous school they addressed the possibility of a false "all clear." How can we know for sure a gunman does not have a gun to the head of the person at the PA? Phil informs us he will think about this and get back to us before Friday.

The remainder of the meeting involves a discussion about providing test-taking skills. Science teacher Ernie Kelsey laments that when he lets students use their books for his exams they either do not bring them or don't bother to open them. David Grasser admits his semester exam is in actuality a discussion of each multiple choice question where he announces the correct answer at the end of the discussion. Students simply have to listen to him give the correct answer and then circle A, B, C, or D on the test. "I got tired of parents and students complaining. This way everyone can get an A," he tells us, "as long as they pay attention."

"Everyone gets an A?" Melissa Fleck asks. "Really?"

"Well, no," David admits. "Quite a few still get the wrong answer because they either don't pay attention or they put their heads down and leave the test blank." Later, David himself spends the last ten minutes of the presentation resting his head on his hand.

FRIDAY, DECEMBER 14

There can be no worse day than this. We learn twenty children and six school personnel are dead after being shot at Sandy Hook Elementary School in Connecticut by a twenty year old named Adam Lanza. One of the adults is twenty-seven year old teacher Victoria Soto who was shot while she tried to shield her first grade students from the gunman. Who else other than this selfless and brave woman should be our national teacher of the year? Reporting for the Associated Press, Matt Sedenksy writes, "[Soto's] name has been invoked again and again as a portrait of selflessness and humanity amid unfathomable evil."

Other educators at Sandy Hook Elementary School duplicated Soto's act of courage and sacrifice. I sit at my kitchen table this evening and read in the Cleveland *Plain Dealer* that Principal Dawn Hochsprung died "while lunging at the gunman in at attempt to overtake him," as did school psychologist Mary Sherlach, who herself was near retirement. Another teacher, Lauren Rousseau, who had been a substitute teacher for many years before landing a full-time job at Sandy Hook, was also killed. Her mother, Teresa Rousseau, said, "Lauren wanted to be a teacher from before she even went to kindergarten" and teaching at Sandy Hook had been "the best year of her life."

Secretary of the Department of Education Arne Duncan writes, "At this time of unbearable grief over the senseless slaughter of 20 first graders and six school staff members, I want to take a moment to thank the many extraordinary educators school leaders and school principals who protected the children at Sandy Hook Elementary School. Words cannot do justice to the courage of Dawn Hochsprung, Mary Sherlach, Lauren Rousseau, Victoria Soto, Anne Marie Murphy and Rachel D'Avino. They made the ultimate sacrifice, literally laying down their lives to protect the children they taught and cared for."

I learn later that the Sandy Hook Elementary School security system, which is a buzzer at the front door – the same system we have at Bayview – accompanied by a camera that requires visitors to be approved to enter the school, wouldn't have stopped suspected shooter Lanza from entering the school, according to Ken Trump, the president of National School Safety and Security Services, which is a Cleveland-based company that advises school districts. Police say Lanza shot his way into the school with a powerful rifle, the same weapon he used to kill all 26 victims at Sandy Hook before using a handgun to kill himself.

That security system is particularly common at most schools, where outside intruders or angry parents are often more of a threat than unruly behavior by students. The buzzer system does have some flaws, such as an unwanted visitor sneaking into the school behind a person who has been allowed access, but they are the first deterrent most schools use.

Bayview High School has a similar system except the secretary who buzzes in all visitors into the school after the doors are locked does not have access to a camera. Nor does she ever leave her desk to view the person entering the school. In addition, although a sign on the outside door cautions visitors to obtain a visitor's pass from the office before continuing through the school, most visitors ignore this rule. This includes parents, siblings, graduates, and friends. At least twice a week I stop an adult in the hallway by my classroom to ask to see his or her visitor's pass, only to receive a blank stare in response and "I don't have one."

I note the irony that our school lockdown planned for today was cancelled due to so many substitute teachers being in the building. Phil Oster reveals to me at the end of the day that he was upset the administration chose to cancel it. And by the way, Phil never tells us how his security crew would deal with a false "all clear."

MONDAY, DECEMBER 17

This is the first day of our school Spirit Week for the winter sports, and today is Wacky Tacky day. In other words, we are supposed to wear clothing that does not match or is out of style. I wear faded jeans, a red t-shirt, and an old, blue windbreaker that used to be my father's with the collar up on one side. I complete this mismatched ensemble with a toothpick in my mouth. In other words, isn't it tacky and even impolite to converse with a toothpick in your mouth?

Jeff Jones sends an email that our staff holiday party will be at Buffalo Wild Wings on Richmond Road after school on Friday. Happy hour. Come if you like. No need to RSVP.

I know already I won't attend. Christopher is wrestling in a tournament this weekend, so that's where I'm heading after school on Friday. I doubt other colleagues will go either – it's the first day for vacation, people are tired, and no one wants to drink alcohol where Bayview parents can observe them.

Our debate today in English 10 is about grudges: "Should we carry grudges in real life?" I ask and then relate this to *To Kill a Mockingbird* where Bob Ewell vows revenge against Atticus Finch, who, in turn, ignores Ewell's threat.

In my period 5-8 block, Peter, a shy boy with a round face and fleshy arms who hardly ever talks, says we shouldn't keep grudges but instantly gets teased by Marcus and Connor because he cannot avoid saying "umm" after nearly every other word.

"Stop that teasing!" I say to the two boys. "It's disrespectful."

Peter watches me to see if I am going to say anything else, and when I don't, he continues talking: "That's umm why I umm don't hold umm a grudge umm. It umm just umm umm makes me umm feel bad umm a lot."

"Consider 9/11 as an example," I add to the discussion. "Should we still have a grudge about that?"

Peter answers before I can call on anyone else. "No umm no, we can't umm change umm umm that now. It's umm umm over."

I wonder if Peter feels the same relief as I do when he finally finishes.

Peter's grade in English 10 has dropped from a C to F this second quarter. I have observed him dip his head face down on his desk. The first time this happened I whispered to him and inquired if he was ill. He was not, but he had no explanation for why he put his head on his desk. He also couldn't explain why he neglected to turn in so many assignments. Phone calls home went unanswered. Extending deadlines for him didn't help either. But he participated today – that's a step in the right direction.

Motivated now by Peter's participation, I ask again: "What about the rest of you? Should we hold grudges?"

"No," Connor calls out.

I let the outburst go and turn to him. Truthfully, I'm grateful for the response. "Why not, Connor?"

He looks at me, seemingly surprised by the follow-up question. "I don't know."

And that's it. No else one speaks up, even after I call on him or her.

In my Honors English class, I ask Derrick Simms, a skinny tenth grader who had been a distance runner on the track team last year, to stay after. "You do such a great job reading *To Kill a Mockingbird* orally in class," I tell him. "You really seem to understand the story and the characters." I pause. "That's why I can't understand why you are failing this class?"

Derrick's lips rise to a slight smile, and he hugs his books closer to his chest. "I don't know, I...." but he does not complete his sentence, and we spend a moment just looking at each other.

"Well, I hope your quiz results improve," I say to break the silence. "You know, if a stranger walked in the room and did not know all the students, he would probably think you were one of the A or B students by the ability you show reading and discussing *To Kill a Mockingbird*."

Derrick smiles again; he enjoys my praise. "Mr. Miller, can I ask a favor?"

"Sure, Derrick. What is it?"

"Will you read my novel?"

I lean back in my chair and stare at him for a moment. "You've written a novel? Really?"

"Well, not really a whole novel...." Derrick smiles again. "Just a couple of chapters."

"I'd be happy to read it, but do you want me to critique it or just read it?"

"What does critique mean?"

"Uh, do you want me to give my opinion about it?"

"Yes, definitely."

"What kind of novel is it?"

"It's about these two planets at war with each other and how one planet tries to stop the other planet from building a super spacecraft machine that can blow up the other planet...and how the captain on one spaceship tries to stop the aliens from destroying Earth."

Okay, so what if he's channeling *Star Wars* and *Star Trek*? So what if he doesn't do his homework? Didn't Ernest Hemingway, a Nobel Prize for Literature winner, drop out of high school? That's why, instead of telling Derrick to stop writing his novel and start doing his homework, I say, "I would enjoy reading your novel, Derrick. Either email it to me or bring in a hard copy."

Derrick is all smiles as he exits my classroom. I watch him go and realize I'm feeling a little envious of him. He's only fifteen but already several chapters into a novel. I'm almost sixty and still on chapter one.

Spirit Week continues tomorrow with Nerd Day. However, that

changes after Melissa Fleck sends this email to every staff member:

I definitely think we should not have nerd day! In light of the weekend I think we ought to teach our students that making fun of the "class nerd" is unacceptable. I can't imagine us allowing our students to let everyone dress as a "dumb jock". There is no difference to me in how these words are used and expressed. Many of these kids who do these shootings appear to be bright boys who are socially isolated.

I suggest we have a green and white day to show our support of the victims and families of Newtown as an alternative.

The response to Melissa is immediate. Via email, four staff members agree, and Gretchen Suchs, who is in charge of Spirit Week, sends another email that tomorrow will be Green and White Day to honor the victims at Sandy Hook Elementary School. Some staff members respond, wondering why green and white have been chosen to represent Sandy Hook. Are we sure those are their school colors? A final email from Mr. Compton clarifies: We are to wear navy and gold on Tuesday, not green and white.

Mr. Compton concludes his e-mail with this:

"When the dog bites, when the bee stings, when I'm feeling sad, I simply remember my favorite things and then I don't feel so bad." Rodgers & Hammerstein

TUESDAY, DECEMBER 18

Because the tragedy at Sandy Hook Elementary School has prompted a concern for safety and security in all schools across the country, we have an emergency meeting in the library before the students arrive. Phil Oster addresses the staff again about school security and our lockdown procedures. He tells us why neither he nor his security staff will carry a gun or taser: If he interceded in a student scuffle, a student could grab the gun or taser and use it against him. According to Phil, the best deterrent to school violence is building relationships with our students and to be more observant of their feelings, especially if they look depressed. We could have guards at each door, metal detectors, even police in the hallways, but none of those measures can guarantee our school cannot be a target of an armed intruder. The experienced teachers in the room know he is right. One of my colleagues says, "They could make a MacGyver bomb if they wanted to; they could really do it."

Former Education Secretary William Bennett said on Sunday's "Meet the Press" that "schools should possibly consider arming certain employees to prevent attacks," and "Let's remember the good things here: the heroism of those teachers and that principal. And I'm not so sure - and I'm sure I'll get mail for this - I'm not so sure I wouldn't want one person in a school armed, ready for this kind of thing."

However, Randi Weingarten, president of the American Federation of Teachers union, advises against arming school employees.

Weingarten says, "Schools have to be safe sanctuaries. We need to actually stop this routine view that just having more guns will actually make people safer. We are opposed to having someone who has access to guns."

At home, I read the newspaper, and, according to the Associated Press, just a few hours before the Sandy Hook shooting, "police in Oklahoma arrested a teenager for allegedly plotting to attack his high school and trying to recruit classmates to help him. Police in Bartlesville, a community about 40 miles north of Tulsa, arrested 18-year-old Sammie Eaglebear Chavez shortly before 5 a.m. Friday on charges of conspiring to cause serious bodily harm or death."

And in Indiana, again according to the Associated Press, police arrested "a northern Indiana man who allegedly threatened to kill as many people as he could at an elementary school near his home, and later found 47 guns and ammunition hidden throughout his home. Von. I. Meyer, 60, of Cedar Lake, was arrested Saturday after prosecutors filed formal charges of felony intimidation, domestic battery and resisting law enforcement against him."

On the television national news President Barack Obama was almost in tears when he addressed the nation over the deaths. "We cannot tolerate this anymore," he said. "These tragedies must end, and to end them, we must change."

I heard this question after the shootings at Columbine, and I hear it today: Are school districts doing enough to protect their students? The *Washington Post* reports, "Safety experts agreed that school practices are uneven and that improvements may be needed in many districts. Still, experts emphasized that preventing a tragedy like Newtown's is far more complex than installing locks or metal detectors."

To be honest, I have no faith in the security measures at Bayview High. I have told my wife Sheryl that if anything happens to me, she should sue the school district for negligence.

By the way, a colleague told us at lunch that Sandy Hook Elementary School's colors are indeed green and white; Mr. Compton was looking at the Newton, Connecticut high school's colors when he emailed us to wear navy blue and gold.

WEDNESDAY, DECEMBER 19

Neither politicians nor the media can let go of the Sandy Hook tragedy. California Senator Barbara Boyer, according to the *Los Angeles Times*, introduced legislation to provide federal funds "to deploy National Guard troops at schools."

As I prepare for our winter vacation (not the nonpolitically correct Christmas vacation or the holiday vacation) and think about the tragedy at Sandy Hook, I catch myself looking more suspiciously at my students. I worry more about those who are failing. *Are they angry? Disturbed? Will they retaliate against me in some way if I give a failing grade?*

Rebecca Mieliwocki, the 2012 National Teacher of the year, notes insightfully that the school personnel at Sandy Hook Elementary confronted the shooter. "No one ran from that gun. That principal, those teachers, and those aids tried to stop this man," she says. "We need to remember that the first responders were actually the teachers."

FRiDAY, DECEMBER 21

This is the final school day before the winter break, and I read more on Sandy Hook in my morning newspaper: According to the *Washington Post*, Virginia Governor Bob McDonnell "said Virginia should consider arming teachers, principals and other school staff." He is not alone in his views. Governor Rick Perry of Texas also believes staff members should be allowed to carry concealed weapons.

And National Rifle Association executive vice-president Wayne Lapierre says in a press conference responding to the tragedy at Sandy Hook, "when it comes to our most beloved, innocent, and vulnerable members of the American family, our children, we as a society leave them every day utterly defenseless, and the monsters and the predators of the world know it, and exploit it." He later adds, "The only thing that stops a bad guy with a gun is a good guy with a gun."

The brutal truth is there is no guarantee that allowing teachers to carry weapons or putting more police in schools will prevent armed intruders, whether they are mentally deranged or not, from getting into schools and harming both staff and students. We have laws already that firearms are prohibited on public and private school property and in school vehicles. But are laws – simple words on a document – enough? For the sake of my colleagues and my students, I have to hope so.

At Bayview High School, today is the final day of Spirit Week, and grades 6-12 and all staff members crowd into the high school gym to hear Mr. Compton introduce our cheerleaders and basketball teams. The boys' basketball team is wearing all black warm ups although our school colors are royal blue and white. I do not understand how this can be until a student sitting near me tells me the boys were given the option of colors for the new warm ups purchased by the Booster Club, and they chose black. I think, "What if they had chosen orange?"

Nevertheless, Mr. Compton muddles his way through the introductions, adding dramatic inflection to his voice with some of the names, mispronouncing other names, and forgetting to introduce two junior varsity basketball players, who then have to walk up to him and ask to be announced. When he does, both their teammates and students in the bleachers laugh.

The cheerleaders then line up to do a dance routine but the sound system in the gym does not work again until the athletic director comes over to fix it. While he fools with the microphone, the girls end up standing at attention in the middle of they gym floor for nearly four minutes, which seems like four hours, listening to the catcalls from restless students in the bleachers.

I leave the pep rally before it is over. I need fresh air. I need to copy a handout for *To Kill a Mockingbird* that I am giving to my students when they return from winter vacation. I need to check my emails one last time before turning off my computer.

Christopher's wrestling tournament is an hour's drive from Bayview. What I really want to do is to get in my car and drive there.

FRIDAY, DECEMBER 28

Today is my birthday. I am fifty-nine years old.

I do not feel like celebrating. My mind is still on the tragedy at Sandy Hook Elementary School, and with about six months before my school year ends, that event makes me hope I retire alive.

I read on-line the school board in Harrold, Texas has decided to allow their teachers to carry concealed weapons. "Our people just don't want their children to be fish in a bowl," says David Thweatt, the school superintendent and driving force behind the policy. "Country people are take-care-of-yourself people. They are not under the illusion that the police are there to protect them." Harrold has no police force and the sheriff's office is seventeen miles away. Rick Perry, the governor, has endorsed their plan. The school board and Thweatt have decided teachers with concealed guns would be a better form of security than armed police in their two brick buildings since any attacker would not know whom to shoot first (there are about 100 students and two dozen teachers). "I'm not exactly paranoid," Thweat says. "I like to consider myself prepared."

"We are trained to teach and to educate," said Zeph Capo, the legislative director for the Houston Association of Teachers. "We are not trained to tame the Wild West." One Harrold resident says, "If something happens, do we really want all these people shooting at each other?"

According to the *Salt Lake Tribune*, "More than 150 Utah teachers and school workers took time off from their winter breaks Thursday to attend a free class on how to carry concealed weapons and respond to mass violence such as the recent shooting in a Connecticut elementary school." Utah is one of two states that already allows concealed weapons permit holders to carry firearms on school grounds. The other state is Kansas. In Ohio, the *USA Today* reports that the "Buckeye Firearms Foundation is swamped with 20 times more applications - from teachers and administrators to custodians and bus drivers - than they have space for in a three-day tactical defense course to be offered this spring."

Arizona Attorney General Tom Horne is proposing a plan where at least one staff member in each of the state's schools can carry a gun. This would be a "voluntary program in which every school could nominate one person to receive free firearms training provided by local sheriffs and the attorney general's office. The individual would be allowed to keep a weapon in a locked place somewhere on campus," according to the Politico news service. Also in Arizona, Sheriff Joe Arpaio has proposed that an armed posse of volunteers be stationed outside public schools.

The Associated Press states that an attorney representing a client known only as Jill Doe is going "to sue Connecticut for $100 million on behalf of a 6-year-old Newtown school shooting survivor who heard violence over the school's intercom system." The attorney says the potential claim is about improving school security and not the money. "It's about living in a world that's safe. The answer is about protecting the kids." The Associated Press adds, "Pinksy's client, whom he calls 'Jill Doe' in the claim, sustained 'emotional and psychological trauma and injury' on Dec. 14 after gunman Adam Lanza forced his way into Sandy Hook Elementary School and gunned down 20 children and six adults inside in one of the deadliest school shootings in US history."

In California, as reported on the NBC Nightly News, a high school student named Courtney Webb was inspired to write a poem in her school journal about the tragedy at Sandy Hook Elementary School, and after a teacher read it, the administration decided to suspend the girl. Webb claims she was just being creative and desired to "start a conversation." Administrators saw her act of creativity as a "threat." First amendment expert and attorney Jonathan Katz says, "This is a bad civics lesson, for students to see someone being suspended in school for her words, especially these kind of words where she could not be sanctioned if she was outside the schoolhouse gates."

Happy Birthday to me, the teacher!

MONDAY, JANUARY 7, 2013

This is our first day back from the winter vacation – I have not used the term Christmas vacation for nearly fifteen years now because many educators consider the term Christmas to be politically incorrect. They are referring, of course, to the separation of church and state. Christmas implies presents and Christianity, and, of course, I do not want to embarrass students who do not receive any gifts or offend those who are non-Christian or even anti-Christian. *Can I say holiday?*

Either way, I tell my students that I have missed them and inquire how they spent the last two weeks away from school. I am always interested to hear if any students went on an exotic vacation or received a great gift.

Tina Wells, who has been suspended twice for fighting in school, tells a story about a fistfight between her stepsisters on Christmas day. It seems an argument over which program to watch on television escalated to screaming and then to fists flying. Autumn shows off her new black Addidas warm up top. Devin, like many others, says, "I didn't do nothin'."

And after I joke and pout that *I* never received a gift from any student, Jamie, who is in my periods 5-8 block, informs me in her matter-of-fact way that I did not get a gift because most students do not like me.

"Really?" I ask, kidding with her. "*No* student likes me?"

"No," she responds immediately. "It's about ninety-eight percent who don't."

"Why don't they like me?"

Jamie's face gets tight; her eyes become slits. "You're kidding, right?"

I decide not to ask her anything else.

The New Year – 2013 – I am told in an article by Justin Reich, who is a fellow at the *Berkman Center for Internet and Society* and the co-founder and co-director of EdTechTeacher, is "the greatest time in history to be a teacher. Never before have educators had available such an extraordinary wealth of resources with which to fashion learning experiences." We teachers "can choose from the *millions of documents* archived online by thousands of libraries and archives around the world, including not just texts but images, audio recordings, film clips, and ephemera." Indeed, according to Reich, we can easily connect via the Internet to other educators and classrooms around the world. This both inspires and discourages me because I view the Internet as a valuable learning tool but still lack the knowledge to use it in more in-depth and exciting ways with students.

John Dewey, I believe, would cheer for the Internet; he would appreciate the notion that we have through technology truly become a nation of learners. However, not all teachers can get on this bandwagon. Reich says, "The rich possibilities of technology raise as much anxiety and dismay as they do excitement. Teachers feel like they don't have time to keep up with the changing technologies and emerging pedagogies."

I start this first day back in the classroom with a review for the test on *To Kill a Mockingbird.* Before the break, I reminded students to finish reading the book and to complete the Vacation Homework Packet. Today I let them examine the five test options I'm giving on the novel and select the test they want to take.

Of course, I am eager to see how much they remember about the novel and whether they enjoyed the resolution with Scout and Boo Radley, so I begin with a freewrite where I call out the name of a minor character like Dolphus Raymond or Mrs. Henry Lafayete Dubose to see how many specific details they can write. Four minutes later I stop them and direct them to exchange papers with a classmate. "What can you add?" I ask and then direct them to begin another two-minute freewrite session on the same character.

I refer to plot events next, like the testimony of Mayella Ewell and Bob Ewell's behavior after the trial, and ask students to rank them: Which single plot event is the most important in the novel?

To make students think analytically, I pose some open-ended questions and have students to write their answers: Who is the novel's greater hero, Atticus Finch or Boo Radley? What event surprised you the most? Why that one? I follow this up with a discussion.

Next is a survey, Who did...? as in Who shot the dog? Who baked cakes for the children? Who believed in magic coins? Students have to answer with the names of characters. I record this as participation points. Students have the option of passing on a question, but I come back to them eventually.

I am constantly checking my students' engagement as I continue the review of *To Kill a Mockingbird* with a visual. Here, students skim magazines (I have all types of magazines on the book racks beneath their desks, including *Time*, *Newsweek*, *National Geographic*, and *People*, among others) to locate pictures that could represent a character, scene, or plot event from *To Kill a Mockingbird*. Of course, they have to explain this connection. I move up and down the aisles checking their work and offering assistance as needed.

Next, I link them with a partner to work on matching character descriptions to characters in the novel and share and compare their answers on the Vacation Homework Packet. I end class and the review by allowing students to see the actual test again and to group with other students who have chosen the same test to discuss possible answers to the questions. Tomorrow is the test day, and students ask for an extension, which I deny.

It is a new year, which means resolutions, and Gretchen Suchs uses the bulletin board in the hallway directly across from our classrooms to put up mini-snowball cutouts that have resolutions from both staff and students on them. I add mine: Stop drinking Pepsi. But even as I staple the paper snowball to the bulletin board I regret this resolution. I fear I will break it before the weekends and regret I did not make a statement about improving myself as a teacher or brag more about my profession.

Because I had read on-line the other day about Julie Conlon, the literacy coach at Melbourne High School in Melbourne, Florida, who declares we need to brag more as teachers in 2013: "The people we meet in a bar or those we sit next to on a plane cannot see into our classrooms to witness the daily flashes of brilliance, inspiration, and enthusiasm that fuel our fires and give us the energy to teach. Instead, they hear the stories on the news and believe them. We need to invite them into our world and tell the stories about the students and the teachers we work beside everyday. Let's show them that what happens between our opening and closing bells is just as significant as what happens on Wall Street. When they hear about what we really do— rather than our complaints of low pay, unfair testing, and kids who really are just kids—maybe then we'll start to see some changes. Changes in the conditions we work in, changes in the pay we receive, and changes in the future for our students—which is really what it is all about."

I stare at my "No more Pepsi" resolution on the snowball and consider ripping it from the bulletin board. Before I do, however, Gretchen comes up behind me and says, "That's really cute, Ethan."

So I leave it.

TUESDAY, JANUARY 8

I read this morning in the on-line *Washington Post* that "the parents of a 6-year-old Silver Spring boy are fighting the first-grader's suspension from a Montgomery County public school for pointing his finger like a gun and saying 'pow,' an incident school officials characterized in a disciplinary letter as a threat 'to shoot a student.'" The parents are appealing the suspension and want the disciplinary action "expunged from the student's permanent record." The *Washington Post* also states "leaders in Maryland and a growing number of states are working to reduce out-of-school suspensions, which have increased greatly in the past several decades and are linked in studies to lower achievement and students dropping out of school."

You think?

The U.S. Department of Education reports that in the 2009-2010 school year over 3.7 million students were given out of school suspensions. This includes Girard Middle School in Dothan City, Alabama where each of its 435 students was suspended at least once.

THURSDAY, JANUARY 10

Another student gets shot today. This time it happens in Taft, California, a mostly agricultural town about 125 miles northeast of Los Angeles. A student armed with a shotgun shot a classmate in a Kern County high school classroom and threatened to shoot others until Ryan Heber, a science teacher, talked him into the putting the gun down. According to the Associated Press, the gunman had "as many as 20 rounds of ammunition in his pocket," and the *USA Today* states he "apparently intended to shoot others." The victim is in critical but stable condition, and Heber, in fact, received a minor pellet wound to his head. In my viewpoint, Heber is another candidate for our national teacher of the year.

At Bayview High School, when the school day ends, all my Honors students file down the aisles and rush to the door. Except for Monique Evans. She is almost hopping from the back of the room to the front. She is all bright smiles and waving arms as she thrusts her *To Kill a Mockingbird* test at me as if showing me she's discovered gold. Monique gives me a hug and thanks me for giving her a B. I reach around her and hug her back, although I actually hug her backpack.

Then I follow Monique and her classmates into the bustling hallway of students who are rushing to the school exits. I need to copy a nonfiction article on weather conditions to see if students can identify it as a technical nonfiction piece, and I on my way to the teacher's workroom I'm slowed by the groups of students ahead of me. I'm almost surprised when I suddenly find myself in step with art teacher Melissa Fleck.

"This is bullshit," she whispers to me.

I glance around at the students to see if any of them heard her. But they're shouting about rides home, the basketball game tomorrow, and stupid detentions, and I think Melissa is angry with them. "They just don't know any better," I whisper back.

She gives me a confused look. "Who? Them?" She's louder now. Her pace slackens. She waves an arm like she's batting away a balloon. "Not the students, Ethan. It's Compton. He's not going to reimburse me for the toilet paper I bought for the bathroom."

"Toilet paper?"

"Yeah, I had to buy it with my own money."

We reach the door of the teacher's workroom, and I stop. Mr. Compton could be inside. He could hear every word we say so I whisper again. "Did Mr. Compton tell you why he wouldn't reimburse you?"

"In the past, the custodians supplied toilet paper for me, but now, according to Compton, I have to buy it myself."

I wince and hope Mr. Compton or Mr. Morgan are not inside the teacher's lounge as I open the door. Thankfully, the room is empty. I turn to Melissa and walk backwards to the copy machine. "Did you fill out a purchase order?"

"Why should I fill out a purchase order? I never had to buy toilet paper before." Her face is tense, her tone incredulous.

"I just thought we always had to fill out a purchase order for classroom supplies."

"He's just being such an asshole." Melissa declares. Then she turns and stomps out.

THURSDAY, JANUARY 17

I attend our second Bayview School District Community forum. Only eight parents attend this time, and since three are couples I calculate that five students are represented here out of total K-12 student population of nearly 950. This evening I am the only teacher who attends this event. The custodians have set up about 120 folding chairs, which makes the gym look deserted. In direct contrast, every school administrator is there, and they all sit behind tables in front of the sparse crowd, each with his or her own nameplate, ready to answer questions.

After Dr. Andrews welcomes the few parents in attendance, the first speaker is the director of food services, a tall, middle-aged woman in black bell-bottom pants and white sneakers. She smiles warmly, but I keep thinking she feels out of place speaking into a microphone without wearing an apron and fishnet cap. Her first words catch me off guard.

"Too many kids are too fat."

Then I get it: child obesity. She's right; our secondary school is full of overweight students. But the Bayview school cafeteria staff is doing their part, she informs all of us, to cut down on calories. We learn that at lunch now our students are only served one percent milk, and the pizza crust is whole grain.

"I probably wouldn't eat that," a parent on the other side of the gym calls out. Still smiling bravely, the food services director claims: "Some of the brave ones have tried it." Then she recommends that parents serve fruit as a dessert at home.

"What kind of fruit?" the same voice blurts out. The woman may be in her late thirties, more likely forty-something. She looks like she squeezed into her long winter coat, and her thick body pushes at the coat's buttons. Her hands rest on a bulky purse in her lap.

The director looks right at her. "Well, any kind of fruit would be acceptable. It's certainly a healthier choice than candy or chips."

"Fruit's expensive," the woman says and looks around to see if any others in the audience agree with her. "I can get two bags of chips at the dollar store for a dollar."

The food director doesn't respond to that; instead she turns to the superintendent who silently nods her back to her seat and then takes hold of the microphone. "I think you all should come in have lunch with your child in our cafeteria," he says, smiling broadly.

Another parent raises her hand. "I seen that food one time. It don't look that good, and most of those kids just throw it into the trashcan anyway. It's a shame."

The director of our food services gives an embarrassed look towards the others on the panel, as if seeking some support. But no other administrator offers any.

The superintendent continues the program by announcing that "China is number one in educational programs...America is number eleven." He does not announce, however, the origin of those statistics. China is number one? *Really? China?*

Then it's the school district's treasurer's turn. She informs us that the passage of the recent levy will now provide $850,000 to the school district over the next six months. Mrs. Carter, the only school board member in attendance, raises her hand and laments that too many residents and businesses in Bayview do not pay their property taxes so the amount of funds the school actually receives could be much less. The treasurer admits that is very true.

"Is it possible," Mrs. Carter declares, "that we might only see half of that total?"

"Yes," the treasurer admits, "but I'm hoping the county and city authorities force compliance from all businesses and homeowners."

"Ha," one father calls out and shakes his head wildly.

The superintendent then introduces the director of special services for students, who perks up in her chair, tugs on the hem of the coat of her green pants suit, and starts to stand. The superintendent, however, starts thanking the eight parents for voting for the levy, even though he can't be certain they actually did, and forgets about the director of special services who still stands nervously behind him. After a minute passes, she, like the rest of us, realizes he's forgotten her and sits down.

"Now, are there any questions?" Dr. Andrews asks.

"Are you doing anything about getting students involved in astronomy?" This question comes from a young man who is sitting with a slender woman on the other side of the gym. In a salesman's voice, he reveals that he runs an astronomy program – something like a science camp – for students at Cleveland State University and he is hoping Bayview' students can take a field trip there. "That's why I'm here," he confesses in closing. "It won't cost that much."

The superintendent stares at him briefly and seems relieved, in fact, when Mr. Horrigan raises his hand. "I think it should be mandatory," Mr. Horrigan proclaims, "that the parents of any student achieving less than a 2.0 GPA must meet with the teachers and principal or they get suspended."

The superintendent tells him that the school cannot mandate parents of low achieving students to meet with teachers. Florida tried this and failed, he says.

Mr. Horrigan notices me and acknowledges me publicly for being one of the few teachers who keeps students' scores regularly updated on our on-line grading system. "What's wrong with those other teachers?" he asks harshly.

Dr. Andrews nods his head. "I will send an email tomorrow to all staff members telling them to keep their on-line grades updated...We're going through a paradigm shift," he adds.

Paradigm shift?

The same woman who complained about the unappetizing cafeteria food now complains about the school website. There is a link for Community Involvement, and she cannot navigate through it either to make a suggestion or to examine the comments made by other parents. Our technology coordinator, Justin Moore, leaves his seat with his laptop and sits next to her to show her what to do. He opens the laptop on his lap, and they both peer down at the screen. The woman politely nods her head at times even when Justin cannot access the site. The woman eventually turns to the superintendent who has been waiting patiently and says, "But even if I can get on this site, how will I know that something will actually happen?"

"Call me," he says.

"I have," she asserts. "You never call me back."

Just before I leave the Community Forum, the father who promoted his planetarium project at Cleveland State University raises his hand and asks again if the school system is interested in sending students to CSU to study the stars and planets. The cost is minimal, he says, waving some brochures in his hands. I leave, however, before I hear the superintendent's response.

MONDAY, JANUARY 21

I begin my journey today towards the Ohio Graduation Test. This is the test every high school student in Ohio must pass in order to graduate. There are five sections (Reading, Writing, Math, Social Studies, and Science), each taken in the morning of single weekday in the middle of March. Standardized tests like this are given in states across the country, often with much anxiety and anticipation from both the students and the teachers.

In Seattle, however, nineteen teachers from Garfield High School announced, as revealed by the *Christian Science Monitor*, they are refusing to administer their state's test, the Measures of Academic Progress Test. The *Monitor* claims the teachers' collective opinion in their press conference that the test "wastes time, money, and dwindling school resources," and that "Garfield's civil yet disobedient faculty appears to be the first group of teachers nationally to defy district edicts concerning a standardized test, but the backlash against high-stakes testing has been percolating in other parts of the country." Teachers at Ballard High School also plan to boycott the Measures of Academic Progress Test.

Should I do the same?

No.

For two reasons: (1) This is my last year of teaching, and I could be fired for violating my contract with the school system by being insubordinate to the administration and (2) I admit I do not have the courage. I resent having to teach to the test, but Dr. Andrews wants to get Bayview out of the depths of Academic Emergency and into the prized stratosphere of Excellent with Distinction. I even remember the

$2500 bonus he promised to share with us if we did.

So I write my list of learning activities on the white board and plug away with my preparations in English 10 for the Ohio Graduation Test. In fact, I begin with the Reading section and explain to students the types of passages they could confront: informational nonfiction, narrative nonfiction, fictional stories, fables, poems, drama excerpts, an editorial, or even a speech excerpt.

I distribute a handout and challenge my students to identify what type of passage it is. Almost all affirm correctly that the article about weather conditions is informational nonfiction. A positive start. I want to make the lesson challenging and interesting, but test preparation is seldom exciting.

William James says in his landmark book for teachers *Talks to Teachers*, "It is nonsense to suppose that every step in education can be interesting." His book was published in 1899, and he believed in using a pop quiz and gold stars as incentives for students. He recommended teachers use different teaching techniques for students' different learning styles instead of mundane lectures (today we would call James' approach differentiated instruction). In addition, James would have been disappointed in our focus on state tests, and in his speeches to teachers he advocated they work to engage students' natural curiosity and connect lessons to "real world" concerns. In short, according to James, teaching and learning are hard work where students have to compete, and teachers have to reward those who succeed.

I continue my review by directing students to compare words like theme, main point, central point, author's purpose, main purpose, and author's perspective, which have been terms that have appeared on previous OGT Reading section tests. We look at an example passage and its questions to emphasize this point. I then deal with other terms they might confront on the OGT: describe, identify, justify, predict, summarize, evaluate, and inference. Here's how I introduce these terms:

"A car has been stolen; describe the car...A suspect has been arrested; identify the suspect...The prosecutor has to explain the arrest to a jury; how does he or she justify the arrest? The suspect appears in court; predict the verdict in the trial...The suspect tells his side of the story; summarize what he tells the judge and jury...The jury discusses the trial in the jury room; how do they evaluate him? Do you think today's legal system is fair? Make an inference."

Here are my students' general responses: Most students describe a Mustang or a Cadillac. Their suspect is typically a young black male. The prosecutor justifies the arrest due to the claims made by witnesses or his fingerprints being found on the car. Most predict he is found guilty and sent to prison. Their summaries involve the suspect simply being at the wrong place at the wrong time. The jury determines the suspect either needs to steal the car to sell it for money for drugs or he wants to go on a joy ride with neighborhood friends. Finally, almost all students infer the American legal system is rigged against defendants, especially those who are poor.

"It's always a black guy who gets arrested," Marcus declares during first period and then folds his arms defiantly across his chest.

"Not always," responds Jeremiah Jackson, who comes out of his rebellious shell for a brief moment, and then returns to staring silently at the floor.

During my lunch break, to find out what other teachers are doing to prepare for the OGT, I surf the web and see a news article about a sixty-one year old teacher at Mariemont High School in Cincinnati is accusing her school administrators of discriminating against her because of she has this rare phobia: a fear of young children.

Maria Waltherr-Willard had been teaching Spanish and French at Mariemont since 1976, and when she was assigned to the district's middle school, her phobia emerged, forcing her to retire in the middle of the 2010-2011 school year. Her lawsuit in federal court claims the school district violated her rights under the Americans with Disabilities Act by transferring her out of the high school to the middle school.

Of course, the school district denies her claim, saying the middle school needed a Spanish teacher. The administration also challenges Walterr-Willard's assertion that the transfer was retaliation against her for complaining to parents the school cancelled the high school French program over her objections.

Her lawyer, on the other hand, says in a letter to the U.S. Equal Employment Opportunity Commission this was "the beginning of a deliberate, systematic and calculated effort to squeeze her out of a job altogether." The lawsuit says Waltherr-Willard has been treated for her phobia since 1991 and also suffers from general anxiety disorder, high blood pressure, and a gastrointestinal illness. She was managing her conditions well until the transfer, according to the lawsuit.

When she was forced to teach the younger middle-school child, her health deteriorated. She was "unable to control her blood pressure, which was so high at times that it posed a stroke risk," according to the lawsuit, which includes a statement from her doctor about her high blood pressure. "The mental anguish suffered by [Waltherr-Willard] is serious and of a nature that no reasonable person could be expected to endure the same."

The lawsuit also says that Waltherr-Willard has lost out on at least $100,000 of potential income as a result of her forced retirement. Patrick McGrath, a clinical psychologist and director of the Center for Anxiety and Obsessive Compulsive Disorders near Chicago, said that he has treated patients who have fears involving children and that anyone can be afraid of anything.

What am I truly afraid of? *Retirement?*

WEDNESDAY, FEBRUARY 6

The boycott of the Measures of Academic Progress Test by Garfield High School and Ballard High School teachers in Seattle, Washington is getting serious support from the NAACP and teachers from across the country. Moreover, three hundred Garfield High School students have received their parents' permission to join the boycott. Nevertheless, the Seattle Public Schools Superintendent Jose Banda announces the test will be given as scheduled.

Here at Bayview High, Mr. Horrigan's email suggests he's upset. Maybe angry.

To Karl Horrigan, Jr.'s Teachers:

Don't think I'm trying to tell you how to do your job. Maybe you think I'm one of those helicopter parents. I'm not. I guess I'm not too popular at Bayview. I've decided Karl will finish this year and then I'm moving him to another school, a better one.

Good luck the rest of the school year. I will stay out of your way from now on.

Karl Horrigan, Sr.

Here is my immediate response to Mr. Horrigan's email:
Mr. Horrigan,

I have never considered your involvement in Karl's academics overbearing; in fact, I remain impressed with your attentiveness to his academic progress. I have two sons and sometimes I regret I have not been more active in communicating with their teachers, especially when I compare myself to you.

If you like, I will continue to follow the academic plan we established earlier.

As I have said before, Karl is most often a very energetic and active student in my class, and I am confident that he will continue to succeed in school due to that reason and due to your active participation in his academics, whatever school he attends.

THURSDAY, FEBRUARY 14

Mr. Compton sends all the teachers this email:
Happy Valentines Day to ALL!!!!!!!!!!!!!!

We have perfect attendance TODAY!!!!!

I count the exclamations points. There are thirteen after ALL and five after TODAY. I wonder why he neglected the apostrophe between the e and the s in Valentine's and chose to capitalize all the letters in ALL and TODAY. My reflection on this subject is brief, however, because as an English teacher I know the answer.

Later in the day, Mr. Horrigan sends me an email:

Thanks for your kind words. I highly respect you as a teacher, which I told to Dr. Andrews, who I have a good relationship with. My issue is with the principal, who apparently doesn't like my parental involvement.

Karl Horrigan

This makes me think of the Gallup poll conducted each year that measures the general population's confidence in American institutions. The military is typically ranked at the top, U.S. Congress is at the bottom, and public schools fall somewhere in the middle. This year, confidence in public schools declined by five percentage points but the irony is that amid all the criticism levied against public schools by legislators this past year 77% of America's parents still gave their school a letter grade of either A or B. Therefore, the surest way to increase support for public education is to advocate that American parents have more children.

THURSDAY, FEBRUARY 21

Devin Jones cannot sit still. He needs a tissue to blow his nose, so he gets out of his seat to yank a tissue from the box on the cabinet. He returns to his seat but a minute later he's on his feet and on his way to the trashcan to throw away the used tissue.

A minute later he's up again, this time to borrow a pencil from my box of recycled pens and pencils. He returns to his seat but when he discovers the pencil needs sharpening, he gets up to sharpen it, and the rest of us have to listen to him sing and dance as he goes to the pencil sharpener.

We're working on using sensory language, so as my directions on how to complete the writing assignment are interrupted by the grating sound of the pencil sharpener, I make this a teachable moment and tell the rest of the class to note the unpleasant sound of the electric sharpener: noisy, grating, harsh, discordant.

After Devin returns finally to his seat and I repeat the directions for him, he starts to write, only to change his mind about what he has on the paper. He is out of his seat again with the crumpled paper in his hand to throw it away, but I step in front of him before he can get half way up his aisle, look up at him to meet his gaze since he is about six inches taller, and reach out my open palm for the wadded up piece of paper. "I'll throw it away for you." I say, smiling.

He looks at me like I am speaking a foreign language but he drops the paper on my palm anyway and returns down the aisle, singing and dancing as he did before. Once there, when he thinks I am not looking, he throws a paper wad at Darrielle who sits a row over.

I stop conferencing with another student on his prewriting and say to Devin, "Pick it up."

"What I do?" Devin asks, an incredulous tone framing his voice.

"You know what you did. Pick up the paper you threw at Darrielle."

Darrielle, in fact, points to the floor where the paper wad landed after it bounced off the shoulder of her purple sweater. Devin grunts loudly, stands again, and saunters down the aisle between the rows of desks to retrieve the marble-sized paper wad. He starts for the trashcan, but I stand in front of him again with my outstretched hand, palm up. As before, he drops the paper onto my palm and wanders back to his desk.

I finish some additional directions on how they should describe the meal they ate the previous evening as a preview for doing a restaurant review later and continue my circuit up and down the aisles to monitor and conference with the students as they write. As I near Devin, who sits looking out the window now, I wonder if I need to call his grandmother again? Give him a detention? Fill out a referral?

In his ASCD SmartBlog post, Mark Barnes explains his "no rules, no consequences" method. This is quoted from his blog:

"What I failed to comprehend in my 'I'm-the-meanest-teacher-in-the-school' approach was that I had created a classroom based on control, and I was alienating my students....They may have, on occasion, acquiesced to my list of demands, but most of the time their compliance came at the price of learning. After all, what child would embrace education in this kind of militant classroom?"

Barnes decided to change the way he dealt with students' behavior:

"A no-rules, no-consequences learning community, based on cooperation and filled with exciting activities and projects engages students and eliminates boredom. When students are working collaboratively, using technology, leaving their seats and, yes, even chewing gum, they are more likely to complete activities and projects and less likely to be disruptive. Rules and consequences, in this bustling, student-centered classroom, are easily replaced with discussions of mutual respect, individual conferences with those who take longer to embrace the controlled chaos that governs the room and rapport-building rather than strictness."

I recognize the distinction between being "controlling" and being in control. I prefer the latter. In fact, I believe in using a cooperative and collaborative approach with my students in many ways, but is there any real solution for preventing mischief, disruptions, or malicious behavior?

I understand Barnes' point, but the class rules from the beginning of the school year are my domain. Whenever a group comes together there have to be guidelines and consequences for the violations of those guidelines. Think traffic laws. Go over the speed limit on a highway and you risk a state trooper's ticket. Consider a baseball game. If a pitcher balks, base runners advance one base. Examine your own contract with the school. Would your principal continually accept you arriving late? Our lives seem linked with rules and consequences. Students need to realize the classroom requires a similar approach. My consequences vary, but I am very serious about how students need to behave in the classroom. Devin Jones, unfortunately, chooses to ignore the rules.

But I decide to let it go with Devin, and today he just continues to stare out the window.

MONDAY, FEBRUARY 25

Farting and a dog whistle are the main events this day in my period 5-8 block. I have no idea which student is passing gas and which student is setting off the dog whistle from a cell phone, and although I can neither smell the fart nor hear the dog whistle, my students are definitely getting annoyed. Even the girls are pulling the tops of their t-shirts or sweatshirts over their noses, and some even change their seats. They point at Connor Reese, but he denies he is the one who farted.

The dog whistle is another story.

"Don't you hear that?" an amazed Jamie asks, and she does not believe me when I say that I do not. Other students begin to laugh.

"What am I supposed to be hearing?" I ask. I set the white board marker on the metal tray, square up to my students, and stick my hands to my hips.

She looks at me wide-eyed. Her jaw drops. "That whistling!"

"I don't hear anything."

"Are you serious?"

"I'm telling you I don't hear anything." I glance around the room and turn my head to see if that improves my hearing.

"He's right." Basketball player Jermaine Bonner sticks up for me. "Old people can't hear the dog whistle."

Dog whistle?

Jamie then explains that the new cell phone apps enable some cell phone users to download a dog whistle sound. I look around again. A dog whistle on a cell phone? No one has a cell phone out or his hands in his pockets.

"Why would you do this?" I say to the whole class because I do not know who is broadcasting the dog whistle sound. "Why is this funny? There is no one else to laugh with because the rest of the class is annoyed. Cut it out."

I eye the whole class left to right, hoping to catch the culprit clicking the off key on his cell phone, but no one moves his or her hand to a pants or coat pocket. The dog whistle sound, however, must have ended because the complaining stops and I can try again to teach persuasion methods they will need to use on a potential writing prompt on Ohio Graduation Test. All goes well for about ten minutes until Connor farts and the shirts are pulled up to their noses again.

THURSDAY, FEBRUARY 28

It is chilly today, and there's a little snowfall – the kind that does not stick but drifts toward the ground and then disintegrates on contact. At the end of the school day, I make copies of my course syllabi and handouts that explain how I evaluate and discipline students to take to the second round of parent-teacher conferences, which lasts from 3-9 P.M. I also collect all my students' Writing Charts from their Writing Portfolios to show any parent/guardian who asks how their child is developing as a writer. The Writing Chart displays categories like Introduction, Organization, Transitions, Conclusion, Style, Punctuation, Sentences, among others, where students can identify their strengths and weaknesses in each category for each writing assignment. It is a revealing document to show young writers where they need to improve, and it also helps me design follow-up lessons for those categories where a majority of students are struggling.

After I return a writing assignment to my students and they have completed their Writing Charts, I will ask, "What do we need to work on?" When several students tell me, for example, they did not check off transitions as a strength, I know to provide a lesson on transitional words and phrases the next day – I am creating a lesson based on the requests of my students, thus creating a student-centered classroom.

As I conference with parents who sit in front of me across my table in the gym, they tell me about the privileges they have taken away from their son or daughter: no more television or laptop or cell phone or I pad. They shake their heads, their shoulders sag, and I try to offer hope about their child's ability to improve. Certainly, with effort and possibly extra credit, any student can improve his or her grade, but I have made this same comment to hundreds of parents during the last 35 years and only rarely has any student become more diligent afterwards.

Mrs. Smith tells me her son David, who is in my English 10 Honors, "hates to read."

"That's unfortunate," I say, "because we do a lot of reading in the Honors class."

Mrs. Collins, whose son Eddie has yet to learn that he should put a period at the end of a sentence and is getting a D in my English 10 class, says, "I don't know what's wrong with that boy. I keep tellin' him he's going nowhere 'less he graduates."

I inform Mrs. Eckle that her daughter Leena sings in class while I lecture, even after I have cautioned her about it. Mrs. Eckle asks, "What songs?"

I pause, then say, "I don't know the songs. Probably something from her choir class. The point, however, is that she cannot sing in English anymore."

"We listen to music all the time at home." She smiles, I imagine, at the memory of Leena singing in the kitchen.

I put Leena's Writing Chart back in the folder. "Okay," I say. "I'm certain that must be wonderful."

At 9 P.M. I look at the list of parents whose names appear on my sign-in paper. There are only twelve names; I averaged two parents an hour during the last parent-teacher conference of my teaching career. As I gather all my leftover handouts and the students' Writing Charts, my good friend Allison Means, who knows I am retiring, says as we leave the gym, "Your last one, you know. You must be grinning ear to ear."

"Not really," I tell her. "I can't shake the feeling I'm not truly helping these people or their kids."

FRIDAY, MARCH 1

On this cold first day of the month in my period 2-3 class Justin does not have a pen or pencil, nor does he have his notebook, so he starts poking the back of the boy who sits in front of him and asking for a piece of paper and a pen. This boy, Isaiah, waves his arm at Justin, like he is trying to pull a knife out of his back, which makes Justin laugh and poke Isaiah's back some more.

I stop my explanation on types of conclusions – make a plea for action, offer a prediction, summarize the main points – that students can use for their persuasion papers and walk over to Justin. I give him a piece of paper and an old pencil and lean over to whisper to him about coming to class prepared and focusing on the lesson instead of teasing a classmate. He smiles mischievously up at me and says, "Okay, Miller, okay."

I walk next to the other side of the room to give a grammar textbook to Eric when laughing makes me turn. Eddie and Isaiah are laughing at Justin who has his hands over his mouth as he runs out of the room. He never makes it to the bathroom. Red vomit spews out before he is five feet out the door, and a trail of red splotches (a fruit drink?) is splattered on the tile floor of the hallway. Justin finally staggers into the bathroom as some of his classmates lurch toward the classroom door to see what happened.

After I call this into the office, Justin returns to class to the cheers of his classmates. Minutes later, John, the custodian, mops up Justin's vomit and sticks a yellow Wet Floor post on the floor.

When the period ends, I stand in the hallway during the class exchange between periods 3 and 4, as the administration expects us to.

I remember Mr. Compton's comments at the third assembly he had with students on school discipline where he re-affirmed the no cell phone, no book bag, and no electronic devices policies at Bayview High School and do my duty and tell a girl passing me in the hallway wearing dangling jewelry and dark jeans to put away her cell phone. Actually, I say cordially, "Would you please put your cell phone away?"

Her response is no response. She does not look at me or acknowledge my request and simply continues down the hall through the student traffic. Maybe, I think, she did not hear me, so I follow her, quicken my pace, weaving between students walking in the opposite direction, and move in front of her so she can see me. "You can't have a cell phone in the hallway," I say in a neutral voice. "You have to put that away." I point to the phone at her ear.

She definitely sees and hears me this time but ignores me anyway and brushes by me, the phone still stuck to her ear. Her back to me now, I am left with two choices: follow her and deliver a consequence for her insubordinate behavior or simply walk away and forget about it. The first option requires effort; the second is an acceptance of defeat. I decide on the former and follow her into David Grasser's classroom and locate her sitting at a desk in the back of the room. I ask her to tell me her name, but she refuses. Then I ask David, who says, "That's Christina...Yeah, she can have an attitude sometimes."

I thank him, look one more time at Christina who looks back with indifference, and return to my empty classroom where I use my school phone to contact first the secretary to get Christina's emergency phone number and then to call the girl's mother. I listen to the mother's introductory message on her answering machine, and after the recorded voice tells me to "Have a blessed day," I leave a message about what happened in the hallway: Christina's use of the cell phone and her insubordinate behavior.

Fifty minutes later, five minutes into my period 5-8 block class, Christina appears at my open door and shouts gruffly, "Come here!" She points at the floor by her feet as if ordering me to come stand there.

Startled by this, I have to pause several seconds before responding. My English 10 students watch transfixed by this new confrontation. "Leave my classroom," I finally demand.

"Come here," she repeats, standing square in the doorway, her tone both imperious and belligerent, her eyes savage and dark. She points again at her feet. I speculate the mother got my message and called Christina.

I take a few steps toward her and look her in the eyes. "You better not give me orders," I say evenly. "And I'm telling you again to leave my classroom."

I want to end this intrusion in my classroom, so I turn slowly away from her to continue passing out a handout on persuasive language – more irony – only to hear my door slammed, which makes some students snicker. "Now I hope we can get on with the lesson," I declare to them, and the class quiets down.

That's why we all can hear a female voice outside the closed door yell, "Motherfucker."

MONDAY, MARCH 4

I learn on the morning television news that 383 members of the Strongsville Education Association have started their strike against the Strongsville Board of Education.

Strongsville, a city on the other side of Cleveland, has a strong teachers' union, but still needs help. Megan Cutler sends an email to us, requesting donations of any amount to help those striking teachers. Megan's email also reminds us, "You better read your contract." Half of us, however, still don't have one because the copy machine broke when a secretary was running off copies.

THURSDAY, MARCH 7

Our principal Mr. Compton gets on the PA at 2:30 P.M. to announce an emergency meeting at 2:40 in the library for all staff members. I finish arranging the desks in my room into groups of four in preparation for cooperative learning on Friday and then head to the library.

Once we are all assembled – although six teachers arrive late – Mr. Compton tells us he wants us to know before the school board makes the official announcement on Monday that he has turned in his letter of resignation effective the end of the school year. He could stop there, thank us, and dismiss us; instead, he feels an urge to explain. "Like any ship on the..." he starts to say, turning his eyes to the ceiling, and the dramatic pause goes on for so long, I say out loud, "Water?"

"Yes," Mr. Compton says, "Thank you, Mr. Miller...yes, on the water...There's a storm..." Again, he pauses, but none of us, including me, know how to finish this statement for him. Neither does he because he leaves the metaphor unfinished.

He raises a hand and lowers his chin, moves a little to his right. "God has destined me to places...." He smiles, lowers his chin now, blinks, and shakes his head slightly, letting us see again the speckles of gray in his hair. "He closes one door; He opens another...I know I'm preaching to you, but that's who I am, that's who Henry Compton is."

I know any reference to any deity makes some staff members uncomfortable. They are big on separation of church and state. You would never hear them say Easter vacation, for instance, only spring vacation.

Mr. Compton glances around the room, his expression a mixture of apology and reverence, and says, "I know Bayview has a way to go...You'll be high on my prayer list."

Which makes me wonder why God "destined" him away from Bayview now. What does it mean that we have "a way to go"? Should we be grateful that he is praying for us? And does he expect us to believe he resigned voluntarily?

Mr. Compton concludes his talk by acknowledging his lame duck status as our principal and thanks us for our efforts. But he cautions us as well: "Just because I have only a couple of months left, you better not run over me; you have to respect who I am. I'm still in charge. I still want those lesson plans every Monday by eight A. M."

MONDAY, MARCH 11

The Ohio Graduation Tests begin today. Specifically, the Reading test. Students in grades 10-12 who have not passed the test must show up by 8:00 A.M. to take the two and a half hour test. It's reading today, math tomorrow, then writing, social studies, and science to finish out the week. Science teacher Jim Simmons and I sit as proctors in my classroom and watch a dozen students – their heads bowed over their test booklets – take the Reading test. They have to read a series of passages, examine four possible answers on a series of multiple-choice questions, and then darken the appropriate circle on the answer document with a number two pencil. Most of the passages are nonfiction, but there is one fable about a teenage boy and a lion in Africa thrown in. As each boring minute slowly ticks away I think of the Seattle teachers who chose to boycott their state test.

Yelling in the hallway prompts all the test-taking students to lift their heads in unison and stare at the closed door. Jim and I look at each other for a moment before I leave my seat and walk quickly into the hallway where I find Adam and Frank, senior varsity basketball players, calling out to a senior girl at the other end of the hall. Seniors who have passed these state-mandated tests have late arrival approval, and Adam and Frank have arrived, in fact, earlier than expected.

Although he now has the girl's attention, Adam yells again, and Frank, the son of a board member, calls out to the girl to text him later.

"Quiet, guys," I demand. "There's testing going on."

"Ahh, Miller, it's cool," Frank says.

The girl is gone, and Adam laughs – *at me?* – and shoves Frank in the arm. Then Frank and Adam turn away from me and face into their open lockers, snickering about something unknown to me. The two boys are about 6' 3" and tower over me at 5' 10". They are starters on our varsity basketball team that is 22-2 and playing tonight for a District championship.

"You need to get out of this hallway," I say to them in a low voice, but they do not respond. They simply finish dumping some textbooks into their lockers and taking others out before moseying, still chuckling, back down the hallway in the same direction where the senior girl had been.

I watch them disappear when they turn at the end of the hallway, and although it is only 10:00 A.M, a game day for varsity athletes in any sport, I used to think, meant having a serious demeanor the whole day. Especially when playing for a tournament championship.

The old-school coach in me believes in that earnest, focused approach during the school day before any competition from the time the athlete got out of bed in the morning to the end of the game that night, and these basketball players show none of that. But they are like that every day in the hallway outside my classroom, and they have already won both the conference and Sectional Tournament titles, so maybe my old-school approach is outdated. I sigh, shake my head, and return to my duty as a proctor for the Reading section of the Ohio Graduation Test.

I watch the local news with Sheryl tonight and see that after months of negotiations and one week of picketing, the Strongsville teachers remain on strike.

TUESDAY, MARCH 12

First, while proctoring the math section of the OGT, I read the sports section of the *Plain Dealer* and learn our varsity basketball team lost the District championship game by twenty points. Then I examine Mr. Morgan's written response to the discipline referral I wrote about Christina, the girl who refused to put away her cell phone. This is what he wrote on the bottom of the referral: "Spoke with Christina and reminded her of consequences."

That's it?

I toss the paper into a box beneath my desk. That is where I throw a lot of the memos and referral responses I receive from any administrator. Since it's March, the box is half full of paper. I doubt Mr. Morgan's meeting with Christina will prompt her to change her rude behavior or to respect me as a teacher in this school.

I have also had a problem with Jamie and Amber, two students in my period 5-8 block class who follow most of the rules but come late to class nearly every day. The problem has been their purses, which are so big they resemble grocery sacks, and Mr. Compton at a recent assembly told students (that was the fourth time this year students heard this dictum) they could no longer carry backpacks or purses into classrooms (they could contain concealed weapons). Although Jamie and Amber exit a classroom only two doors down from mine at the end of period 4, they do not put their over-sized purses in their lockers; instead, they walk up to Mr. Morgan's office, drop their purses there, and then return to my class with a pass from him. So each day, Jamie and Amber stroll into my classroom typically four to five minutes after I have started class, disrupting the lesson.

During my lunch period I catch Mr. Morgan standing at the secretary's desk just outside his office and by coincidence Jamie and Amber are there, too.

"This is wonderful," I say, grateful for the good fortune to address the issue with all parties present. "What a great coincidence." I look past the girls at Mr. Morgan. "I need to talk to you about the girls here and their purses."

The girls swivel their heads towards me, their faces a mix of curiosity and displeasure, and I note with interest that both have the straps of their purses slung over their shoulders. The three of them listen to me recount Mr. Compton's policy about book bags and purses (what he announced at the assembly). I point to the girls' large purses, explain my wish to be consistent in enforcing the policy, and then lament that the girls' constant late arrival to my classroom disrupts my lesson.

"I give them a pass," Mr. Morgan says quickly. He adjusts his eyeglasses and moves the papers he is holding from one hand to the other. I sense when he looks away that this conversation annoys him, and the girls, in turn, roll their eyes and look indeed just as bothered.

I, however, refuse release them from this obligation. "I know you give them a pass, but at issue here is that their late arrival every day disrupts the class, as I have to stop what I am doing, get them caught up, and then get everyone back on task again." I gesture with one hand toward the girls. "Can't they simply put their purses in their lockers?" My eyes are only on Mr. Morgan now.

"We don't have locks on our lockers," Jamie interrupts, shifting her purse strap on her shoulder. I glance at her and think, aren't they violating the school policy right now?

"I've seen some kids' lockers," Mr. Morgan adds, chuckling. "They have so much junk in there, I'm surprised anything fits in them."

I look back at him, wondering how the status of any student's locker matters here, and say, "I'm just complying with the policy that

Mr. Compton has about book bags and purses. The girls should leave their purses in their lockers instead of having to walk all the way to your office and then back to my classroom."

"He's right. They should leave their purses in their lockers." It is Mrs. Moore, the secretary, who says this from her desk. "Don't they have locks?"

Mr. Morgan does not answer her question. Instead, he repeats, "They've been leaving them in my office, and I've been giving them passes."

I glance out the window and notice that clouds and a flurry snowfall have replaced the sunshine we enjoyed earlier in the day. More importantly, I get it now that the issue will not be resolved and decide to bring closure to it. "How about this?" I offer. "How about I just ignore Mr. Compton's book bag and purse rule with all my students – not just Jamie and Amber – but *all of them*? That way I can be consistent and the girls can show up on time." I am being facetious, even sarcastic, but Mr. Morgan does not react as I anticipate.

In fact, my offer makes Mr. Morgan's mood change immediately. He smiles, stands a little straighter, and exclaims, "That works for me."

Jamie speaks up, seeking clarification. "So we won't get in trouble for bringing our purses?"

"Not any longer," I say to her, adding drama to my voice. I even smile. "I am simply not going to enforce a school policy for that class anymore." I emphasize this for the assistant principal, who is partly in charge of school discipline, and I turn directly to Mr. Morgan to make sure he understands. "Is that okay? I should just ignore a school rule?"

"If it makes everyone happy," he answers. And to emphasize this in turn, he adds as he turns his back on me and the girls and walks into his office, "Happy, happy, happy!"

WEDNESDAY. MARCH 13

Tonight I attend the Bayview Cultural Commission book club meeting. The event has great promise: Bayview students and adults sitting and talking about a selected book they have all read. For the elementary school, the book was *Rules* by Cynthia Lord, a novel about an autistic child. For middle school students, it was *Rocket Boys* by Homer Hickam whose excellent memoir profiles his motivation along with several high school friends to build rockets, and for grades 9-12, the selection was *Cry, the Beloved Country* by Alan Paton, a novel about the early stages of apartheid in South Africa and a Zulu pastor's tragic quest to reunite with his son.

My English/Language Arts colleagues and I had promoted the books in our classes, offered extra credit to those students who read them, and, of course, encouraged students to attend the discussion session, which is held just four blocks from the school at Faith United Church on Richmond Road, beginning at 7 P.M.

I show up at 7 P.M., the scheduled time for the discussion, but there are only five other adults there, all of them standing in the foyer/hallway of the church and chatting about some movie they all saw recently. I join them but I cannot participate in the conversation because I did not see the movie. However, I ask where our book discussion will take place and Mrs. Williams, a former school board member, points to the church's fellowship hall down the hallway. I glance where she is pointing and notice that the fellowship hall is empty except for four white tables and folding chairs set in a circle.

I amble into the fellowship hall and sit patiently on a metal folding chair and glance occasionally at the movie-discussing group in the foyer. Lois Jennings, who is a teacher at the elementary school, arrives and after being greeted by the others, eventually walks into the fellowship hall and sits next to me. The book discussion is supposed to begin at seven, but even by 7:20 there are still no more than six other adults there. It is not until 7:35 P.M. that the entire group – about fourteen in total – finally comes into the fellowship hall and takes seats on the folding chairs around the white tables where they plop down their books. The average age of the group, I estimate, is around 65. Even the mayor of Bayview joins us, wearing a black suit and a tie that depicts the American flag.

Unfortunately, despite the incentive of extra credit and our pleas to attend the event, not one student from any of the three schools (elementary, middle, or high school) shows up. The book talk, however, goes on, and maybe the fact that no student came is a positive because they may have been shut out of the conversation which is dominated by two adults: the church pastor and the leader of the Bayview Cultural Commission, an older man named Robert Schmidt.

Across from me, a white-haired gentleman, who must be in his late seventies at least, spends almost the entire session with his eyes down, picking at his book with his fingernail, trying to remove a price tag stuck on the cover. He looks up only briefly several times but then resumes his task with his fingernail on the price tag. Six other people hardly say a word either. When the pastor asks one elderly woman her impressions of the novel's resolution, she admits, smiling timidly. "I didn't get that far into the book. I didn't finish it."

The pastor, I can tell, enjoys these sessions. He looks to be in only in his thirties but has already a start on a receding hairline and sagging paunch above his belt. His comments reveal he has also read about the life of Alan Paton and researched some facts about the colonization of South Africa by the Dutch. When the pastor reveals what he learned from his research, the older man finally stops picking at his book's price tag and utters something about the Boers in South Africa. "I think they were farmers," he adds.

247

The others stop and stare at him for more than a moment until the pastor asks, "Do you mean the Boer War?" The older man, however, does not respond to the question. Instead, he turns to the woman sitting next to him and mutters, "They were the white people."

Undaunted by the outburst, the pastor regains his composure and declares his understanding of the theme of Cry, *the Beloved Country*, "It's all about power...who's got the power."

"And racism," Mr. Schmidt asserts. "How the Blacks suffered in South Africa."

No one disagrees with them or offers another interpretation.

I surprise myself by announcing to the group, "What I find especially interesting is the title ...the comma after cry seems to indicate direct address, as it seems Paton is appealing to the citizens of South Africa, his 'beloved country,' to cry...to feel sadness."

The pastor and Mr. Schmidt only glance briefly at me before flipping through the pages of their books to look for other quotes they previously highlighted.

Finally, near the end of the evening (8:45 P.M.), Roy (I can see his name tag), who tells us he works part-time at the Bayview Public Library, strokes his white beard and complains that no students attended the book talk. "This would have been better if the students were here. Where are they tonight?" he asks this of no one in particular, although I sense he expects Lois or me to respond.

I do not, however, offer an answer. Undaunted by the lack of response from Lois or me, Roy then alleges that a possible consequence of children not reading enough is an increase in the prison population in the United States, especially by young black males. Roy reminds us that he is Jewish and that "we are still fighting the Holocaust, you know. Black people, Jewish people...it's all the same."

Mr. Schmidt tries to lessen the focus on Lois and me and says that maybe the Commission had not done enough to encourage the students to come. The pastor adds that the problem could be our "entertainment culture" and kids just are not as entertained by books as they are by the Internet, television, and video games.

At 9 P.M. the pastor announces the meeting must come to an end, and I help him and Mr. Schmidt stack the tables and chairs in a corner of the fellowship hall. Before I leave, Mr. Schmidt stops me and asks, "So what do you think we can do, Mr. Miller, next year to get the kids to come?'

I stand in front of him and try to eliminate the resignation in my voice. "It's like I said last year. Let's pick a book the kids have to read for school. That way they might be more encouraged to attend the book club."

I sense that my comment disappoints Mr. Schmidt because he says, "Yeah, I guess we just need to try something else."

I do not have the heart to tell him I am retiring.

THURSDAY, MARCH 14

Devin Jones is at it again. Today in my period 5-8 block class, although his assigned seat is now the first desk in the front of the room now, he enters and takes a desk in the back and begins to sing. Actually, he mixes his lyrics with buzzer-sounding grunts. I tell him to sing after class has ended, and he rolls his eyes and responds, "Okay, B."

"Thanks, B," I say immediately in response, and this makes several students laugh.

Devin pretends now to smoke a joint, pinching his thumb and pointing finger in front of his mouth and loudly sucking in his breath. He wants to make sure Connor Reese notices this so he calls across the room to the other boy. "Gettin' high, man."

I stop again our oral reading of Act I, Scene 3 of *The Tragedy of Julius Caesar* and say, "Stop that" to Devin.

"Why you messin' with me, B?" he demands, lifting both arms to emphasize his frustration.

I still do not know what B stands for, but I use it again because it seemed to connect with him (and his classmates) the last time. "Well, B, it's because you're being disruptive. We can't focus on the reading with you pretending to smoke marijuana, making that hissing sound."

The question excites him. "Who says I'm smoking a doobie?"

Now *I* am feeling frustrated. "Just follow along with the play, will you?"

"I'm not the only one, ya' know. Tell them." He gestures with one hand to the rest of the class.

I do not know who the "them" are because he has been the only disruptive student in class. Nevertheless, to humor him, I turn to the rest of the class. "Be quiet," I caution them in a dramatic way, "unless you're reading a part or participating in the discussion." Then I turn to Devin. "Is that okay, B?"

Again, the other students chuckle, making an annoyed Devin fume at his desk in the back of the room.

At the end of the day I meet privately with Donna, our school treasurer, in her office to discuss my intent to retire at the end of the school year. She closes her office door and advises me to meet certain deadlines and to submit my retirement application to the State Teachers Retirement System [STRS] as soon as possible to lessen any delays in getting my application processed. She shows me what my severance pay will be and even lets me use her phone to call the STRS to have them send me some more financial information.

We lament together the challenges of working for the Bayview Local School District, and Donna tells me that no other school district operates like this one. "This board of education is out of control," she tells me. "They treat us like we are their servants." She then confides in me that she also plans to retire herself in August.

FRIDAY, MARCH 15

I am absent today – another mental health day. Although the absent rate differs from district to district, the Education Department reports that 5.3 percent of teachers nationwide are absent on any given day. Their report also states that the cost of hiring substitute teachers is four billion dollars annually, which is about one percent of total K-12 spending. The truth is that teacher absences increase in the spring, which bothers some administrators who point to the private business sector where only 73% of employers provide sick leave along with paid vacations.

I am not physically sick but I need a day off to rest due to the fatigue I have developed working with teenagers, who themselves enter my classroom with their own sniffles and illnesses. According to the American Nurses Association, compassion fatigue is "a combination of physical, emotional, and spiritual depletion associated with caring for patients in significant emotional pain and physical distress." The same conditions are found in the classroom, and dealing with needy students each day even before I teach a lesson takes a mental toll. To me, this day off is not a luxury but a necessity.

Still, I do some schoolwork. I sit alone at the kitchen table while my wife is at her daycare job and my sons are in school, and evaluate the Act I quizzes students turned in the day before. Using my laptop I even check my school emails to keep updated. When I do, I see that the superintendent has sent an email to the entire staff asking us to welcome another new physical education/health teacher, who is now the fourth p.e./health teacher hired this year. He replaces Jeff Jones who replaced the 300 pound gentleman who replaced another teacher whose name I have forgotten. In his email, the superintendent assures us, strangely, that this new teacher's references have been thoroughly checked.

MONDAY, MARCH 18

The Ohio Graduation Test is behind us now, and my students and I can now more earnestly get back to the business of teaching and learning. This week we will focus on Act II and III of *The Tragedy of Julius Caesar*. I have the desks arranged in a circle so students can see and hear their classmates orally read and discuss Shakespeare's famous play.

In addition, I tell my students that I will be evaluating them based on their level of participation, either by reading out loud or answering questions, including our debates about the characters: Is Cassius a true friend to Brutus? Should Brutus join the conspiracy based only on what he thinks Caesar *might* do as emperor? Does Caesar deserve to die for being arrogant and ignoring all those who try to warn him that he is in danger?

In hopes of making *The Tragedy of Julius Caesar* relevant, I pose a topic for another debate: Should our government order the assassination of another country's leader? The best examples are Ronald Reagan's missile attack on Muammar Gaddafi's house in Libya, George W. Bush's personal war against Saddam Hussein, and then the famous SEAL Team Six assassination of Osama bin Laden in Pakistan. To provide some background, I show students a clip from the movie "Zero Dark Thirty." The students seem disinterested by all of this – some have never heard of bin Laden, they have no recollection of George Bush as President, and they have no idea where Afghanistan or Pakistan are on a map. Originally, I thought they would find this information both entertaining and informative. Alas, they do not; only three students make a single comment to this debate.

The actor Tony Danza spent a year teaching high school English in Philadelphia, and his days in the classroom were filmed as part of a reality television series. He wrote a book about his experiences titled *I'd Like to Apologize to Every Teacher I Ever Had: My Year as a Rookie Teacher at Northeast High*. Danza wrote: "We can't want them to get an education more than they want it for themselves." He acknowledges that teachers must engage students but adds: "It strikes me that what we really need are students engaged in their own education."

I drop the debate activity, and since Shakespeare's language can be confusing I spend time to demystify it by translating some lines, explaining the colloquialisms, and making analogies until they can handle the dialogue on their own. In fact, some students start to complain that I am doing too much translating as we read.

The desks are arranged in a circle so we can see and hear each other read, and I let Jenny Wilson, one of the girls who was suspended for fighting in the first quarter, play Julius Caesar refusing the crown. She sits in a chair with wheels in the middle of the circle and three times pushes away an imaginary crown offered to her by a classmate standing next to her. After we conclude the role-play Jenny asks if she can still sit in the chair and I say yes. Jenny then spends the final minutes of the class period twirling and rolling in the chair as if on a carnival ride.

Later, after eating dinner with Sheryl, I learn from a television newscast that on the west side of Cleveland, hours and hours of negotiations between the Strongsville Education Association and their board of education failed to produce a contract; therefore, the Strongsville teachers' strike continues. The board of education, in fact, declares they have given their "last, best offer."

TUESDAY, MARCH 19

I stop in Ander Klyszewski's classroom during my free period to see how he is feeling. He has missed nearly two weeks of school with a back ailment. Like me, Ander is one of the oldest teachers on staff. Unlike me, Ander served in the military and even had a tour of duty in Iraq. He wears a suit and tie every day to school and has complained frequently to me about the disruptive behavior of his sixth graders.

I find out today that though his back still bothers him, he feels compelled to return to school because of the poor work his students had been doing during his absence. A colleague had been bringing their work home to him, and when he saw the substitute had been giving them all A's, he checked their assignments more closely and discovered that ninety percent of their responses were incorrect. The substitute had only cared that they had turned in a paper.

Ander tells me that sitting makes him uncomfortable, so he leans against his desk and says glumly, "My wife tells me I should quit."

"Are you going to?" I sit at one of his student's desks and lean my elbows on its flat surface. I am indeed very curious about his answer. My retirement plans still remain a secret to my colleagues.

He shakes his head. "I could walk in tomorrow and tell them I'm done," he answers, and for a moment his face darkens as he surveys the empty room, as if seeing the faces again of the students at their desks. "There's just too many of them who don't want to learn."

I know the *them* he refers to are his students. "I see the same thing at the high school level," I say, hoping he recognizes my empathy.

Ander continues lamenting: "I spend half my day correcting

behavior." He peers at the ceiling, blinking, as if remembering incidents. "That's a disservice to the rest of the students and to us."

He is correct, of course, and we get quiet, both of us, it seems, thinking about our students and their behavior in our classrooms.

At the end of the school day I walk up to Megan Cutler's classroom and, since she is my union president, I show her a letter to the superintendent that announces that I plan on retiring at the end of the school. She reads it silently and slowly, then looks up, smiles, and says, "You'll be missed."

WEDNESDAY, MARCH 20

I am really curious what my English 10 Honors students will think about the novel *Dicey's Song*. I have assigned them to read it out of class while we read *The Tragedy of Julius Caesar* in class. I begin by asking the class to brainstorm social skills with me – initial greetings, table manners, friendly conversations – and lead into the problems we might have with others who might lack social skills. "How do we acquire our social skills?" I ask, and they respond with the answers I expect: from parents, friends, television, movies.

"What if a child grew up without parents, friends, or television?"

The room gets silent, and the silence makes some students in the back start private conversations about people they know who they think have no social skills. To get them back on track I introduce them to Dicey Tillerman, the protagonist of *Dicey's Song*, who as a thirteen year old is forced to come live with her grandmother along with her three younger siblings. Unfortunately, Dicey has no social skills and no friends.

Hands go up, and most of their questions are about Dicey: Why doesn't she have any friends? What does she do if she doesn't have any friends? If she lives with her grandmother, where are her parents?

Instead of answering their questions, I wink, distribute the novels to my students, and allow some time for them to examine the front and back covers. Then I start reading the opening chapter of *Dicey's Song* out loud, changing the inflection of my voice for dialogue, even stumbling over some words as I find myself rushing. After several minutes, I stop and ask, "What do you think about it so far?"

Most express some interest so I direct the students to write 4-5 questions they want answered before they are done reading the book. After I collect their papers, I express my optimism they will enjoy *Dicey's Song* and even tell them about novels I read as a teenager that changed my life: *On the Road* by Jack Kerouac, *The Adventures of Huckleberry Finn* by Mark Twain, and *QB VII* by Leon Uris, the first novel I ever read – although I don't tell my students this – that described sex between a man and a woman.

I allow the remaining class time for sustained, silent reading as I hope to continue developing their reading stamina. Karl Horrigan, Jr., and volleyball player Tierra White, however, try to sleep.

FRIDAY, MARCH 22

This is our last day of school before spring vacation. The school day over, Devin Jones comes into my classroom and places without comment his textbook on my desk and a paper from the office that verifies he is withdrawing.

"What school are you going to?" I ask as I sign my line on the paper. I see that all his other teachers have already signed this document.

"Not going to any new school...just dropping out. I'm seventeen now."

I put my pen back on my desk, stare up at him, and when I finally realize I've lost control of my lower jaw, I close my mouth only to open it again and ask, "Are you sure you want to do this? There's still time to improve your grade."

"I'm failin' everything." He pushes the textbook toward my hands.

I don't touch the textbook. "Devin, I don't think this is the right thing for you to do."

He looks to the classroom door, sways a little, and groans. "What's the point," he says as a statement, not a question. "I'm screwin' up. I can't help it."

"Devin, you-"

He swipes the paper off my desk. "I gotta go, B."

So I stand, shake his hand, take the textbook, and wish him luck.

Goodbye, Devin.

FRiDAY, MARCH 29

My wife has the television news on when I come downstairs for dinner, and we both watch a NBC Nightly News report that the superintendent of the Atlanta school system and 34 other administrators and teachers have been charged with cheating on standardized tests. According to the NBC news broadcast, "teachers operated in a culture of fear that forced them to change answers on students' tests in order to push up scores." Ironically, Beverly Hall, the Atlanta superintendent, was the National Superintendent of the Year in 2009 and hosted at the White House by Arne Duncan. Now she faces up to 45 years in prison.

When we switch to the ABC World News, their broadcast about the Atlanta school system declares, "The indictments are the latest page from a now three-year-long education that's shaken the faith of parents of schoolchildren. At one point, nearly 200 teachers from 44 schools were accused of changing student answers to improve scores on federally required standardized tests." The teachers in Atlanta claim they were forced to give or change answers on students' tests.

But school administrators cheating on standardized tests is not confined to Georgia; an El Paso, Texas superintendent is in prison for removing some students from class to improve his school's test scores. Is it really possible that these are the only two cities where cheating happens?

The local news broadcast reveals the Strongsville Education Association has reached the fourth week of their strike.

My wife doesn't argue when I turn off the television.

TUESDAY, APRIL 2

This is our first day back at school after spring vacation. I check my emails, and I note this one from Mr. Compton:

Greetings Staff:

Welcome Back!!!!!!!!!!!!!

I hope you had a wonderful Spring Break with family and friends.

As we enter into our last quarter/final grading period of the 2012/2013 SY, lets help our students become more in acknowlegment of their self awareness. Students require advanced work in key areas related to personel growth, which has been called the executive function of self-awareness. Such competencies include discovering and capitalizing upon learning strengths, goal setting and acheivment, and complex decision-making.

Lets make April and May our goal to tap in to our students learning style and continue to move our students to excellence!!!!!!

Have a Wonderful Week!!!!!!!!!!!!!!!!

As an English teacher, I am disturbed by all the exclamation marks, the punctuation errors, and the misspellings. As an educator, I am puzzled by "Students require advanced work in key areas related to personel growth, which has been called the executive function of self-awareness. Such competencies include discovering and capitalizing upon learning strengths, goal setting and acheivment, and complex decision-making."

What does this mean?

This evening I watch the ABC News, which shows the implicated Atlanta teachers, principals, and administrators surrendering one by one at the county jail. The prosecutors say superintendent Beverly Hall is most responsible, firing teachers who failed to cheat and giving handsome bonuses to those who did. Hall defends herself saying she and her staff say didn't know teachers were cheating.

The news about education gets worse. The Associated Press reports about an Iowa teen and his family who are suing a school district and its administrators in Bedford, Iowa because school officials neglected to protect the boy from other teens who bullied and assaulted him. The lawsuit alleges "he was subjected to persistent bullying by other students at his Bedford high school. They say it culminated in last October's attack, in which two students pelted him in the head with footballs, leaving him with severe brain injuries that required surgery to remove a blood clot and with permanent disabilities."

WEDNESDAY, APRIL 3

At our Professional Learning Community meeting after school today, I sit with five colleagues, all of us English/Language Arts teachers from the high school and middle school in the library to discuss the use of student data that is supposed to drive our instruction. We are doing this because the Ohio Department of Education has labeled our school as an "Academic Emergency" school. This means we need to develop strategies to improve our students' academic performance; the English Department is looking at how effectively our students can identify the main idea of a reading passage.

Our conversation shifts to students' reading skills. Get an image of your favorite, older aunt and that is Betty, who teaches Bayview's gifted students. She says, "Kids these days just can't stay focused for any length of time to read anything." She looks around our small group as if asking one of us to agree with her.

Some of us pick up on her cue and nod our heads probably just to placate her. Greg, a second year reading teacher and our school's baseball coach, stops checking his text messages, looks up, and says, "They just don't like to read." He snickers as if he just told a joke.

More polite head nodding follows, and after 11th grade English teacher Rebecca Leever suggests we look at the data we collected from our classes, Cindy Greenlee complains she did not know she had to bring her students' data; she left it in her classroom. "When were we told to bring it?" she demands.

"In the email," Rebecca politely responds.

"What email?" Cindy asks. Her eyes narrow, as if she has been the victim of a terrible prank. She sits up straight in her chair.

Rebecca responds quickly but tactfully. "I sent it before we left for spring break."

Cindy just shakes her head. "I don't remember it." She then offers to go to her classroom and get the data, her students' scores on a sample reading assignment, and Rebecca tells her she can. Cindy, however, never leaves her seat.

Suddenly, Betty gets up and leaves. She doesn't apologize, she doesn't explain, she just walks away. I watch her exit the library and then focus again on my colleagues' conversation. We are going to complete a "Five Step Plan" to analyze the data we have. Greg checks his cell phone again, Cindy just glances around the room at the other groups, and I recall with some irony that three years ago another administrator ordered us to complete a "Six Step Plan."

THURSDAY, APRIL 4

I sit at my desk on this sunny but cold morning before period one checking my emails when David Grasser comes into my classroom and tells me Bob Hundly is dead. After teaching social studies for over 30 years, Bob retired from Bayview High School about eight years ago, had a stroke two weeks ago, and, as David has just learned, died yesterday. David is smiling, which surprises me, but I do not say anything. Maybe this is how David shows shock because there is certainly no humor to Bob's death. Then he leaves as abruptly as he arrived, leaving me to return to my emails.

Later, as I begin my period 5-8 class, Charkita asks me from her desk if she can get her literature book from her locker.

"No," I say immediately. This is our fourth week on *The Tragedy of Julius Caesar* and students should know certainly by now to bring their literature book to class. If I allow Charkita to get her book, then I could not expect any student to bring his or her book. It's about being responsible. I would have chaos. *Right?*

Charkita's mood darkens. "That's why no one likes you," she proclaims, staring at me. "You're such a prick."

I feel my face grow hot and almost on instinct I take a step toward her before I stop myself and lean a hand on an empty desk in the first row to steady myself. I return her stare, count to ten, and then back up to my front table. I even amaze myself when I say, "Let's begin Act IV."

The other students glance quickly at each other, and there are some gasps and quiet laughter before they open their literature textbooks and dutifully turn to the correct page. I ask for volunteers to read orally the characters' dialogue, and Connor, Jenny, and Jamie raise their hands.

I prep the scene – Antony, Octavius, and Lepidus are discussing the rogue Roman senators they plan to kill – and read the stage directions, while the three of them speak the lines of Antony, Octavius, and Lepidus in Act IV:

ANTONY

These many, then, shall die; their names are prick'd.

OCTAVIUS

Your brother too must die; consent you, Lepidus?

LEPIDUS

I do consent--

OCTAVIUS

Prick him down, Antony.

I stop the oral reading right there, move a little closer to Charkita's desk, and say, "See, everyone, that's how *that word* is supposed to be used. Got it, Charkita?"

This makes the entire class laugh, and someone says, "Girl, he got you...for sure."

At the end of class during my lunch period, I make Charkita stay and sit next to me as I call her father. When he answers, I tell him what Charkita said, and he gets immediately apologetic – a positive sign. He then expresses gratitude when I say I will not turn in a discipline referral for Charkita (knowing Ellis Morgan, what good would it do anyway?).

"Thank you. Believe me," he declares firmly, "I will talk to Charkita, and she won't talk like that again in your class."

I remind him that earlier in the school year, Charkita had been an engaging and typically enthusiastic student. She raised her hand during discussions, and she had been progressing adequately until the second quarter. "I miss those days," I tell him.

Maybe he remembers, like I do, that in December, Charkita was caught smoking reefer in the parking lot and was suspended for ten days. In January, in her math class she punched a boy in the neck after he knocked her purse off her desk. That got her suspended again.

When she returned after the second suspension she was off-task so often, she typically missed my directions. Of course, I spoke several times to Charkita after class and asked her what had happened to the on-task student she used to be. I even gave her some extra credit handouts, but she never turned them in.

And now this outburst today.

I finish my conversation with Charkita's dad and give the receiver to her. Mostly, she says "Okay...okay...okay" before handing the phone back to me. I hang up and dismiss Charkita to her lunch period, feeling grateful that the dad was on my side. Parents are not always so supportive.

I remember when I first started teaching English and coaching varsity wrestling at my first school. Even though I worked really hard, I admit I was less than competent as both a teacher and a coach. My diligence, though, hardly mattered to Mr. Fredericks, the father of one of my wrestlers.

Mr. Frederick's son David was a 185-pounder wrestler who was one of those decent but lazy athletes. In several matches David would complain of an injury to get the official to stop the match for a minute whenever his exhaustion on the mat forced him to need a breather. At the Woodmore Invitational in January that year in his semifinal match, David was winning against a strong kid from Cardinal High School until the third period when his opponent scored a takedown and took a one-point lead. David suddenly pointed to his nose and asked the official to stop the match. The official did stop it and checked David's nose as David whimpered and gestured toward his nostrils. I walked on the mat and joined the official in examining David's nose. "What's wrong?" I asked.

David pointed to his thin nose. "It's bleeding," he moaned, his chest heaving.

I looked at the official, he looked at me, and then we both went back to looking at David's nose. "No, it isn't," I said to David.

"Yes, it is," he asserted and began wiping his nose with a finger.

Again I traded glances with the official who said, "I don't see any blood, young man. Can you continue wrestling?"

David, forced now to either default the match or continue, nodded his head and returned to the center of the mat. He eventually lost by eight points.

After the match I returned to the bleachers, sat down with my scorebook, and was immediately joined by David's father, who slid down the bleachers next to me. He sat quietly next to me for a couple of minutes as I busied myself with my scorebook.

Then he tapped my forearm. "Why didn't you do something to help David when he got injured?" he demanded.

"But he wasn't injured, Mr. Fredericks," I said.

Mr. Frederick's large head seemed to expand like a balloon. His forehead reddened, he squared his shoulders to me, and he took some quick breaths. "How do you know he wasn't injured?"

"I checked him," I said, keeping my tone matter-of-fact. "So did the official. There was no nosebleed."

His face got tense. He clenched his lips. His eyes darkened. "Are you fucking with me? Are you really fucking with me here?"

Although he was sitting right next to me, I pretended I did not hear him. "What?" I desperately wanted to believe he was kidding with me. What did he mean: *Was I fucking with him?*

He raised his voice loud enough that the spectators sitting in front of us swiveled their heads to look at us. "I would kill you," he growled, "if you were fucking with me. I don't let the unions fuck with me at my business, and I ain't gonna let *you* fuck with me."

Clear now he wasn't kidding – this was no joke – I did not respond. Instead, I got up and left the stands – I walked, shakily in fact, to the lobby area outside the gymnasium, feeling a little bewildered but mostly worried by Mr. Frederick's threat. *Was he serious? He would kill me? Really kill me?*

I guess being called a prick is not so bad.

FRIDAY, APRIL 5

This is Good Friday, and according to the Associated Press story in my morning newspaper, Jesus is in the news because the superintendent of the Jackson City, Ohio school district declared "a Jesus portrait that has hung in a southern Ohio school district since 1947 was taken down Wednesday because of concerns about the potential costs of a federal lawsuit against its display...The decision was made after the district's insurance company declined to cover litigation expenses. He said the faculty adviser and two student members of the Hi-Y Club, a Christian-based service club that the school says owns the portrait, took it down at his direction." The state ACLU chapter and the Freedom from Religion Foundation sued on behalf of a student and two parents.

My end-of-day routine today resembles almost every other day during the school year. Before I leave my classroom I wet a towel in the nearby bathroom, return to my classroom, and wipe my white board. Then I check my emails, delete all the advertisements from textbook companies and wrestling camps, and turn off my computer. I return to the now dry white board and write the next day's lesson activities (for Monday, April 8) on it, along with the Common Core academic standard we plan to accomplish. Then I stuff my black, leather briefcase with *The Tragedy of Julius Caesar* Act V quizzes, put on my jacket, and get ready leave my classroom.

Just before I exit, I turn and look one more time at the empty classroom. Is it clean? Are my novels and biographies neatly arranged on the bookshelf? Has a student left a purse or jacket in the room? Are my blinds at halfway? Suddenly, I overhear some girl in the hallway yell, "Shut the fuck up!"

I decide to wait, hoping this girl takes her potty mouth somewhere else. I take a seat at a student's desk and watch the clock above the door. I wait, in fact, several minutes, and after I move into the hallway, it is empty. This makes me sigh with relief.

The Bayview High School choir room is near the exit, and when I near the glass doors that lead outside, I hear our choir practicing in the music room. They are repeating over and over the lyrics, "We will worship the lord" which makes me think of the Jackson City, Ohio school district lawsuit.

I go outside on this sunny and warming afternoon and discover the parking lot is nearly empty of cars, which means almost all of my colleagues have left for the day. They probably were in their cars ten minutes after the kids left. It's Friday, and two days away from Bayview High await all of us. Walking toward my car, I too look forward to the weekend.

MONDAY, APRIL 8

Mr. Compton's Monday morning email tells us...

1. Extraordinary teachers have great **passion** for their work...Be passionate.

2. Extraordinary teachers have a craftsman's ability to choose the best tools for each particular task...They have the courage to accept risks and defy conventional wisdom.

3. Extraordinary teachers excel at creating **exciting** classroom environments; their classroom is their stage and they relish the opportunity to perform for their students—not necessarily for laughs or popularity, but to excite a student response toward learning.

4. Extraordinary teachers **connect** exceptionally well with students...They know that under-standing, acceptance, compassion, and fairness carry much weight with children. They comprehend the importance of a teacher's character and credibility and try to be good role models.

5. Extraordinary teachers **challenge** students to reach their full potential. Students are worked hard and held responsible for finishing assignments on time and for delivering quality performances. Such teachers have high standards, which are not compromised. Their motto seems to be, "I welcome any and all to my classes, but don't sign up unless you are serious about learning."

6. Extraordinary teachers get extraordinary **results**...These teachers receive accolades from students, colleagues, and parents.

BHS teachers are indeed extraordinary. Thank you all for striving each day to demonstrate what preeminent, exemplary, exceptional, highly effective, outstanding, and acclaimed teachers do. We are truly a family of teachers, and we learn from one another how to become even more proficient in our craft. At BHS, teachers are extraordinary because we *Teach with Passion* each day!

Have a positively wonderful week!!!!!!!!!!!!!!!!!!!
Am I an extraordinary teacher?

I do some research on-line and discover Mr. Compton plagiarized these statements from Jeff Zoul's website entitled "Teach. Learn. Lead. Repeat." Zoul, however, goes uncredited in the email.

When I have my lunch period, I walk over to 9th grade teacher Gretchen Suchs' classroom and give her a handout listing a series of Elizabethan terms, like thou and thee, with their modern definitions so she can use them when she covers *The Tragedy of Romeo and Juliet*. Gretchen thanks me, eyes her open door discreetly, and whispers, "I've applied for two jobs." She actually closes her eyes and puts her palms together, as if praying, when she says this. "I have to get out of this handicapped, dysfunctional school."

I return to my room, open a bag of pretzels, sip from a 20 ounce Pepsi bottle (I know, my diet is terrible and I didn't follow through on my New Year's resolution), read in the newspaper that over on the west side of Cleveland, the Strongsville school board refuses to meet with the Strongsville Education Association since they have already issued their "last, best offer." The strike, therefore, continues.

TUESDAY, APRIL 9

Gretchen Suchs is absent today – maybe she's at a job interview – and Jack Mason, a twenty-something who is substituting for her, wanders into my classroom during the lunch period we share. He used to wrestle so he knows me. His short-cropped hair, square face, and solid frame suggest he has a military background and after I ask, he tells me he spent two years as a correctional officer before he went back to school to get a teaching degree. He tells me he did his student teaching at a high school in Cleveland where in the fall, students tripped fire alarms at least three days a week. This would get them outside where they could settle neighborhood conflicts with fistfights, and if a teacher attempted to break up the fight, they would try to beat him up too In short time, the teachers stopped interceding. In fact, they even stopped leaving the building during the fire drills altogether.

"There's no teaching going on," Jack reveals, "only managing."

I am very curious. "How do the teachers do that?" I ask. "Manage, that is."

"Mostly worksheets," he explains. "But when I took over the classes as the student teacher, I'm not a worksheet kind of guy. I'm more conversational – you know, lecture and discussion – so that caused some problems. The kids weren't used to that."

Jack also is a substitute at Ontario High School, which is a small, wealthy suburban school south of Cleveland. He contrasts the Cleveland high school and Ontario High School this way: "The worst thing I ever observed at Ontario was one kid giving another kid the finger, and I called him out on it. He got a two day suspension, and when he came back, he apologized to me." He shakes his head wearily, the way a much older person would, and adds: "Cleveland city kids, all they know is sickness and slums. I'd tell them, 'You can make your life hell or ask for help.' Those kids grow up, and they'll either be their brother's keeper or his killer. I was hoping to be an agent of change for them, but they looked upon me with indifference. They had no interest in hearing anything I had to say. I was there for only two months; many of them have to endure that school, that environment for four years."

Jack leaves to eat a sandwich, and I exit my room and walk to our teachers' workroom to make some copies. On my way, I see assistant principal Ellis Morgan stalking the hallway a hundred feet away from me. He's waving his arm when he passes an open doorway and calling out into the classroom. His voice is a blur to me, and when Rebecca Leever and Megan Cutler come up behind him, he turns, says something to them, and shakes their hands with great enthusiasm.

When I get closer, he reaches out, shakes my hand, too, and says, "This is my last day here. They're kicking me out." He smiles when he says this, but I sense he's upset. "They're kicking me out," he repeats. "Thanks a lot. Goodbye, Bayview!" He continues down the hallway past me, still waving into the open doorways, yelling "Goodbye," and glancing around for some more hands to shake. Indeed, by the end of the school day, we learn that Ellis Morgan is not returning to Bayview High School because the superintendent fired him. I guess someone else will have to do the data-driven schedule for next year.

I'm amused this evening, as I eat some beef stew for dinner alone (the boys have a late baseball practice and Sheryl is shopping), by a story in *The Wall Street Journal,* which reveals that experimental robot instructors will be used in public schools in Los Angeles and New York this year. In Los Angeles, a robotic dragon will be used to teach first graders about healthy lifestyle choices, while in New York, a robot will be programmed to make errors when working with children that the students can then correct. Robot instructors actually started in South Korea in 2009 with robotic English instructors in more than twenty schools.

Alas!

THURSDAY, APRIL 11

In my period 5-8 block, pretty, dark-haired Amber Phillips, sitting in the back of the room, starts shouting something at me I cannot understand. She waves her hand, looking frightened, and beckons me to come to the back of the room.

I am in the middle of previewing the play *Twelve Angry Men*, gearing up, in fact, to have the students examine the list of juror characters, but I rush to Amber and look at her waving hand. "What's wrong, Amber?"

Amber's response is a shriek and more hand waving. "Look...look at this...look at this." She points to a paper stuck to the gray metal side of the radiator. "It's stuck."

Oddly, the radiator's dented air circulation fans have sucked the paper against a vent. Jenny continues to point at the paper and squeal.

"Interesting," I say and swipe the paper off the radiator.

FRIDAY, APRIL 12

We have another awards assembly for our students in the gym, and just after Mr. Compton hands out the first perfect attendance award to a ninth grader, he admonishes the boy for going in the wrong direction with his certificate. "Toren, you're not listening! The ninth graders stand *over there*." He points to his right, and the ninth grader named Toren walks over to the top of the key on the gym floor as Mr. Compton directs him with his pointing finger. A bunch of students laugh.

Jamie, my student who kept coming to class with the oversized purse, is helping Mr. Compton. Jamie hands out the certificates as he calls the names of students. Suddenly, she starts arguing with some other girl in the first row of the bleachers. Because I'm sitting near the top of the bleachers, I cannot hear what they are arguing about but Jamie keeps shaking her head and raising her hands in frustration as Mr. Compton continues to call out names. She even sticks out her tongue at the girl.

Chen Lee's name gets called, of course. He is achieving all A's, including an A+ in my English 10 Honors class. He is of Chinese descent (I have taught both his older sisters) and a diligent and always on-task student. However, Chen seems reluctant too often to participate in discussions and debates in class. He's shy and tenses when I call on him. He might be the shyest student I have ever had in class. Even now, after receiving his Honor Roll certificate, Chen stands stiffly on the gym floor in the middle of the line of sophomores with his head down, adjusting his glasses as his eyes focus on the flimsy certificate in his hands.

The school board mandated that Mr. Compton make this awards ceremony more formal and prestigious. His interpretation of that mandate was to order 400 cupcakes and juice boxes for students who earn awards in grades six through twelve. In the bleachers, most students – even the Merit and Honor Roll award winners – look on with apathy, even with the incentive of the cupcake and a juice box. As the assembly ends and the students straggle out of the stands, they drop their napkins, empty juice boxes, and cupcake wrappers in the bleachers. Even worse, they begin throwing half-eaten cupcakes at each other.

Mr. Compton has already left the gym, and Phil Oster can't identify exactly who is throwing the cupcakes in the mass of students, so more cupcakes get thrown, hitting students near the door in the back of their heads. I can't tell who is throwing the cupcakes either.

During my lunch break I read in a newspaper that, according to the Associated Press, "New York school district officials have placed a high school English teacher on leave for having students pretend to be Jew-hating Nazis in a writing assignment. The teacher at Albany High School caused a storm of criticism after having students practice the art of persuasive argument by writing a letter to a fictitious Nazi government official arguing that 'Jews are evil.'"

TUESDAY, APRIL 16

Students have to attend the fifth discipline assembly of the school year in the gym. Mr. Compton repeats for the fifth time that students are not allowed to have cell phones in the hallways. "Thirty-three days is all you have left." He shakes a finger at them. "And I don't want to see tenth graders in the tenth grade next year...Don't go playin' with me now." Then he checks a paper in his hand. "And make sure you pay your fees. There's even some seniors who have $1000 in fees, and they aren't graduating unless they pay them."

Next, Mr. Compton introduces a young, spindly-looking man leaning against the gym wall, who is, I estimate, a little over five foot tall and about 120 pounds, and announces he is the offensive coordinator on the new football coaching staff. Mr. Compton has forgotten his last name so, as he waves him over to the podium, he calls him Tyrone and asks him to say his last name.

"*Terrell*...Williams," the young man mumbles, correcting Mr. Compton.

"Tyrone Williams!" Mr. Compton announces proudly into the microphone as if he has just solved a riddle, and Terrell/Tyrone steps forward to the podium.

"Just want you'all to know you'all can come out for the team," Terrell/Tyrone continues to mumble. A sophomore girl raises her hand and asks if she can come out for the football team. He pauses and then answers, "Yeah, you'all females can come out, too."

More girls start waving their hands at him and giggling; they all shout out, asking where they can sign up. Terrell/Tyrone looks up

280

nervously at them and his eyes widen as even more girls start waving their hands or stand up to get his attention. Mr. Compton gestures him away from the podium, and Terrell/Tyrone Williams seems grateful to return to his spot against the wall.

WEDNESDAY, APRIL 17

After school, in our weight room, I observe the other two new assistant football coaches exhort about a dozen boys to lift weights to get ready for the next football season. They are directing the boys to dead lift, bench, and squat whatever amount of weight they can handle. One coach in particular stands only a foot away from one boy who is squatting about eighty pounds and yells, "Georgia's comin', South Carolina's comin', LSU is comin'. One more rep. C'mon, now. They comin' with scholarships. "Notre Dame comin'. You gonna get one. One more rep now."

Georgia? LSU? Notre Dame?

Scholarships?

When I look more closely I see that the assistant coach who is yelling about colleges and scholarships is wearing both gym shorts and sweatpants, but for some reason he's dropped the sweatpants to his ankles, as if he was standing in front of a urinal. As the boy he's screaming at finishes his set, he growls at another boy to grab the bar.

I move to the rack of dumbbells and hope he doesn't start yelling at me. I lift two forty pound dumbbells off the rack and move off to a corner of the weight room to do some sets of curls, hoping to stay invisible to both the coaches and the boys.

Across the room another coach says to a stubby five-foot freshmen boy who is dead lifting seventy-five pounds that if he keeps working hard Jim Tressell will give him a scholarship to Ohio State, forgetting that Tressell lost his job as head coach at Ohio State University last year.

Thirty minutes later, I finish my workout and leave the school, my briefcase full of novel study projects to grade.

FRIDAY, APRIL 19

As I pass her classroom this morning, I say hello to fellow English teacher Rebecca Leever and notice the frustration and exhaustion in her face that cannot be hidden by makeup or maybe even a good night's sleep. I step inside her classroom and ask, "What's wrong?"

"I can't take it here anymore," she admits.

"It's not that bad, is it?" I say more as a statement than a question.

"Yes, it is. Maybe you don't see it."

"We're not as bad as some Cleveland schools," I argue. The general belief is that the Cleveland schools experience many more problems with daily attendance, academic performance, and student discipline than suburban schools like Bayview.

"We almost are," Rebecca laments. "Ethan, my students don't do their reading outside of class. They don't follow directions. They won't study. And they yell in the hallways."

I do not say anything at first. I have to think about this. "Maybe we need some different strategies. Maybe we're not teaching them the right way."

Rebecca's eyes go to the ceiling and then back at me. "Ethan, you can say that because you can see the light. Aren't you retiring?"

"Yes," I say. "But I'm not certain how bright that light is."

MONDAY, APRIL 22

The school day begins with news running around that there still is no settlement in the teachers' strike in Strongsville. They are beginning their eighth week on strike and have even picketed the homes and businesses of school board members. We did that, too, when we were on strike five years ago. The rumor was that the Strongsville school board was going to hold out until the summer and try to break the union. All of us in the Bayview School District empathize. Megan Cutler, our union president, knows teachers' unions across the country realize that public schools are at a crossroads. Whether they will even exist decades from now is uncertain.

In my classroom, my period 2-3 English 10 class Erica, who sits next to Marcus, suddenly points to the back of his shoulder and says, "There's a bug on you, Marcus."

This news panics Marcus. He jumps out of his seat and begins flailing with his arms toward his back. He's twisting and turning and jumping to remove the alleged bug, and while I watch stunned at these wild gestures, his classmates laugh. They even stand at their seats to get a better look at Marcus, who first rips off his sweatshirt and then his t-shirt to stand naked from the waist up in front of the classroom, still jumping and swiping with his hands, which makes his fellow students laugh even harder. I can only watch this stunned and speechless. Finally, when Marcus is convinced he has removed the insect, I calmly say, "Okay, put your shirt on now. The bug is gone."

Marcus does so, and the laughter subsides. Students return to their seats. We start to read *Lord of the Flies* again.

Irony.

WEDNESDAY, APRIL 24

Today during the period exchange between periods 9 and 10 right outside my classroom door I catch junior Carla Hilliard saying, "Shut the fuck up, Rickie!" in the hallway to Rickie Miller, a senior football player. Carla does not know I am behind her and continues, "Stay the fuck away from me." She is smiling, almost laughing, in fact, as she says this, and she is surprised when I tap her shoulder.

"Carla, you can't use that language..." I start to say.

She turns hard, making her gold earrings jingle, and looks at me incredulously. "Didn't you hear what *he* said?"

Behind me, I hear laughter from other students. "No, I didn't...I suspect he bothered you in some way, but...."

Beatrice, another former student, interrupts this time, and she speaks to Carla without even looking at me. "Don't listen to him," she declares, meaning me. "He won't do shit about it."

Beatrice, a senior who I had in class two years ago, was constantly a problem: She called out in class, every day she demanded I let her go to the office, she constantly used her cell phone, she teased her classmates, and all my calls to her mother had no effect on her insubordinate behavior.

I look at her and then back at Carla. I feel hopeless here, so all I say is, "There you go, Carla." I gesture with my thumb towards Beatrice. "Here's a good role model for you."

This makes the group around Beatrice and Carla laugh, and Beatrice first looks bothered but then joins them.

FRIDAY, APRIL 26

I give a quiz on *Lord of the Flies* author William Golding. Students had to research Golding's background and find out why he would write a story about British schoolboys crash landing on a Pacific island during a war. The intended answer to the quiz is that he was a teacher at a British school and had served in the Royal Navy during WW II. His ship patrolled Pacific islands.

Marcus writes this as his answer: *Because back in world war II he was a survival and were stranded just like they boys in the book and he felt hey he been through it before and he want too tell people his story but in his own words perspecte.*

WEDNESDAY, MAY 1

Our new assistant principal, a lantern-jawed woman with mouse-colored hair named Tonya Billingsly whose previous experience in education was as a substitute teacher, meets with the entire staff in the library. She does not have a license or certificate from the ODE to be an administrator, but that does not matter to the Bayview school board. Before we begin our PLC work, Mr. Compton asks her to stand and say some words to introduce herself. As directed, she stands from her seat and shakes her head at the thought she has in her brain. Then she says, "Kids cutting class...We have to stop it somehow. They just can't walk out of school anymore."

Most of us stare off into space or shuffle homework papers in front of us on the library tables. I deduce my colleagues, like me, cannot be certain this is a statement or a question, so no one responds, and the long-legged Ms. Billingsly sits down. She, too, starts shuffling the papers she has on her table.

David Grasser gently taps my right shoulder, leans towards me, and whispers, "What if you went to bed tonight, then woke up in the morning and realized you were only at year five here, that the last thirty years were all a dream?" He chuckles softly, pokes my arm again, and then leans back on his own chair before I can answer.

I have just about one month left in my career as an English teacher at Bayview High.

WEDNESDAY, MAY 8

As usual, part of the Bayview staff has our weekly PLC meeting after school, this time in Gretchen Such's classroom, to decide on a writing rubric to be used across the subject areas. The meeting begins at 1:15, and is scheduled to conclude at three o'clock, certainly enough time I speculate for about twenty teachers to identify the criteria for a writing rubric.

Our new Spanish teacher, the fourth one this school year, is a dark-haired woman with coppery skin who looks like she is actually from Spain. She arrives late and says nothing the whole meeting.

Next to me, social studies teacher Jack Johnstone surfs the web on his laptop. Sixth grade teacher Ander Klyszewski texts on his cell phone.

Computer teacher John Santora, who is sitting on the other side of the classroom, jokes and makes side comments to Jennifer Stimson (I know this because, although I cannot hear him, I see Jennifer laugh several times).

The rest of us argue about the language of this rubric because it has to be generic enough to be applied to all the subjects but specific enough to be functional for students. This academic argument eventually makes Jennifer, a math teacher who is leaving at the end of the school year to join her husband in Baltimore, call out in frustration, "Let's just complete this damn thing so we can turn it in on time. It's not going to make any difference."

Except for Gretchen who is sitting at her desk, we are all sitting at students' desks, and I swivel in mine so I can look directly at Jennifer. "Do you really think this won't make a difference?" I ask.

She sighs and pushes her brown bangs off her forehead. "The problem is that no matter how this turns out, it still is all about teacher discretion, how each of us interprets what the kids write. What is well-organized to me might not be to someone else, so the actual document itself doesn't really make any difference."

Sixth grade teacher Ander Klyszewski continues texting on his cell phone.

I swivel back in my seat and stare again at the screen in the front of Gretchen's classroom where the rubric is displayed via a projector. I have to digest Jennifer's comment before I can respond. *Is she right? Does anything we do really make a difference?* Shakespeare's *Macbeth* again.

Suddenly, interim assistant principal Tonya Billingsly comes in and asks if we need the handout Mr. Compton was supposed to copy for us. Gretchen tells her that we do, but then Ms. Billingsly admits she does not know where the handout is. She leaves and never returns.

Melissa Fleck, our art teacher, works on some papers and then leaves at 2:00 P.M. In turn, without a word, Cindy Greenlee walks out at 2:10 P.M. Neither of them returns either.

I point at the screen where half of the writing rubric is displayed. "I want to finish this," I say to no one in particular. "Let's figure out the rest of the criteria."

THURSDAY, MAY 9

At the very beginning of my English Honors 10 class, Monique, who used to talk constantly in my class, comes to my front table where I am arranging some papers and asks in a concerned voice, "Mr. Miller, are you retiring?"

Other students file past us to their desks, and I look her in the eyes and let go a small smile. "Yes."

Her dark eyes widen. She straightens her small body and almost demands, "No, you can't retire...You have to wait until I graduate!"

"That's two years from now," I tell her. "I'm too old right now. I doubt I could last that long." I say this last statement as a joke, but Monique does not laugh or even smile.

"You're not that old...What are you?"

"Old enough to know better, but not old enough to stop." I grin again for her.

She pauses. "Stop what?" Her forehead crinkles, and then she goes to her seat.

FRIDAY, MAY 10

This warm and sunny day concludes Teacher Appreciation Week, and the superintendent sends us all an email that he has provided a cake for us in the lounge. During my free period I go to the lounge to check out this cake.

The cake has a chocolate inside with white frosting, and already several pieces somehow have been cut out, which surprises me since next to the cake box there are no plates, no napkins, and no forks. Even a knife to cut the cake is missing. My only immediate option is to scoop out a piece with my bare hand, but then I think of the calories and sugar and my expanding waistline and leave it alone. Crumbs litter the table, which makes me think of Mr. Buckman, our maintenance supervisor, and his request to us that we not leave a mess in our classrooms.

On my way back to my classroom, I glance into Rebecca Leever's room. She's sitting at her desk spooning yogurt into her mouth.

"Have you seen the cake?" I say. "When Mr. Buckman sees the mess, he'll have a fit."

Rebecca rests her spoon inside the yogurt container. "Probably not," she says. "I'm not certain whether he quit or got fired, but he and Dr. Andrews had an argument about the toilet paper Buckman ordered. Supposedly, Dr. Andrews didn't like it, and Buckman said he was trying to save the school district some money." Rebecca smirks at the story and digs her spoon again into the yogurt container.

I'm glad her classroom is empty. "He got fired...over toilet paper? Seriously?"

"This is Bayview, Ethan," Rebecca sighs. "Nothing should surprise us anymore."

Two periods later, Mr. Compton and Ms. Billingsly enter my block 5-8 class unannounced, they both smile, and Mr. Compton apologizes for interrupting. He then abruptly asks the students their impressions of me as their teacher. Jenny Wilson, who is failing my class and likes sitting on the radiator rather than a desk, astonishes me and says, "He pushes us to do our best."

"He's cool sometimes," Connor Reese says from the back of the room.

"C'mon, be honest," I say to the class.

"He's funny," someone else announces from the other side of the room.

"Wonderful, wonderful," Mr. Compton exclaims and hands me a $3 gift card for Baker's Square restaurant, reminds the students that this was Teacher Appreciation Week, and leaves with a still smiling Ms. Billingsly.

The school day concludes with a spring sports pep rally in the gym, and a problem surfaces immediately: for the umpteenth time this school year, the volume on the microphone goes in and out. The coaches then have to introduce the players on the baseball and softball teams by yelling out their names when the microphone goes out. This is followed by some games – a relay race, a contest where four senior boys who have to put on a wig and then an old prom dress over their clothes (the loudest applause from the students in the bleachers determines the winner), and then a dodge ball game, which prompts math teacher Gordon Davison, who is sitting next to me in the bleachers, to say. "A lot of schools have outlawed this game."

Amid the noise, I turn to look at him. "Really? How do you know that?"

"I read," he declares as if this is an obvious fact.

"Where did you read it?" I am a reader, too, but this is the first time I have ever heard this news about dodge ball being outlawed. I still feel Gordon is teasing me.

But he is not. Gordon shrugs, his eyes still on the students playing dodge ball and screaming at each other. "I can't remember where I read it."

I return to watching the students on the gym floor hurling nerf balls at each other and realize this is the last pep rally I will witness at Bayview High. I turn to science teacher Ernie Kelsey, who is sitting on the other side of Gordon, and ask, "How many years again have you been teaching, Ernie?"

"Seven," he answers.

"If you teach for thirty years and count a pep rally for each sports season, you have sixty-nine more of these." I smile and add, "Eighty-four if you go thirty-five years like I have."

Ernie laughs, although I wasn't really joking, and leans his elbows back on the bleachers.

MONDAY, MAY 13

We are in the final chapters of *Lord of the Flies*, and my period 2 English 10 students struggle to read silently. This is an endurance test for them – it's spring, the weather is warm, school is almost over – and they keep turning in their seats to talk. I cannot detect the exact contents of their conversations, only the annoying mumbling followed by laughter. Only Anna, a Vietnamese girl who is an English Language Learner student, reads quietly.

We all hear the muted sounds of some movie coming from Gretchen Such's classroom next door, and this prompts Leena Eckle to look at the wall that divides our two rooms and call out, "What movie is that?"

"I don't know for sure," I tell her. "but it sounds like *Romeo and Juliet*. Please try to avoid the distraction and just read *Lord of the Flies*."

Suddenly, Justin raises his hand but does not wait for me to call on him. He just exclaims, "I think I read Shakespeare had a male partner. Does that mean he was a homosexual?" Justin looks at me, and his expression is open and serious as if he is ready to have a thorough intellectual discussion about Shakespeare's sexual preferences. But his question makes other students giggle, put down their books, and start to chatter. Now they, too, want to talk about Shakespeare supposedly being gay.

"Quiet down," I insist. "What you probably read, Justin, is that Shakespeare had a male *business* partner." I even repeat this. "He had a business partner in the Globe Theater. That's what you probably read. There is no evidence that Shakespeare was gay."

Justin looks surprised. "Mrs. S said he was gay. Are you sure he wasn't?"

I do not want to argue and I wonder now how Gretchen introduced Shakespeare last year. *She told them he was gay?*

I downplay Justin's question and tell the students, "Either way. Okay, everyone, let's get back to reading."

Michael Small keeps getting out of his seat to spit into the trashcan. The first time I ignore him; the second time several of his classmates go "Ewwwww," and I give him a look that attempts to show I am both bewildered and exasperated by this. Is he sick? Is there a nasal problem? Allergies? After his fourth trip to the trash, I stop him on his way back to his seat ask, "What's the problem here, Michael? Are you sick?"

"I want to get rid of this taste in my mouth," Michael says, pointing at his open mouth, and I notice that he is puckering up to spit again.

"Well, you can't keep spitting like this. It's an annoying distraction. Just swallow it and rinse your month with water when the period ends."

Michael glares at me, displeased with my suggestion, but I am, in truth, grateful that he returns to his seat and stays there. I also make a mental note to find out what Gretchen Suchs is teaching her students about Shakespeare.

TUESDAY, MAY 13

Middle school teacher Cindy Geenlee and I share the same lunch period, and today she peeks her head inside my door and asks if I am busy. I am just responding to parents' emails, so I stop to find out what she needs.

Cindy walks hurriedly to my desk, sets a paper on it, and smiles. "My kids' Christian school is having money problems that tuition can't cover," Cindy says, "so I'm seeking donations." She points at the paper resting on my desk. "Will you?"

The paper has the school name at the top and two sets of lines – one for names and the other column for the dollar amounts. Five other teachers' names and their pledges are already listed.

I feel cornered here. "Sure, I guess. How much?"

"It's up to you...I'll take anything."

I examine the names already on the paper. One colleague pledged ten dollars, another $2.50. I print my name and put $5.00 on the right hand column. "When do you need the money?"

Cindy looks surprised by my question. "Well, right now, if you have it."

"I don't have it. I'll have to bring it tomorrow."

"That's fine. I'll come back to tomorrow. Is this period okay?"

"Sure."

Paper in hand now, Cindy smiles a final time and leaves my classroom, leaving me to wonder why a public school teacher would send her children to a private, albeit parochial, school.

WEDNESDAY, MAY 15

Former college basketball coach Al McGuire said, "I think everyone should go to college and get a degree and then spend six months as a bartender and six months as a cabdriver. Then they would really be educated."

Maybe he is right, but last night at our Senior Awards Program (I did not attend this event), several groups, like the Booster Club, the Bayview Garden Club, and the Kiwanis Club awarded scholarships to graduating seniors. Their intent, of course, is to provide some assistance to these seniors for their college tuition costs. The truth is that the $250, $500, and even the $1000 scholarships can only pay for the cost of their textbooks now. Most of our seniors go to Ohio colleges – at least those who do attend college.

As I stand again in the hallway between classes today, several senior students walk by, offering me congratulations. Senior football player Tommy Lower, in fact, stops, congratulates me, and shakes his head, as if in disbelief. "All that coaching you did, Mr. Miller. All those state champions... wow, that's impressive." Before he walks away, I thank him although I do not know for sure why Tommy and some other seniors are, in fact, congratulating me. Has news spread about my retirement?

I find out why they are congratulating me during my lunch period after the athletic director catches me by chance in the hallway and informs me that at the Senior Awards Program last night I was awarded the Award of Merit from the Ohio High School Athletic Association.

"Really?" I ask.

"Yes, I'll get an aide to bring you the plaque."

"Okay, thanks...But how come no one told me ahead of time? I would have attended the Senior Awards Program last night to receive it."

"I don't know." The athletic director just frowns and keeps moving down the hallway.

FRIDAY, MAY 17

I tell a senior who is wearing a ball cap to remove it, and he says, "I'm a senior, you can't do nothing to me no more." He smirks, turns his back on me, and jogs away down the hallway.

At the end of the school day, social studies teacher Jack Johnston joins me in my classroom for a parent-teacher conference. In actuality, this meeting is not with the parent of Derrick Simms. Instead, we meet with his older sister, a thirty-something woman whose thick arms, legs, and neck make me think she played rugby in her past. The sister's name is Barbara, and she explains, "Our mom couldn't handle something like this."

Having this conference somewhat surprises me because starting in the first quarter for weeks and weeks I tried contacting his mother, but the first number Derrick gave me was not a valid phone number. I checked the phone number with the office and learned this was the same number they had. I tried again in November but experienced the same results. I sent home letters and progress reports but never received any response. Now it is May. What dramatic change would Derrick's mother or sister expect now?

Derrick, a cordial and cooperative fifteen year old who still hasn't showed me his science fiction novel, sits across from his sister and listens while I explain to her that he has regularly neglected to complete his homework and projects in my English 10 Honors class. "How many times have we talked about this?" I ask him in a solemn voice.

Derrick stares at his desktop and says, "A lot."

"So why don't you do it?" his sister demands harshly. "What's wrong with you?"

Derrick looks right at her. "Nothing."

"He's getting a C in my class," Jack says and then folds his arms across his chest over his black windbreaker. He is ready to leave and get to his other job at a bowling alley. "He's doing okay, I guess," he adds. Then he exchanges glances with Derrick's sister and gets quiet.

I tell Barbara that my first conversation with Derrick was after his absences in the first quarter where we discussed his make up work. These assignments were never turned in. We even discussed, I add, Derrick moving from the Honors class to regular English 10, where the work was not as comprehensive, but he declined.

Derrick remains silent. Three adults surround him, and the only positive comment he has heard so far is that he is performing "okay" in social studies.

I offer, therefore, that he is an excellent oral reader and is quite insightful when we discuss literature in class, especially *To Kill a Mockingbird*. I add that I am surprised he does poorly on quizzes and tests, even though he has had the opportunity to examine the test before taking it.

"He lets you see the test?!" the sister exclaims. In fact, she almost yells this. "When I was in school, we never saw the test before we took it...And this man lets you see it? And you still fail?"

"Yes," Derrick says glumly. He knows what is coming next.

His older sister turns on Derrick and says angrily, "You just lazy, Derrick. You lazy, that's all there is to it."

MONDAY MAY 20

I have ten total workdays left on my contract as an employee of the Bayview School District. I am, obviously, nearing the day when I leave Bayview High School for good. I could say forever because I sense that after I walk out of this school, I will never walk back in.

And then I will disappear.

I also suspect that within a year I will be forgotten.

Not unlike my seventh grade math teacher who at first just yelled at us when we were late to class or misbehaved. A month or two later, he was grabbing boys by their shirt collars and yanking them out of their seats for chewing gum loudly. And in the spring, we became convinced he was sick when one day we saw him chasing an 8th grade boy down a hallway, brandishing a wooden paddle, and yelling at him to stop and bend over, until, convinced he couldn't catch him, he threw the paddle at the boy's back. He missed, and the paddle clattered on the tile floor. Another teacher witnessed this, and we never saw him again. As I stated, I can't remember his name.

At the end of the school year, possibly at the end of a career, teachers – and their students, in turn – should feel a sense of accomplishment and satisfaction. We should all walk out of a school on a warm and sunny June day and feel a great sense of reward for all that we achieved in the last nine months together.

Unfortunately, the sad truth is I do not feel I have accomplished anything. I feel more regret and frustration for what I have failed to achieve with my students. If I'm such a good teacher, why do some students still fail my class? In past years, I needed the summer to regain my enthusiasm and confidence and revise my lesson plans to make them more engaging for students, but today I worry that all that tweaking of my lessons may have helped some students, but possibly not enough.

I would like to think I have made a difference in my students' lives, that they will remember what I taught them and find that instruction valuable. A colleague long ago told me that if I helped one student, that was enough. I disagree; helping only one student is not enough.

My experiences are not unique. Jordan Kohanim taught high school English in Georgia and received the NCTE/SLATE Affiliate Intellectual Freedom Award, from the Georgia Council of Teachers, an affiliate of the National Council of Teachers of English, in 2011. In her article "Why I Left Teaching," Kohanim writes in her *Get Schooled* blog of the *Atlanta Journal-Constitution* on June 22, 2012, "I was disgusted."

Her tenure as an educator was probably more challenging than mine, and her story is very compelling: "My classes were big. If I worked six-hour days with no breaks, it would take 28 days to grade my students' 159 essays. I was an English teacher. My kids had to write. I had to grade. And I actually enjoyed grading, but 159 students? That was too much. Twenty-eight days to grade those essays was too much.

"And I did it alone. I neglected my family and myself. I gained weight from too much fast food on the way home from school...I rarely saw my husband and, when I did, I was so exhausted that talk of family was put on hold.

"That's what this boils down to: The needs of my family come first. I have given so much to other people's families. I have fought hard to always do the right thing. To be honest, after seven years, I'm tired. I can't do this job halfway. I just can't. It's too important. It means too much.

"Maybe I could have found a different school. Maybe I should have to moved to a private school. I believe I will be happier for having quit teaching. I will make more money. I will have more time. I will no longer sacrifice myself for the sake of others' children. I would like to go back someday when the system finally figures out how lucky it is that people are so dedicated to teaching.

"...I walked away from a profession that I loved dearly. I viewed teaching as a calling. But I lost my faith along the way, and that meant it was time for me to leave."

I imagine Kohanim is like me and came to school an hour before it started and left one hour after it was over. I imagine she sincerely cared about her students and her school district. I imagine her family heard her laments about her school each day at the dinner table, if she got the opportunity to eat with her family. And I imagine she looked forward to retirement, much like I have for the past three weeks.

WEDNESDAY, MAY 22

Brandy comes into my classroom at the end of the school day to chat. I had Brandy in class last year, and she was always an energetic and conscientious student, one of those kids who is always smiling and who finds almost any lesson interesting. This year she is taking cosmetology and English at a vocational school. Today, back at Bayview to pick up her 9th grade sister and while she waits for her, she simply wanders around my room, glancing at books on the bookshelves, the handouts on the front table, my notes on the white board. Then she stops and looks at me. "You know, Mr. Miller, you're picky, but that's good."

I lean back in my desk chair and look at her. "A lot of students would disagree with you, Brandy."

"They may hate it now," she says, "but later, they know it's good...I wish I had you again."

"Well, thank you, and I bet you're doing a great job again in your junior English class at the vo-ed school."

Brandy scowls a little and examines a handout on my table. "My teacher now, she doesn't know what she's doing."

I try to offer a compromise. "My students probably think I don't know what I'm doing either."

"No, Mr. Miller, they just don't know yet how good they got it with you."

MONDAY, JUNE 3

The last work day for teachers.

My last day.

In the library two hours before lunch, the entire staff meets a young man named James Thomas. He will be the new principal for Bayview High School for the 2013-2014 school year. Currently, he is an assistant principal in the Cleveland Municipal School District. Ironically, Mr. Compton has the task of introducing him to us in the library, and the irony is affirmed when, as Mr. Compton takes a seat, Mr. Thomas congratulates him for his "great work at Bayview."

In his opening comments, Mr. Thomas likens the relationship between a principal and his staff to a marriage. What he actually says is, "I want our marriage to be a great one." Mr. Thomas reveals that he is an ordained minister, that his career in education is only four years old, having spent two of those years at a charter school, and that his father was murdered when he was ten.

When he opens the floor to questions, I raise my hand, prompting some colleagues to chuckle. Everybody knows now that I am retiring. Nevertheless, I ask, "Other than student achievement, what is your priority for Bayview High School?"

He answers without pause. "Making sure kids go to class. If they are not in class, they're not learning."

Ander Klyszewski asks about discipline, and Mr. Thomas says he needs to explore the policies but admits, "I'm not a 'I gotcha guy.'"

Although I do not know what he means by this, I do not ask for clarification. Nor do any of my colleagues, including Ander.

After Mr. Thomas ends the meeting, we return to our empty classrooms to finish our end-of-year tasks like putting books back into storage, completing forms, and cleaning up our rooms. I have already finished all these obligations, so I sit at my desk and breathe the warm, musty classroom air as I wait for my exit conference with Henry Compton, who is meeting, in fact, with every teacher on this last work day, where we turn in the key to our classroom door, a form listing our classroom inventory, a print out of our student grades, another form listing lost textbooks, our summer mailing address, and a form identifying our professional development plans. I don't bother to complete the last form. It's official. The school board has accepted my retirement.

At 11:00 A.M. I meet with Mr. Compton who takes my forms and adds his signature at the bottom of each page before turning to me and telling me he has to ask me a series of survey questions.

"What questions?" I worry that this will be both time-consuming and pointless. The truth is he is *leaving* and I am *retiring. Why bother?* I then inquire, "Why do we have to do this?"

"It won't take too long," he answers and begins to click the mouse to his computer.

"But what's the point?" This comes across, I sense, as too aggressive, even somewhat inconsiderate, so I soften my tone and add, "Is someone else demanding you do this?"

This time he rests his elbows on his desk, raises his hands as if signaling a successful field goal, and rolls his eyes before grinning sadly and answering with a slow head nod. I infer this to mean the superintendent has demanded he ask these questions. And I know something is amiss immediately with the first question.

"Why have you decided to leave the Organization?"

The Organization?

Once again, I am convinced that either Mr. Compton or Dr. Andrews copied a generic exit interview and neglected to change Organization to Bayview High School.

"Oh, yeah." Mr. Compton answers the question himself and types this on his computer keyboard. "You're retiring."

He continues the survey: "How was your relationship with your manager?"

My manager? I discover I have been leaning forward with my hands gripping the edge of the seat of my plastic chair, and now with this question I slump back in my seat and release my grip.

My manager? This question confuses me for two reasons: (1) Is Mr. Compton my manager or Dr. Andrews? (2) If Mr. Compton is my manager, how do I answer honestly with him sitting right in front of me?

Either way, I say, "I think we had a good rapport." This is a lie but with only an hour left in my career here I let it go.

"What are your views about the management and leadership in general of the Organization?"

I feel both more prepared now but more disenchanted. "I have no views."

He types and then clicks the mouse. "Did you receive adequate feedback about your performance day-to-day and in the performance development planning process?"

"No."

"Describe your experience of the Organization's commitment to quality and customer service."

I want to scream my feelings of frustration and distress; instead, I simply say, "I never knew who the customer actually was."

Mr. Compton's eyes are on the computer screen. "Do the policies and procedures of the Organization help to create a well-managed, consistent, and fair workplace in which expectations are clearly defined?"

In my head I hear bowling pins crashing into the pit and think of a dozen circus clowns jumping out of a miniature car, of students farting in my class, of Honor Roll and Merit Roll certificates being folded into little squares, of microphones that don't work, and girls fighting in my classroom. "I do not know," I answer.

"What did you dislike about your position in the Organization?"

"I have no opinion."

Mr. Compton continues through his list of questions, and I repeat I have no opinion for questions about the school facility, professional development options, and my future personal and professional goals.

He manipulates the mouse with his right hand again, clicks, and then takes his eyes off the screen to look at me. "Can you offer any comments that will enable us to understand why you are leaving, how we can improve, and what we can do to become a better Organization?"

I'm still slumped in my chair. This is my moment, I recognize, to let him have it. I can inform him of everything I think is wrong with the Bayview School District – the incompetence of the administrators, the dysfunctional meetings, even the disruptive and disrespectful students. My response would take probably take an hour.

Instead, I sit up in my chair and tell him, "I have nothing to say."

Mr. Compton finishes typing my final answer on his computer, prints off two copies that we both sign, hands one to me, and shakes my hand. We wish each other luck in a way where neither of us sounds sincere, and I exit his office.

I return to my classroom and check all the cabinet and desk drawers a final time. They're empty, and everything seems in place for the teacher who will replace me. The bulletin board is clean, and my teacher's desk drawers are also empty except for leftover paper clips, a stapler, scissors, and a box of staples.

Satisfied everything is in order – again, most teachers like closure – I start my march through the hallways to say goodbye to several colleagues: Jack, David, Ernie, Ander, Megan, and, of course, Allison.

Then I leave the school and walk onto the parking lot with my two English colleagues, Rebecca and Gretchen. Gretchen carries a shoebox of some of my personal items for me while I carry a cardboard box of notebooks that contain my lesson plans. I ask them – I tease actually –

if I should turn and take one final look at Bayview High School.

Rebecca gives my shoulder a little shove. "No," she says, walking next to me. "Keep going."

This makes us all laugh, and as we near my car I wonder how to say goodbye. What is the etiquette for an occasion like this?

"What are we going to do without you, Ethan?" Gretchen asks, and although she is behind me I hear the sadness in her voice.

I keep my back to the two women, unlock my car doors, and put the box and my briefcase on the passenger seat. I still don't know what to say or do. When I turn to take the shoebox from Gretchen, I notice that she and Rebecca are tearing.

"How are we going to get along without you?" Rebecca asks. She swipes her hand beneath her eyes.

"Easy," I tell them. "It will be great for you both next year. A new person means a different approach and not the same old same old anymore. I bet you'll enjoy the change."

"It won't be the same." Gretchen rubs her eyes and stares for a moment at the moisture on her finger.

I smile for them and stand straight. "No, it won't, but that's okay. I'll miss you two. I really will. I made it through this last year thanks to you two."

We hug, they step away from my Ford, and I get in my car and drive away. On the highway home I listen to "Moon River," my favorite song, and it is finally then that I cry, too.

Purchase other Black Rose Writing titles at *www.blackrosewriting.com/books*

and use promo code PRINT to receive a 20% discount.

CPSIA information can be obtained at www.ICGtesting.com
Printed in the USA
BVOW06s2148271015

424478BV00009B/75/P